AF478119

Literature and the Renewal of the Public Sphere

Cross-Currents in Religion and Culture

General Editors:
Elisabeth Jay, Senior Research Fellow, Westminster College, Oxford
David Jasper, Professor in Literature and Theology, University of Glasgow

The study of theology and religion nowadays calls upon a wide range of inter-disciplinary skills and cultural perspectives to illuminate the concerns at the heart of religious faith. Books in this new series will variously explore the contributions made by literature, philosophy and science in forming our historical and contemporary understanding of religious issues and theological perspectives.

Titles include:

Harold Fisch
NEW STORIES FOR OLD
Biblical Patterns in the Novel

Susan VanZanten Gallagher and M. D. Walhout (*editors*)
LITERATURE AND THE RENEWAL OF THE PUBLIC SPHERE

Philip Leonard (*editor*)
TRAJECTORIES OF MYSTICISM IN THEORY AND LITERATURE

Lambert Zuidervaart and Henry Luttikhuizen (*editors*)
THE ARTS, COMMUNITY AND CULTURAL DEMOCRACY

Carolyn Jones
THE FICTION AND CRITICISM OF TONI MORRISON
Making Myths

Elizabeth Clarke
REWRITING THE BRIDE
Authorship, Gender and 'The Song of Songs' in the Seventeenth Century

Stephen Happel
GOD'S JOURNEYS IN TIME
Co-operation between the Divine and Creation

Cross-Currents in Religion and Culture
Series Standing Order ISBN 0–333–79469–9
(*outside North America only*)

You can receive future titles in this series as they are published by placing a standing order. Please contact your bookseller or, in case of difficulty, write to us at the address below with your name and address, the title of the series and the ISBN quoted above.

Customer Services Department, Macmillan Distribution Ltd, Houndmills, Basingstoke, Hampshire RG21 6XS, England

Literature and the Renewal of the Public Sphere

Edited by

Susan VanZanten Gallagher

and

M. D. Walhout

In memory of Lionel Basney, 1946–1999

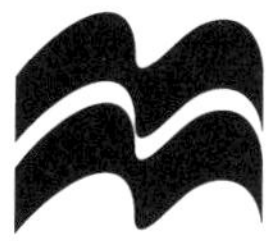

 First published in Great Britain 2000 by
MACMILLAN PRESS LTD
Houndmills, Basingstoke, Hampshire RG21 6XS and London
Companies and representatives throughout the world

A catalogue record for this book is available from the British Library.

ISBN 0–333–74690–2

 First published in the United States of America 2000 by
ST. MARTIN'S PRESS, INC.,
Scholarly and Reference Division,
175 Fifth Avenue, New York, N.Y. 10010

ISBN 0–312–22672–1

Library of Congress Cataloging-in-Publication Data
Literature and the renewal of the public sphere / edited by Susan
VanZanten Gallagher and M.D. Walhout.
p.   cm. — (Cross-currents in religion and culture)
Includes bibliographical references and index.
ISBN 0–312–22672–1
1. Literature and society.   2. Literature—History and criticism–
–Theory, etc.   3. Authors—Political and social views.   4. Public
interest.   I. Gallagher, Susan V.   II. Walhout, M. D., 1959–   .
III. Series.
PN98.S6L585   1999
809—dc21   99–33527
                                                        CIP

10   9   8   7   6   5   4   3   2   1
09   08   07   06   05   04   03   02   01   00

Printed and bound in Great Britain by
Antony Rowe Ltd, Chippenham, Wiltshire

Contents

Acknowledgements

Over the past ten years a diverse assortment of scholars has gathered together each summer to read and talk about the relationship between the study of literature and Christianity. This informal band eventually received funding from the Calvin Center for Christian Scholarship in order to put together this book. Many people have contributed to the congenial discussions and animated debates that inform the essays included here. Those of us who have written and edited these essays express our gratitude to other participants in this long conversation, including Nancy Arnesen, Matthew Beaverson, Stephanie Paulsell, Lawrence Cunningham, Nick Wolterstorff, Ron Dooley, Wendy Ver Hage Falb, Gail Kienitz, Don Marshall and James Olthuis. We also express our appreciation to Ron Wells and Donna Romanowski, from the Calvin Center, who provided gracious hospitality, along with logistical and financial support. Finally, a special thank-you goes to Teri Hull Owens, without whom this manuscript might never have seen the light of day.

An earlier version of Chapter 3 appeared as 'Dostoevsky and the Ethical Relation to the Prisoner', *Renascence*, 48.4 (1996) 259–78.

An earlier and shorter version of Chapter 13 appeared in Dutch translation in *Levensecht en bescheiden* (Kampen: Kok Agora, 1998).

An earlier version of Chapter 14 appeared as 'Sacrifice and the Public Sphere', *Contagion*, 5 (1998) 57–73.

Grateful acknowledgement is made to the following for permission to reprint previously published material: W. H. Auden: 'Funeral Blues'. From *W. H. Auden: Collected Poems* by W. H. Auden, edited by Edward Mendelson. Copyright 1940 and renewed 1968 by W. H. Auden. Reprinted by permission of Random House, Inc. 'Stop All the Clocks'. From W. H. Auden, 'Twelve Songs', *Collected Poems*, edited by Edward Mendelson, rev. ed. Copyright 1991. Reprinted by permission of Faber and Faber.

Preface

This book is the product of the Calvin Center for Christian Scholarship (CCCS), which was established at Calvin College in 1976. The purpose of the CCCS is to promote creative, articulate and rigorous scholarship that addresses important theoretical and practical issues. This present volume is the result of the ideas and work of an interdisciplinary working group of scholars concerned with the role of religion and literature in 'the public sphere'. Under the leadership of Clarence Walhout, Mark Walhout and Susan VanZanten Gallagher, the group met over the course of several summers here at Calvin College. The CCCS was glad to be their host and to provide funding for their work. We on the CCCS staff called them 'our Habermas group'.

Their work, and this book produced under the leadership and editorship of Susan VanZanten Gallagher and Mark Walhout, is informed by some of the seminal insights of Jürgen Habermas. While not limited to discussing Habermas, the group of scholars bring the important implications of Habermas' thought to bear upon their own desires to seek the role of religion and literature in a renewed public life. We believe the book will make a valuable contribution to the important debate about the nature, and future, of democratic life. The Calvin Center for Christian Scholarship is honoured to be the sponsor of this project.

Grand Rapids
Fall, 1998

Ronald A. Wells
Director, CCCS

Notes on the Contributors

Lionel Basney teaches in the English Department of Calvin College, Grand Rapids, Michigan.

Janet Blumberg teaches in the English Department of Seattle Pacific University, Seattle, Washington.

James Champion teaches in the English Department of Seattle Pacific University, Seattle, Washington.

Paul J. Contino teaches in Christ College, Valparaiso University, Valparaiso, Indiana.

Glenn W. Fetzer teaches in the French Department of Calvin College, Grand Rapids, Michigan.

Susan VanZanten Gallagher teaches in the English Department of Seattle Pacific University, Seattle, Washington.

Alan Jacobs teaches in the English Department of Wheaton College, Wheaton, Illinois.

Colin Jager is finishing a PhD in English at the University of Michigan, Ann Arbor, Michigan.

Pamela Corpron Parker teaches in the English Department of Whitworth College, Spokane, Washington.

Michael Vander Weele teaches in the English Department of Trinity Christian College, Palos Heights, Illinois.

Clarence Walhout taught in the English Department of Calvin College, Grand Rapids, Michigan.

M. D. Walhout teaches in the English Department of Seattle Pacific University, Seattle, Washington.

Lambert Zuidervaart teaches in the Philosophy Department of Calvin College, Grand Rapids, Michigan.

1
Introduction: The Public Muse

M. D. Walhout

As we approach the end of the twentieth century, the air is filled with lamentation over the decline of public life. Civility has vanished, we complain; the streets are meaner than ever. Voter apathy and cynicism run rampant, while workers are subjected to continuous lay-offs and mergers. The spirit of community, we are told, has given way to cultural warfare or narcissistic self-absorption. As for public information and entertainment, what responsible editor or serious producer can possibly compete with the global media empire of Rupert Murdoch? Meanwhile, intellectuals have begun to regret their diminished status and influence outside the academy. A call for the return of the 'public intellectual' has been issued, and academicians like Stephen Carter and Martha Nussbaum have responded with general-interest books like *The Culture of Disbelief: How American Law and Politics Trivialize Religious Devotion* (1993) and *Poetic Justice: The Literary Imagination and Public Life* (1995), insisting that religion and literature can make a vital contribution to political and economic life. At the same time, thanks to the widespread perception of crisis in public life, academic research on the so-called 'public sphere' is growing.

It is in this context that references to the work of Jürgen Habermas, the eminent German philosopher and social theorist, have begun to appear in the English-language press. Consider, for example, a column in the *New York Times* by Victor Navasky, long-time publisher of *The Nation*, the oldest and most prominent magazine of the American Left. Adopting the confessional mode, Navasky admits to buying most of his books nowadays at Barnes & Noble, the national chain of 'superstores' known for their vast shelves and fresh coffee, rather than the small independent booksellers he patronised in years past. 'I am impressed', Navasky declares, by the fact that when privatization is in the air ..., these chains seem intent on taking private space into the public sphere. Jürgen Habermas, the German philosopher, has described the public sphere as that place between the governmental realm and the private realm where people can hammer out the issues of the day through rational discourse. He traces the history of this realm, which began with the rise of commerce, to the salons, coffee-houses, and so-called table societies of the 17th century. These were places for court gossip and political discourse. In other words, they were institutions that contributed to the sort of culture without which democracy suffocates.

'I am not suggesting', Navasky hastens to add, 'that Leonard and Stephen Riggio, who run the Barnes & Noble bookstores, had Professor Habermas in mind when they decided to encourage the consumption of food, drink, and intellectual fare on their premises'.[1] What Navasky is suggesting, I take it, is that late capitalism is not entirely hostile to the sort of democratic culture Habermas describes.

Navasky was undoubtedly thinking of an early work by Habermas, *The Structural Transformation of the Public Sphere*, published in Germany in 1962. This book documents the rise and fall of the bourgeois or liberal public sphere, which sprang into being as a result of the rapid expansion of commercial and literary activity in eighteenth-century Europe. Designed to facilitate the free circulation of information and ideas, this sphere served the interests of the rising bourgeoisie as it challenged hereditary aristocracies and absolute monarchies for control of public opinion and, ultimately, the state itself. By the twentieth century, however, the enfranchisement of the working classes, combined with the manipulation of public opinion through the mass media, had virtually destroyed the social conditions under which the bourgeois public sphere had flourished. As a result, the public sphere was becoming little more than a carefully orchestrated caricature of itself – or so it seemed to Habermas in 1962. Unfortunately, the English translation of *The Structural Transformation of the Public Sphere* did not appear until 1989 – well after the social upheavals of the late 1960s and, in a neat historical irony, just as the Berlin Wall was collapsing under the weight of public opinion.[2] By that time, Habermas' pessimism regarding the future of the public sphere had come to seem unnecessarily bleak – not only to liberals, but to the New Left as well.

Perhaps the most trenchant New Left critic of *The Structural Transformation of the Public Sphere* is the American social theorist Nancy

Fraser, who charges 'not only that Habermas idealizes the liberal public sphere but also that he fails to examine other, nonliberal, nonbourgeois, competing public spheres'. Drawing on the revisionist historiography that has emerged since the 1960s – much of it aimed at recovering the counter-histories of workers, racial and ethnic minorities, and women – Fraser questions four assumptions of the bourgeois public sphere described by Habermas:

- The assumption that it is possible for interlocutors in a public sphere to bracket status differentials and to deliberate as if they were social equals
- The assumption ... that a single, comprehensive public sphere is always preferable to a nexus of multiple publics
- The assumption that discourse in public spheres should be restricted to deliberation about the common good, and that the appearance of private interests and private issues is always undesirable
- The assumption that a functioning democratic public sphere requires a sharp separation between civil society and the state[3]

Against these assumptions, Fraser contends that social inequality persists informally in the public sphere even though formal exclusions have been abolished; that it is often useful for subordinated social groups to form what she calls 'subaltern counterpublics' in order to rally their members and train them in the arts of publicity; that it is sometimes necessary to make economic, domestic and other so-called 'private' matters public in order to promote social justice; and that too rigid a separation between civil society and the state is incompatible with participatory democracy.

Habermas' response to such criticism has been to sketch a more adequate model of the liberal public sphere, acknowledging the impact of 'new social movements' like feminism and the European 'green' parties while continuing to insist upon the limits of public opinion. In *Between Facts and Norms*, he defines the public sphere as 'a network for communicating information and points of view' that eventually 'coalesce into topically specified *public* opinions'.[4] In modern societies, this network – thanks to the development of the mass media – extends far beyond the face-to-face communication that characterises private life. For this reason, it is a convenient tool for those who would use money or power to manipulate public opinion. Nevertheless, the modern public sphere still belongs to what Habermas calls the 'lifeworld' – the world of everyday life in which cultural values, social solidarity and personal identity are formed – as opposed to the autonomous 'steering systems' that dominate modern society, namely the market and the state. Such steering systems are made necessary, Habermas admits, by the sheer complexity of modern economic and political problems, which overtax the public's limited problem-solving capacity. Yet attempts to solve these problems by systemic means – by means, for example, of the welfare state in the West or the free market in the East – have produced various crises in the lifeworld: loss of meaning, anomie, psychiatric disorders. That is why the public sphere continues to play a vital mediating role in modern society. In Habermas' terms, the public sphere functions as a *sensor* for the economic and political systems, alerting them to potential crises in the lifeworld, even as it serves as a *barrier* to corporate and governmental intrusion into the lifeworld.[5]

The institutional precondition for a genuine public sphere, Habermas observes, is a vibrant civil society made up of associations (churches, political parties, labour unions) and social movements (feminism, ethnic subcultures, the ecological movement) that are free from government as well as corporate control. Where such associations and movements are weak or non-existent, the media of public communication will be controlled by the state (as in totalitarian societies) or by business interests (as in democratic societies where civil society is still in its infancy or has entered a period of decline). A society in which such associations and movements are strong, on the other hand, is capable of sustaining a variety of 'autonomous public spheres', each of which, though limited by locale or topic, remains open in principle to the others. That is why Habermas continues to speak of a 'universal' public sphere embracing the many 'partial' public spheres found in civil society.[6] Of course, not all modern associations and social movements are democratic in character; witness the rise of fundamentalist movements that are at once modern and authoritarian. 'A robust civil society', Habermas admits, 'can develop only in the context of a liberal political culture and the corresponding patterns of socialization, and on the basis of an integral private sphere; it can blossom only in an already rationalized lifeworld', that is, a lifeworld in which cultural traditions are open to criticism.[7]

As he did in *The Structural Transformation*, Habermas continues to distinguish the 'political' from the 'literary' public sphere. The function of the political public sphere is to alert those in power to problems in the political and economic systems. But such problems are first experienced privately by the individuals who are the clients and consumers of those systems. As Habermas notes, 'Problems voiced in the public sphere first become visible when they are mirrored in personal life experiences. To the extent that these experiences find their concise expression in the languages of religion, art, and literature, the "literary" public sphere in the broader sense, which is specialized for the articulation of values and world disclosure, is intertwined with the political public sphere'.[8] Thus Habermas attributes an important political function to religion, art and literature, all of which serve to translate private experience into public discourse.

Although Habermas assigns religion to the literary public sphere, he does not mean to imply that it is, like art and literature, a specialised form of discourse. On the contrary, he supposes that religion, along with education and the family, is the very foundation of social life. 'Specialized systems of action and knowledge that are differentiated within the lifeworld', he claims,

> fall into one of two categories. Systems like religion, education, and the family become associated with the general reproductive functions of the lifeworld (that is, with cultural reproduction, social integration, or socialization). Systems like science, morality, and art take up different validity aspects of everyday communicative action (truth, rightness, veracity). The public sphere, however, is specialized in neither of these two ways.[9]

What distinguishes religion from art and literature in Habermas' mind, then, is that it continues to perform everyday functions that are necessary for the reproduction of the lifeworld – the transmission of cultural values, the maintenance of social solidarity and the formation of personal identity. Art and literature, by contrast, constitute for Habermas a specialised branch of modern culture governed by 'veracity' or sincerity, one of the fundamental values transmitted by religion (as well as by education and the family).

That religion will always be necessary for the reproduction of the lifeworld is, for Habermas, a dubious assertion.[10] Yet religion, as José Casanova of the New School for Social Research has reminded us, is playing an increasingly prominent public role in the modern world. In *Public Religions in the Modern World* (1994), Casanova observes that the 'new religious movements' of the 1980s, including the Solidarity movement in Poland, the Brazilian People's Church, and the Moral Majority in the United States, offer compelling evidence of the 'deprivatisation' of religion – a sociological phenomenon that runs counter to the theory of secularisation as it has developed since the Enlightenment. That theory, Casanova explains, embraces three separate theses: the *marginalisation* thesis, which holds that religion is in permanent decline because it is incompatible with modernity; the *privatisation* thesis, which holds that religion is compatible with modernity, but only when it retreats to the private sphere; and the *differentiation* thesis, which holds that modernity requires the separation of secular spheres (the state, the market) from the religious sphere. The new religious movements of the 1980s, Casanova argues, prove that the first two theses, at any rate, rest on a weak empirical foundation. Not only is religion on the rise in many societies, but it is reclaiming a public role in those societies.

In light of these developments, the secularisation theses can be seen as veiled prescriptions that religion *should* be marginalised, privatised and differentiated. For this reason, Casanova offers a normative as well as an empirical defence of public religion. The key to Casanova's argument is his acceptance of the third thesis, which prescribes a differentiation of secular and religious spheres leading to the disestablishment of religion and the guarantee of religious freedom. Affirmation of such differentiation is, for Casanova, the condition of legitimacy of public religion. 'This condition is met', he insists, 'and, therefore, the deprivatization of religion can be justified in at least three instances':

> a) When religion enters the public sphere to protect not only its own freedom of religion but all modern freedoms and rights. ... The active role of the Catholic church in processes of democratization in Spain, Poland, and Brazil may serve to illustrate this instance.
> b) When religion enters the public sphere to question and contest the absolute lawful autonomy of the secular spheres and their claims to be organized ... without regard to extraneous ethical or moral considerations. The Pastoral Letters of the American Catholic bishops questioning the 'morality' of the arms race and of the state's nuclear policies, as well as the 'justice' and inhuman consequences of a capitalist economic system, ... exemplify this second instance.
> c) When religion enters the public sphere to protect the traditional lifeworld from administrative or juridical state penetration, and in the process opens up issues of norm and will formation to the public. ... The public mobilization of the Moral Majority and the Catholic public stand on abortion in support of 'the right to life' are examples of this third instance.[11]

Not only is public religion justified in these instances, Casanova hints, but it may well be necessary to prevent the self-destruction of modern society. 'It would be profoundly ironic', he concludes, 'if, after all the beatings it has received from modernity, religion could somehow unintentionally help modernity save itself'.[12]

If religion and literature both speak what Habermas calls an 'existential language' – a language in which personal experience achieves public expression – then perhaps literature, too, can help modernity save itself. The question is whether literature, like religion, has been privatised in the modern world – and, if so, whether it, too, is capable of 'deprivatisation', of re-entering the public sphere. These questions have been posed by Terry Eagleton in *The Function of Criticism* (1984), which marks the first application of Habermas' concept of the public sphere to the history of English literary criticism.[13] Contrasting the public role of eighteenth-century arbiters of taste like Addison and Steele with that of today's book reviewers and academic critics, Eagleton declares 'that criticism today lacks all substantive social function. It is either part of the public relations branch of the literary industry, or a matter wholly internal to the academies'.[14] Nevertheless, Eagleton concludes his survey on a hopeful note, celebrating the birth of a new social movement that has changed the publishing industry and the academy as well as society at large. 'In a striking historical irony', he observes, 'a marginalization of the "intimate" realm closely related to the decline of the public sphere has led to a fresh resurgence of that realm in the form of a new counterpublic sphere: that of feminist discourse and practice'.[15] In other words, the increasing penetration of the state and the market into domestic life – the traditional sphere of feminine influence – has forced women to 'go public' with their concerns, thereby reinvigorating criticism.

The concept of a 'feminist counterpublic sphere' has been taken up by Rita Felski and other feminist critics.[16] Thus far, however, only a handful of critics have attempted to analyse the interplay of literature and religion in the public sphere. One of these critics is Robert Detweiler, whose *Uncivil Rites: American Fiction, Religion, and the Public Sphere* (1996) purports to uncover 'an ancient religious comprehension' that is still 'operating in the contemporary American public realm'.[17] This primitive religious mentality manifests itself in such ritualised behaviours as scapegoating, seduction and abandonment, and apocalyptic violence – rituals which, as Detweiler points out, shape the narrative structure of many fictional representations of public events and issues, including Robert Coover's *The Public Burning*, with its depiction of McCarthyism; Toni Morrison's *Beloved*, with its depiction of sexual abuse; and Philip Caputo's *Indian Country*, with its depiction of the Vietnam War. By exposing the archaic rituals underlying contemporary history, Detweiler suggests, these novels subvert the power of religion in American public life. But what enables them to do so, he adds, is yet another ritual with a religious origin: the ritual of confession, in which characters open their hearts to readers.[18]

Detweiler's approach is a postmodernist version of what used to be called 'myth' or 'archetypal' criticism, which treats works of literature as variations on a handful of themes found in ancient religion and the collective unconscious. What makes *Uncivil Rites* unique is Detweiler's extension of such criticism to politics itself – his suggestion that American public life is riddled with archaic religious impulses which need to be 'demythologised' through fictional representation. The chief limitation of this type of criticism – apart from the plausibility of more mundane explanations of American history – is that it emphasises the vestiges of *premodern* religion in contemporary public life at the expense of the specifically *modern* forms of public religion described by Casanova. Take Casanova's example of the Moral Majority (or its successor, the Christian Coalition). From Detweiler's perspective, such religious movements exhibit a primitive compulsion to externalise evil and demonise the Other. For Casanova, on the other hand, they represent a legitimate protest against the intrusion of the state and the market into the traditional lifeworld. While these explanations are not necessarily incompatible, they derive from different approaches to the study of religion: one from historical anthropology and Jungian psychology, the other from contemporary social and political theory – more specifically, from the work of Habermas. The first approach, with its emphasis on primitive religion, is readily transferable to the study of literature, if not public life. The question is whether the second approach, with its emphasis on modern public religion, will prove to be as fruitful for literary criticism as it has been for social and political theory. Our hope is that the essays in this volume will begin to answer this question.

The essays that follow are arranged in order of generality, beginning with close commentaries on particular texts and ending with general analyses of literature's place in the public sphere. In the opening essay, Lionel Basney re-reads *King Lear* as a critique of the contemporary public sphere – or, more accurately, of the economic and political conditions on which that sphere depends. These conditions, Basney contends, have produced a sense of cultural dislocation that finds its image in the dislocated world of *Lear* – a world in which communal bonds of love are dissolved, in which public resources are used to private advantage, in which subalterns are reduced to a condition of mere subsistence. Through its egregious representation of these dislocations, *Lear* snatches the ideological blinders from the public sphere, reminding us of the human cost of our technological civilisation and the importance of preserving communities of obligation.

Like Basney, Paul Contino draws a literary classic – *The Brothers Karamazov* – into the arena of contemporary public discourse, relating the humiliation of the imprisoned Dmitri to the inhumanity of the modern criminal justice system. At a time when the rights of suspects and prisoners are under fire and prison construction has become virtually the only public project taxpayers are willing to subsidise, Dostoevsky's novel becomes an urgent plea for a more humane approach, one in which even convicted criminals are attended to as persons. For Dostoevsky, the model of such an approach was the Christian practice of confession, however antithetical to the penal procedures of the secular state.

In his reading of Melville's classic tale 'Bartleby the Scrivener', Clarence Walhout explores the ethical question embodied in the title character, namely, the question of our responsibility for those who are unable or unwilling to function within a capitalist economy. What Bartleby's society lacks, Walhout hypothesises, is a public sphere in which this ethical question can be asked and possible answers debated. The institutions that might have supported such a sphere, notably the church, merely transmit the individualist ideology that underwrites laissez-faire capitalism. What 'Bartleby' cries out for, Walhout concludes, is a recovery of the utopian dimension of religion as a source of social criticism and political change.

Finally, Pamela Corpron Parker examines Elizabeth Gaskell's *The Life of Charlotte Brontë* as a contribution to the emergence of a female counter-public sphere, a sphere in which female public identity can be forged. By publishing the details of Brontë's private life, Gaskell also publicised the dilemma of the female author, torn between the conflicting demands of domestic life and professional ambition. Gaskell's response to this dilemma, Parker shows, was to defend female authorship as a sacred calling, counselling the feminised Christian values of mercy, sympathy and tenderness in opposition to the harsh masculine judgement on Brontë during her lifetime.

The next cluster of essays is somewhat broader in scope, surveying the careers and *oeuvres* of particular writers who have sought to enter the public sphere. Alan Jacobs begins with a somewhat pessimistic assessment of the power of literature to reconstitute the public sphere. Reviewing W. H. Auden's experiments with working-class forms of drama, song and light verse in the 1930s, Jacobs concludes that Auden's dream of forging a unified culture for a new era of social democracy was doomed to failure. Not only did Auden lack the talent for dramatic composition, but, more importantly, he lost faith in the socially transformative power of poetry itself. Like T. S. Eliot before him, Auden came to the conclusion that it was not the poet's job to reconstruct society, but the theologian's – a conclusion that freed him to pursue the less ambitious, more intimate verse of his later years.

Next, Michael Vander Weele analyses the enormously influential short stories of Raymond Carver as reflections of the decline of public life in the United States. After comparing Carver's famously spare style to the rhythms of working-class speech recorded by Studs Terkel, Vander Weele examines the way Carver's narrators typically invite the reader to help make sense of the tale, only to withhold meaning in the end, illustrating both the need for and the absence of shared discourse in individualistic America. Only in a few stories, notably 'Cathedral' and 'A Small, Good Thing', is meaningful communication between teller and auditor realised. The conditions of such communication, Vander Weele suggests, are also the conditions of a genuine public sphere – including meaningful economic and religious association, as theologian John Calvin, writing long before Weber and Habermas, affirmed.

In her essay on the contemporary Native American writer Sherman Alexie, Janet Blumberg explores the tensions that arise when 'subaltern' writers gain access to the public sphere of the dominant society – a sphere from which subaltern populations have historically been excluded, or admitted only at the expense of their ethnic or cultural identities. For the larger public, Alexie's suspicion and anger towards whites can appear, as Blumberg testifies, to forestall communication. For Alexie himself, on the other hand, the public's embrace can feel suffocating to the extent that it is premised on the commodification of Native American culture. Yet it is through these very tensions, Blumberg reminds us, that both writers and public spheres develop more expansive and democratic identities.

Lastly, James Champion contrasts the shallowness of contemporary American culture – including its market-dominated public sphere – with the ontological depth revealed in the work of Denis Johnson. Resisting the relentless commodification of human beings, Johnson pushes both poetic and narrative forms toward the limits of expression, thereby intimating a world beyond the reach of market – a world accessible in moments of imaginative experience, but impossible to capture in stable form. Inasmuch as such moments tend, in Johnson's poems and fictions, to be moments in which absence is negated, they mark him as a latter-day mystic and 'apophatic' theologian, seeking God, as Champion puts it, in the 'gaps and lacunas' of perception and thought. It is through this *via negativa*, Champion suggests, that religion must go in order to renew a sense of mystery in our public culture.

The final cluster of essays is still broader in scope, examining historical and theoretical dimensions of the public spheres in which literature is performed and criticised. In his essay on contemporary French poetry, Glenn Fetzer reviews the debate over the so-called 'crise de vers' in the post-war era – a debate prompted by the difficulty of contemporary verse and the shrinking market for poetry. What the debate reveals, Fetzer suggests, is the creative dissonance at the heart of French culture – a dissonance that is mirrored and magnified in contemporary French poetry. Thus what might appear to be the demise of a public for poetry turns out to be, paradoxically, a mark of the pluralism and openness of French culture.

Susan VanZanten Gallagher examines the process by which public spheres develop in postcolonial societies. Taking South Africa as her example, Gallagher shows how both literature and religion have contributed to the emergence of a public sphere in the post-apartheid era: first by supplying a language of protest against apartheid, then by forging a new, pluralistic South African identity. Some works, such as the popular apartheid-era township drama *Woza Albert!* have fulfilled both of these functions: initially part of the 'theatre of resistance', *Woza Albert!* continues to be performed in the post-apartheid era as part of the 'theatre of development'. The great promise of the new South African public sphere, Gallagher concludes, is that it will retain its multi-racial, non-exclusionary character, enabling South Africa to avoid the retributive violence that marks the emergence of many postcolonial states.

My own contribution to the volume examines the role played by Edward Said, the distinguished Palestinian literary critic and political activist, in the international turmoil that engulfed Salman Rushdie after the publication of *The Satanic Verses*. On the one hand, Said proved to be one of Rushdie's most outspoken and courageous defenders, upholding secularism and assailing fundamentalism in a variety of venues. On the other hand, he considered the 'Rushdie Affair' to be a reaction to Western domination of the global public sphere, with its caricatures of Islamic 'terrorists' and 'fundamentalists'. The problem, I argue, is that Said's rhetoric perpetuates the secularist/fundamentalist dichotomy, rather than recognising the importance of public religion in mediating the conflict.

The penultimate essay in the volume is Lambert Zuidervaart's analysis of 'new genre' public art – art that challenges the modernist ideal of the autonomous work, together with the institutions of high culture that perpetuate it. Deliberately crossing traditional borders between work and audience, between high art and popular culture, new genre public art embodies the creative tension between the modern ideal of authenticity and the equally valid ideal – anathema to modernists – of social responsibility. By opening the institutions of the art world to non-traditional audiences and inviting their active co-creation of the work of art, Zuidervaart contends, 'new genre' public art projects a new, more democratic culture.

The volume concludes with Colin Jager's attempt to vindicate Hannah Arendt's theory of the public sphere as a space of conflict, suffering and sacrifice – conditions of public life that have, Jager observes, been neglected by more sanguine theorists in the Habermasian tradition, such as Seyla Benhabib. It is only by acknowledging such violence, Jager argues, that we can hope to realise the utopian public sphere envisioned by Benhabib, one based on dialogue and solidarity. And that, ultimately, is why literature is necessary to the public sphere. Drawing on Arendt's concept of storytelling, Jager argues that stories of sacrifice, by making suffering public, also make forgiveness possible – without which the violence of politics would render public life impossible.

The publication of this volume of essays – in so far as it contributes to the 'deprivatisation' of Christianity in the literary public sphere – is itself an expression of modern public religion. As Christian literary critics, we cannot help but observe that the *marginalisation* of criticism – its transformation into a specialised academic discipline – has coincided with its *secularisation*. Once critics revered literature as a source of spiritual consolation and moral order in a post-Christian culture; now they analyse it as a product of linguistic codes and ideological contradictions. To the extent that this transformation has put an end to the Arnoldian religion of culture, it has no doubt been salutary for criticism. The same goes for the new critical interest in *cultural difference*, which marks a historic opening-up of the publishing industry as well as the academy to African-American, working class, gay and lesbian, and other 'subaltern counterpublics'. In this context, it is worth noting that religion, like race, class and gender, remains a key sociological variable in the literature and politics of most modern societies. But our attention to such variables – like that of Marxists, feminists and other 'engaged' critics – is not merely an attempt to rescue criticism from political irrelevance. Above all, it is a matter of conviction: the conviction that Christianity, through the literary traditions and works it has shaped, continues to be a prophetic resource for modern public life.

Notes

1 'Buying Books: Theory vs. Practice', *New York Times*, 20 June 1996, p. A13.
2 J. Habermas, *The Structural Transformation of the Public Sphere*, T. Burger and F. Lawrence (trans.) (Cambridge: MIT, 1989). Habermas' 1964 encyclopedia article on the public sphere was translated into English in 1974 ('The Public Sphere: An Encyclopedia Article', *New German Critique*, 1.3 [Fall 1974] 49–55).
3 N. Fraser, 'Rethinking the Public Sphere: A Contribution to the Critique of Actually Existing Democracy', in *Habermas and the Public Sphere*, C. Calhoun (ed.) (Cambridge: MIT, 1992) pp. 117–18.
4 J. Habermas, *Between Facts and Norms: Contributions to a Discourse Theory of Law and Democracy*, W. Rehg (trans.) (Cambridge: MIT, 1996) p. 360.
5 J. Habermas, *The Philosophical Discourse of Modernity*, F. Lawrence (trans.) (Cambridge: MIT, 1987) p. 364.
6 Ibid., p. 360.
7 Habermas, *Between Facts*, p. 371.
8 Ibid., p. 365.
9 Ibid., p. 360.
10 J. Habermas, 'Transcendence from Within, Transcendence in this World', in *Habermas, Modernity, and Public Theology*, D. S. Browning and F. Schüssler Fiorenza (eds) (New York: Crossroad, 1992) pp. 226–48.
11 J. Casanova, *Public Religions in the Modern World* (Chicago: Univ. of Chicago Press, 1994) pp. 57–8.
12 Ibid., p. 234.
13 Writing before *The Structural Transformation of the Public Sphere* had been translated, Eagleton drew on P. U. Hohendahl's analysis of the literary public sphere in *The Institution of Criticism* (Ithaca: Cornell Univ. Press, 1982). Hohendahl, whose essays on Habermas have appeared regularly in such English-language journals as *New German Critique* and *New Left Review*, deserves much of the credit for bringing Habermas' work on the public sphere to the attention of English-speaking critics.
14 T. Eagleton, *The Function of Criticism* (London: Verso, 1984) p. 7.
15 Ibid., p. 118.
16 R. Felski, *Beyond Feminist Aesthetics: Feminist Literature and Social Change* (Cambridge: Harvard Univ. Press, 1989).
17 R. Detweiler, *Uncivil Rites: American Fiction, Religion, and the Public Sphere* (Urbana: Univ. of Illinois Press, 1996) p. 5.
18 Ibid., pp. 207–10.

2
Enacting the Bonds of Love in *King Lear*

Lionel Basney

Reading is always adaptation, but some texts are more adaptable than others to certain cultural moments. So *King Lear* to ours. The remarkable fact is not only the quantity of discussion the play inspires – that may be just follow-the-leader – but the philosophical and even theological reach of the discussion. To put the matter simply, we feel compelled to quiz *Lear* about the forms of traditional civilised life, the duties and obligations that have long mediated between our actions and our understanding of the world. *Lear* was once read as a triumphant if wrenching vindication of these forms. Now the play is commonly read as an equally wrenching exposure or evacuation of them. In either mood, however, what inspires our reading is the depth of our own cultural dislocation.

The traditional moral ties of child to parent or subject to sovereign, what K. R. Monroe calls 'canonical expectations',[1] are taken for granted in hundreds of western fictions. But *Lear* does not take them for granted. It meets our actual dislocation with an imagined dislocation, perhaps even more profound, of its own. The play opens (as Coleridge noted) as if it were a fairy tale: once there was an old king who had three daughters. ... Being elderly and male, a parent and a king, Lear epitomises the authority of canonical expectations. Therefore, when he exerts this authority toward the wrong ends, the errors that cost him his own security and sanity seem to put the entire fabric of this social world into question. If a king cannot grasp the basic requirements of a polity, then what is a king and what is he for? If a parent sets out to be worse than a cannibal to his own child, then what are families and would we do better to abandon them and the kinds of loyalty that hold them together?

While Lear emerges from his collapse into a state of aboriginal licence, where he is child and shaman, the social world itself falls apart. This collapse is registered by the play's language, though the familiar generalisation that 'language fails' is too general. Shakespeare's dramatic writing is nowhere more powerful, but what it shows above all is how the *characters'* language fails. In *Lear* the structures of common humanity that allow people to make sense to each other have been damaged and perverted; there seem to be no dependable networks of loyalty, no circles of sympathy, no practical consensus. Deeply beautiful and accurate speech occurs, along with radical acts of love. But the social context has disappeared. Such words and actions are exceptional, or, in something like the New Testament sense, scandalous. They occur in a wasteland.

But isn't this our own predicament? The brutal selfishness Lear releases into his kingdom is like our relentless use of public resources for private advantage. The collapse of Lear's polity reminds us of the impotence of ours: we have relativised our cultural norms to gain individual autonomy, only to find that any consensus allowing for broad common action seems beyond hope. We have no arena in which to debate the direction and meanings of our practical culture. Yet the economic and technological powers we cannot interpret proceed without restraint and are terrible in effect.

It is, of course, such an arena that Habermas' public sphere is meant to supply. His is a discursive commons depending only on the norms of communication itself and not, therefore, on canonical expectations about morality or social roles. What has troubled many about the public sphere, however, is that it cannot account for its own privileges. It seems to depend on special political and economic conditions that are themselves not innocent. Habermas recognises that the secular state and market that gave us (or some of us) material security and a democracy of information and opinion also aspire to colonise and commodify these gifts. State and market obey their own mandates, which say that the lifeworld, like everything else, must be brought under state and market control. The public sphere meant to protect the lifeworld exists at the sufferance of forces that put the lifeworld in danger.

There is an obvious anachronism in reading our cultural predicament, and Habermas' response, in the vicinity of *Lear*, since *Lear* is a pre-modern play. But *Lear*'s representation of the testing of canonical expectations is so extreme that the text seems to question the preconditions of any society, not merely pre-modern ones. *Lear* deals, in particular, with three dimensions of society relevant to our predicament. It concerns, first, the lifeworld itself. Though the play opens with a political error, the division of the kingdom, politics then recedes to a kind of middle background. What transpires in the foreground is individual and domestic, physical and psychological life – parents and children, physical need and torment, adultery and social aspiration, illness and cure. The confusion of the state plays in and through the articulations of personal life.

Lear concerns, second, the voice of the 'subaltern' or socially invisible person. In this, *Lear* is not unique among Shakespeare's plays. This theme is an inheritance from medieval dramas such as the Towneley *Second Shepherds Play* and ultimately from a long Augustinian strain of Christian political thought.[2] Much of *Lear*'s Pyrrhic goodness, much of what moral realism persists, is owed to characters with no names, to the banished and victimised. The eighteenth-century public sphere was a bourgeois institution, but *Lear* suggests how the inapt, the culturally deprived, can speak in the public sphere, can speak without having their speech distorted or co-opted.

The play concerns, finally, nature itself and its meaning as a condition of the lifeworld's existence. Habermas has little room for this theme, largely because he concurs with Adorno and Horkheimer (and with late Marxists such as Frederic Jameson) that capitalism has abolished nature as an analytical category.[3] In *Lear* nature asserts itself, as elemental force and as the condition of subsistence, and is wedded to the theme of the subaltern. For it is the subaltern – *Lear*'s servants and tenants, the Californian migrant worker, the Palestinian labourer in Israel – who provides subsistence labour for society. To speak as *Lear* allows the subaltern to speak is to admit the voice not only of an excluded class but of an excluded reality basic to all cultural life.

'My very deed of love'

As a play, *Lear*'s unpacking of canonical expectations is accomplished by formal means – perhaps most of all by disproportion of effect. Lear's disproportionate fury generates the shock of the opening scene and, by extension, of the whole plot, for his outburst against Cordelia initiates the consequences that will finally encompass her death. Violence balloons from insufficient or coincidental causes. Explanations are impossible. If we sense this, it is clear also to the characters – to some with limited grasp, like Gloucester, and also to those, like Edgar, whose understanding grows. The sense of disproportion is not incidental. The action as a whole seems to force on us a fundamental disproportion, between the obligations the characters owe one another and the effects of failing to pay. Obligations are stated and staged in the first scene, then refused or traduced, and the consequences comprise, in a sense, the rest of the play – family conflict, anger, brutality, psychosis, war, adultery, murder, suicide and accidental death. But the effects seem too large. Or – to put it the other way around – the obligations seem too simple, too spare, to control the forces that produce such havoc.

The opposite of fulfilled obligation in *Lear* is not only heartache; it is the disappearance of humanity. 'Monster ingratitude' (1.5.39) is 'more hideous' than the 'sea monster' (1.4.257–9); Goneril 'bemonsters' herself, says Albany, who fears that 'Humanity must perforce prey on itself / Like monsters of the deep' (4.2.64, 50–1).[4] A daughter becomes an entity 'in corrupted blood', a bacterium (2.4.225). The mouth tears the hand for proffering food (3.4.15–16). Nature will not acknowledge the causes of such effects.

The obligations set forward in the play are taken, then, to be (in some sense) constitutive of humanity. They are natural to us – not that the physical order dictates or even models them to us, nor that they are instinctive, but that outside them humanity is not itself. The obligations the play appeals to are relatively few and anthropologically basic: parent/child (male/female and male/male), master/servant (including feudal superior/dependent), sovereign/subject, guest/host. These are the primary forms in the play of our canonical expectations about human life. Not that the play affords them any unambiguous enactment. These obligations are claimed, challenged, rejected, pretended, misused, revised. They are in evidence negatively, through the effects of their loss.

This fact in itself, however, implies to some readers that these obligations do not 'constitute humanity', or that any 'humanity' they might constitute would be merely an ideological construct. Jonathan Dollimore, for instance, takes *Lear*'s upheavals to mean that 'the cherished norms of human kindness ... have no "natural" sanction at all'; the play's 'catastrophic redistribution of power and property' shows that power and property are the *conditions* of any human kindness we might aspire to.[5] But it is hard to see in what the 'catastrophe' consists, if human kindness is not to be a criterion; and it is equally hard to see why success (considering that Dollimore takes the 'redistribution' to be 'catastrophic') should be the criterion instead. Dollimore oversimplifies: the obligations of human kindness are not *either* natural and inevitable *or* artificial and arbitrary. They are *natural and not inevitable*. The play's claim is not that these obligations guarantee happiness or even decent conduct, but rather that in view of the precariousness of human life they are humanity's identifying mark and stay. It is not, with them, success. It is, without them, nothing: monstrosity.

Many readings of *Lear* offer that as the burden of the play: nothing, moral cheat or metaphysical absence. But it is as easy to exaggerate the play's denials as its consolations, and equally sentimental. What the play seems to offer is a more mixed and uncomforting predicament: enormous danger, fragile stay. This quality is felt from the first scene. Announcing his retirement, Lear divides England and assigns a third to each of his daughters, pending her public profession of love for him. Lear's action puts the issue of obligation in two ways: he requires his daughters to fulfil their obligation to love him by obeying an obligation to speak this love. But the second requirement clearly falsifies the first. It enforces what can only genuinely be offered, a profession of private devotion, and enforces this in the presence of an exorbitant public reward. The inevitable result is to turn whatever private devotion the daughters feel into public manoeuvre. Rhetorical success, measured by Lear's gratification, will be repaid not only with wealth but with the power to dictate the conditions of public life, the power to make a new kingdom in the shell of the old, to become the new Lears.

Goneril and Regan respond by fulfilling their obligations, which is how they and Lear (probably in different ways) see what they do (1.1.282–3). They provide, that is, doses of hyperbolic love-language, to which Lear responds almost automatically, by awarding them the kingdom. But the older daughters' frankly cynical 'obedience' puts Cordelia in an impossible dilemma. As in a fairy tale, she is virtuous, and her virtue demands that she articulate honestly the facts of her relationship with her father. What Cordelia does, however, is unexpected: she raises the issue of obligation itself in an unprotected, almost stark way. She states the moral framework of what she has to say. Clearly, as S. L. Goldberg remarks, Lear wants something more spontaneous than this.[6] So do we. We might like Cordelia better if she answered Lear with some impulsive tenderness. But the language of explicit feeling has been monopolised and traduced by Goneril and Regan. Their laboured flourishes occupy the space where Cordelia might have used an endearment. In this mode she can say just what she does say: nothing.

But those readers who insist on the force of the 'nothings' that reverberate between Lear and Cordelia never quote what Cordelia goes on to say. This omission leaves the impression that she feels no love or will not profess it. But she does both:

> Good my lord,
> You have begot me, bred me, loved me. I
> Return those duties back as are right fit,
> Obey you, love you, and most honor you. (1.1.95–8)

In her predicament Cordelia articulates, more schematically than she will (or will need to) again, the priority in her mind of obligation as a form of love. The language sounds contractual but is not: a contract is concluded on the basis of self-interest and can be withdrawn on the same basis. Cordelia means obligation as the unretractable offer of care – reciprocal according to pattern, but if not reciprocated then obligatory none the less. The basis of this obligation is not self-interest, nor the self's security against exploitation, but the intent to constitute a community of care.

This is not, however, what Lear wishes to hear. Goneril and Regan's rhetoric has released him from reciprocal obligations by winding him into a self-regarding cocoon: 'I am alone felicitate', Regan has said, 'In your dear Highness' love' (1.1.75–6), which provokes Cordelia's dry response that Regan may owe her husband some regard (99–100). Cordelia envisions – or, actually, recognises – community, and her vision is consequently practical in a way Regan's is not. It is realistic in the practices it implies. First, Cordelia articulates a specifically daughterly love in contrast to her sisters' ambivalently erotic vows. Second, Cordelia reminds Lear that their relationship has a history that will necessarily affect the future. Third, she reminds him that this history is not of words only but of actions, of commitments fulfilled in doing. And, finally, Cordelia points out that such actions are reciprocal and therefore that Lear may owe her something harder to pay than a slice of the kingdom. By bringing her profession of love to the test of obligation, Cordelia sketches out the practice of love – what it entails, what it may expect, how it is to be enacted.

Lear, of course, will not reciprocate. Cordelia's speech sends him into hysteria. He no longer wishes to be obliged. The retirement he plans will afford him kingly status without kingship; he will inhabit the representation 'king' without doing a king's work. He assumes that the behaviour of those around him will continue to reflect this identity back to him – 'The name and all th' addition to a king' (1.1.136). This is what a king who acts like a king may expect. But Lear rejects the practice; he will become a consumer of representations. It is not long, however, before the residual content of these representations begins to wear away. 'Who is it that can tell me who I am?' he demands, rhetorically, assuming that everyone can, and the Fool catches the very quality of the exhausted representation by responding, 'Lear's shadow' (1.4.227–8). Having repeatedly tried to elicit the expected response from a world now numb to him ('I think the world's asleep', 47–8), Lear begins to threaten: 'Thou shalt find / That I'll resume [my] shape' (307–8). But of course he cannot. His shape depends on acknowledgement, and this depends on – in fact, is constituted by – the reciprocal obligations he has rejected. If he will not be a king, Goneril and Regan, at least, will not be subjects to make him one.

'The basest and most poorest shape'

Lear is full of the vocabulary of relationship and obligation, but after Act I this language is increasingly distorted and exploited. Lear's insistence on 'shape and duty' turns increasingly into outcry, as he mimes and begs for acknowledgement. Apart from Lear, the forms of obligation become the property of characters on the make. Maligning his elder brother, Edgar, Edmund scripts himself lines about the bond of child and father and receives the recompense of his lie in the same vocabulary ('you have shown your father / A childlike office'. 'It was my duty', 2.1.104–6).

Lear has lost the good of this language; his enemies use it mendaciously. This does not mean, however, that faithfulness and care have been removed from this world. All assurance of good is indeed removed from Lear, but not from us, since we witness the expedients goodness adopts to survive. In Kent and Edgar loyalty and care are active, though to continue they must go underground. The disguise of goodness is the principle of Lear's new kingdom. The disguise, further, is social, and consists of humiliation and self-humiliation. Kent, banished in the first scene, returns to protect Lear, but to do so he must descend from his standing as an earl into Iago's role, the bluff, cynical, quarrelsome soldier, and from there into the humiliation of the stocks, which make him, as the Fool points out, a fool (2.4.85).

But Edgar is the play's crucial example of strategic relocation, because his descent changes Edgar himself. Disowned by Gloucester, his father, through Edmund's conspiracy, Edgar disguises himself, first as poor Tom the homeless beggar, then as an anonymous but valiant bumpkin (Act 4), and finally as a nameless knight-avenger (Act 5). Poor Tom is the crucial identity. As Tom, Edgar is a chorus; even more than the Fool, Edgar is a character who acts and comments, alternately active and passive in relation to others. According to

Robert Weimann's influential analysis of Shakespeare's stage, Edgar/poor Tom occupies both *platea* (downstage) and *locus* (upstage); he can be involved in the action and yet share the audience's distance from it, a complexity of positioning that reaches its peak in Lear's mock trial in Act 3.[7] And this complexity affects Edgar: seeing the action from different vantages, a victim at one moment and an avenger at another, Edgar is the play's main figure of moral growth. Events make him 'pregnant to good pity' (4.6.226) even as he struggles to refine his growing awareness and act appropriately. It is of consequence for the play as a whole, finally, that Edgar is not a detached or cynical chorus (like Iago or Falstaff) but a sympathetic expositor who, like Cordelia, feels the force of obligation.

Two things about poor Tom, Edgar's beggar-role, have been clarified by recent scholarship. One is that Edgar is being simply accurate to the social landscape of 1608 when he describes the class he is joining:

> The country gives me proof and precedent
> Of Bedlam beggars who with roaring voices ...
> Sometimes with lunatic bans, sometimes with prayers,
> Enforce their charity (2.3.13–14, 19–20)

Though statistics are lacking or confused, it is clear that such beggars were many in Shakespeare's England and that they were visible, obtrusive and persistent in 'enforcing' that 'charity' which was still understood in theological terms as a debt of piety. The second fact about poor Tom complicates this picture: the Bedlam beggar was a role the poor, and the con man, could play for profit. Most of Edgar's pretending – the nakedness, the insanity, even 'Tom's a-cold' (3.4.57) – can be found in pamphlets about fraudulent begging. But this does not necessarily invalidate the role as a sign of social fact, as William Carroll points out: 'The self-mutilations of fraudulent beggars ... become the self-confirming stigmata of those excluded from society; they write their humiliation at large on their skins as an acceptance of what the social order has already inscribed them to be'.[8]

Edgar's participation in this role is more complicated yet. Though as poor Tom he is without his normal resources as the heir of an earl, Edgar has been inscribed one of the aristocracy. He does not 'accept' poor Tom but adopts him, hides in him. Edgar exchanges his powerlessness as persecuted Edgar for a powerlessness which allows him to wait, to learn from 'known and feeling sorrows' (4.6.225), to prepare for the moment of action. For Edgar the role is a *kenosis* – not a recording of what society has done to him, but an emptying of himself to register what society (and his own class) does to others. Even fraudulent beggars are telling part of the truth; Edgar confirms this truth by submitting to it.

This reading of poor Tom complicates, as well, our reading of his encounter with Lear in Act 3. For Tom is clearly not, in a simple sense, what the deranged king takes him for – not really 'the thing itself' (3.4.105), essential humanity, not even a true sign of Edgar who stands before him. Tom is the sign of a cultural result. Still, the encounter is important for Lear's change of self. To know oneself in this world, one must know that one is, partly, a 'poor, bare, forked animal' (106), a lesson taught by many Christian and classical moralists. Tom is a sign of the 'nature', the experience of bare subsistence, which Lear and others have ignored in pursuing their gratifications. Lear will never practise whatever this encounter might imply for kingship. It is Edgar, ironically, appropriately, who will be king – though, again, the play ends before we see what poor Tom will have taught him about justice in practical politics.

As an economic and social sign, Tom is 'basest'. Theatrically, however, he is far from 'unaccommodated'; the Quarto title page makes clear that he was one of the play's main attractions. Similarly, Shakespeare has reserved the play's turning-point for characters with a stage life of about ten lines and so minimal in characterisation that they have no individual names, which is the culmination of the thought that the obligations that constitute humanity are few and primitive. These anonymous figures appear in the scene of Gloucester's maiming, which is obviously the play's climax for sheer undisplaced agony. For its first seventy lines or so, the scene has an explosive, spasm-like quality, as the malice in Goneril and Regan bursts through their decorum all at once ('Hang him instantly'. 'Pluck out his eyes', 3.7.4–5), and Cornwall's self-releasing, self-relishing cruelty ignores Gloucester's pathetic attempts to assert the tie of guest and host (31–2, 40–2). But this cruelty simply confirms what we have sensed in Cornwall and the sisters all along; theatrically, it is a release of the implicit. The unexpected event is the intervention of one of Cornwall's servants:

> Hold your hand, my lord!
> I have served you ever since I was a child;
> But better service have I never done you
> Than now to bid you hold. (75–8)

It is one of the telling oddities of *Lear*'s construction that this brief, almost incidental moment is crucial to the plot as a whole. This moment sets in motion the defeat of evil in Act 5: Cornwall's death makes Regan and Goneril direct rivals for Edmund's attention, and Albany's discovery of this rivalry leads him to credit the disguised Edgar. The Servant initiates whatever small justice the play affords us. As a character, of course, he is almost negligible. But by intervening in Cornwall's violence, he does first of all what Cordelia and Kent have also done – reminding the wrongdoer of an established relationship and obligation. Like them, the Servant faces a dilemma: he has served for so long in conventional ways that he hardly fathoms now what he is doing. Still, ethically, it is quite clear: he will perfect 'service' by serving his master's best ethical interests. He will be a 'good servant'.

Regan and Cornwall, of course, understand 'service' in terms of mere power. Servants take orders and extend their master's grasp. The Servant has not existed, as a moral entity, for Regan at all, and now in her surprise she instinctively degrades him: 'A peasant stand up thus?' (83). But he is not a peasant (or a 'villain', Cornwall's near-synonym); he has standing in a ducal household. He ennobles himself by facing Cornwall sword in hand; Regan reinstates him, so to speak, by stabbing him in the back. In his brief rising, however, the Servant has presented an alternative to other 'servants' in the play, such as Oswald, who out of self-interest do what they are told. Oswald, says Kent, 'bite[s] the holy cords atwain / Which are too intrinse t'unloose' (2.2.75–6). What Kent means, I think, is that these cords can be broken only by an 'outside' violence that destroys the integrity of the whole structure of obligation at once. The bonds are 'holy' (in *Lear*'s undogmatic way) because they exist at the centre of human life. There is no way to loosen them without destroying that life.

Unlike poor Tom, the Servant is not a *kenosis*: he does not empty himself, but fulfils his familiar obligation in a way that contradicts its routinised form. One may be a servant, that is, like Oswald, though one breaks the holy cords; one may also be a servant by defying one's superior.[9] It might be argued (it would seem a logical conclusion from Dollimore's reading) that Oswald cannot be blamed for doing what power requires. But the Servant cancels that rationalisation; he fulfils his servanthood by acting against power. Even so he is not a pattern for all *Lear*'s nameless characters. They enact a variety of responses to formular identities. The Knight (1.4) and the Gentleman (3.1) are hardly more than interlocutors; Edmund's Captain (5.3) is a lesser

Oswald. The Old Man of 4.1, however, justifies his conduct specifically in terms of his routinised role; he has long been a tenant of the Gloucester estate. In Lear's new kingdom, Gloucester warns him, his loyalty and charity may cost him, but the Old Man is attending to his moral indebtedness and will risk the suffering (4.1.49–50).

In such figures the 'subaltern' speaks, and it is worth pausing to test the meaning of this. The fundamentally romantic faith in the validity of primitive or proletarian versions of social experience has engendered many radical critiques both of political discourse and of the political investments of critical discourse. As Gayatri Spivak has argued, however, the more thorough the critical disinvestment in language, the harder it is to imagine how, or that, the subaltern can speak or hope to be heard.[10] But *Lear*'s nameless characters are not wholly determined by their social identities. Having an identity so formular that its only name is the name of a social place or function does not mean saying one thing only or acting in a wholly determined way. At the same time, the formular identity is not merely cancelled out or transcended. It is the social form of the character's expression without determining its content. The Servant acts as he does because he is a servant; if he were not a servant, his action would not mean what it does. But his social identity circumstances his action, so to speak, without determining it. He acts through it, as Cordelia does through hers, toward a larger ideal of care.

'Crowned with rank fumiter'

The most troublesome presence in *Lear*, however, is neither humanity nor society but nature. The text's persistent habit is to associate the constitutive obligations with 'nature' in one of its traditional senses ('loyal and natural boy', 2.1.84). Taken at face value, this seems to introduce an uncritical quantity whose use (like that of 'providence' in religious readings or 'nothing' in sceptical ones) is to distract us from the play's actual scrutiny of commitments and power.

But *Lear*, as so often, seems to anticipate our difficulties – not so much to resolve as to enrich them. Edmund is certainly right when, at the beginning of his career of deception and betrayal, he rejects some 'natural' things (like astrological influence or the curse of his illegitimacy) as in fact only 'plague of custom' (1.2.3). But what Edmund opposes to the stars is the definiteness and fixity of his own moral nature (1.2.134–6). And he does not want to do away with the mechanisms or norms of custom: he just wants to make them work for him rather than against him. We can grant him the dubiety of many 'natural' norms without granting that he is therefore justified in falsifying his 'childlike office' (2.1.106) to betray his father to Cornwall. Edmund's own nature (or 'blood') rebels against it (3.5.23–4).

But the problematic quality of nature has more to do with our cultural predicament than with the text's complicated uses of the term. For it is our culture, not Shakespeare's, that holds nature's illegibility as a necessary doctrine. This is clearest when we turn to nature as physical or environmental phenomena – the 'sheets of fire' and 'bursts of horrid thunder' that 'Man's nature cannot carry' (3.2.46, 48). All our cultural institutions and practice (including those of literature and criticism) support and are supported by a violently extractive economy. It is a constant reassurance to this economy to think of nature in (superficially) Wordsworthian or Darwinian terms – as an uplifting prettiness or a distant, unstable aggregate of materials and forces. These fictions provide the ideological blindness we need to exploit nature as the consumer economy requires.

Lear helps us to remove these blinders. It does so by setting nature in direct relation to the survival, suffering and well-being of human bodies. Nature is repeatedly associated with subsistence needs. Poor Tom 'eats the swimming frog' and 'drinks the green mantle of the standing pool' (3.4.128, 132–3) because he has nothing else. Lear's half-skewed perception that in his destitution Tom 'ow'st the worm no silk' (3.4.102–3) might be connected with his acute riposte to Goneril (2.4.266 ff.) about the relation of 'need' to full humanity to suggest much about the metabolism of nature and culture. And in his early madness Lear sees the poor's lack, their exposure to nature, as evidence that he (and by extension his kingship) has failed his obligations (3.4.28 ff.).

The point the text repeatedly implies is less theoretical than practical: behind all evolved patterns of consumption stands the unavoidable requirement of subsistence; behind subsistence are two other requirements, an accessible and adequate nature, and cultural forms that restrain consumption. Nature logically precedes culture because culture cannot survive without it. In practice, of course, we approach nature in cultural terms. But this does not mean that any culture is as 'natural' as any other. A culture that destroys nature can replace it with nothing.

This 'nothing', the failure of provision for human existence, is the true nothing that haunts *Lear*'s entire action. The natural obligation might be defined as one whose fulfilment allows human life to flourish within the limits of nature. *Lear* projects three possible states in relation to this flourishing: destitution, or the failure of subsistence; a hubristic culture without regard for nature; and a culture fitted to nature and co-operating with its health-giving power. Cordelia's lines about Lear in his madness imply the entire pattern:

> Alack, 'tis he! Why, he was met even now
> As mad as the vexed sea, singing aloud,
> Crowned with rank fumiter and furrow weeds,
> With hardocks, hemlock, nettles, cuckooflowers,
> Darnel, and all the idle weeds that grow
> In our sustaining corn. (4.4.1–6)

In the picture Lear is not crowned with gold, the symbol of culture's predominance over the entire world of human experience, or with cultivars ('our sustaining corn'), but with weeds that are nature's own preserve and have no use in human economy. Fumiter is nature's poor Tom. It is the thunder that will not peace at Lear's bidding (4.6.101–2). Raw nature has helped to teach Lear what he is outside of dependence and obligation, 'unaccommodated'. But this is not a human condition. Left here, Lear will die. (So will poor Tom.) He can be restored to health only by the gifts of the farmer and the doctor, the 'sustaining corn' and the 'simples operative' (4.4.14). Then Cordelia and Kent will crown him again with the crown of human culture.

'O you are men of stones'

Bearing the body of Cordelia, Lear enters the final scene with this cry. The play's violence has passed like a tornado: maimed Gloucester, preserved from suicide, has died of natural causes; Cordelia has returned from France to find and heal Lear, but failed to restore his kingdom; Cornwall, Edmund and Lear's older daughters are all dead. We are still on the battlefield; all the living principals are present, in addition to three (and then four) characters without names. To whom is Lear's cry addressed? Twice he will arraign the people on stage for unresponsiveness, for paucity of feeling. If they were not stones, they would howl at his command, with cosmic effect. But it is not impossible that the line includes us as well. The openness of Shakespeare's stage to the audience makes this probable. Lear entering upstage, his cry passes through the stage company, violating the *locus/platea* divide and the divide between stage and audience. We are all men of stones. None of us can respond adequately.

Discussion of this moment in the play has been dominated, however, not by Lear's cry but by Kent's response: 'Is this the promised end?' (268) – that is, the end of the world. The question seems not to have a clear answer. This is not a Christian apocalypse, since good characters and evil, 'sheep and goats', lie side by side on stage; nor does the moment have the scope of a pagan apocalypse, a *Götterdämmerung*, since good characters remain and the scene's pathos depends on Shakespeare's careful modulations of feeling. Kent's question seems to be formal rather than substantive. It brings to mind the issue of the *play*'s resolution, its final moral 'take' and its aesthetic completeness. That the two issues are interdependent has been clear since the time of Johnson, who understood the aesthetic success of the ending to rest on the question of whether Cordelia's death is morally acceptable. If it seems gratuitous, we are facing both a frustration of moral order and the disunity of a plot which seems to have 'promised' a restoration.[11]

Johnson's incisive statement of the crux has led, through many readings, to the dualism we noted earlier: two currents of interpretation, affirmative and negative. Either we find a way to recuperate the meaning of Cordelia's life from the accidental horror of her death, and thus can argue that the play concludes with a realisation of order, or we take this horror to be the final answer that voids all the smaller justices and charities the play affords. Yet it may be that the play's final vision is not either/or. Like a morality play, *Lear* may be designed to break out of its aesthetic confines and to raise questions neither reading nor watching can answer. The dualist answers inadequately the complexity of *Lear*'s form and of its version of our moral predicament. The ingredients of consolatory and nihilist readings can be found earlier, in Edgar's generalising about how 'The worst returns to laughter' (4.1.6), and then, instantly, Gloucester with his bleeding face. But more is going on in the final scene, almost uniformly ignored by critical discussion. Here is the nameless Old Man, faithful to Gloucester and charitable toward poor Tom in the face of a persecution we can hardly underestimate, given Gloucester's lost eyes.

Lear is constantly reminding us with convincing representations of obligation, faithfulness and care, without allowing us to take the kind of comfort from them that we want. There is a vivid frustration in this. But it is the frustration, we see (if we persist), of a desire that was false to begin with. We either want Cordelia's goodness to triumph, or we want the play to show us that it was not goodness. Either justice is done wholly, satisfyingly, or justice is impossible. But it is more probable that Cordelia's goodness and Albany's justice are goodness and justice, *and* that they succeed in part, Pyrrhically. This is the condition of their practice.

In this they represent all 'canonical expectations' in response to the demands of human survival. But the upshot is not that all forms and duties are morally equivalent or equivalently useless. Cordelia's faithfulness in her daughterly obligations does not, in the end, save either Lear or herself. But it provides an intelligible alternative to the unworkable schemes of her sisters. The anatomy of obligation in *Lear* ends then not with a simple analytical scheme but with a complex practical predicament. It accepts that culture is structured by forms and duties, though it shows us clearly that these are often the vehicles of folly and injustice. The play does not claim that forms and duties are themselves the substance of moral practice. They are shapes of opportunity. But moral practice must have its shapes. One cannot 'be good' just by 'being good': goodness waits on its enactment, and there are certain basic obligations in which this enactment is urgent, required. Failure here means both moral and practical failure. Faithfulness does not guarantee practical success; it does sustain our knowledge of 'humanity'.

Kerala

Habermas' theory of the public sphere is designed to meet the challenges of modern self-consciousness within a fragmented polity. No intact community, tribe or traditional culture would need a public sphere. It first evolved from the early movements of technological culture, and exists now (in so far as it may exist) to help the lifeworld negotiate its needs within this technological culture, grown now to global scope and almost limitless invasive power.

The value of reading Habermas in *Lear*'s vicinity, as I suggested earlier, is to see more clearly how the demands of the lifeworld structure and extend what might be discussed in the public sphere and who will be admitted to the discussion. This extension is important because the public sphere, oriented toward the material prosperity and universal information apparently promised by the global economy, tends to keep out of sight things that question this economy – issues like the ethical basis of our practical culture and the state of nature itself.

Not that our evaluation of the global economy will be, in any simple way, determined by our scepticism about its treatment of nature or the subaltern. We cannot simply reverse this economy's direction or heal the damage it is doing. For one thing, many of us believe that the advances in health care, food supply, literacy, social equality and political justice clearly needed in many parts of the world depend on the expansion of western technological culture. Does *Lear*'s pre-modern world, with its slate of known obligations and its intimacy with nature, correspond to anything in our post-modern predicament? Is a traditional culture imaginable now, and would it be desirable if imaginable?

Some people, however, are beginning to suspect that crucial social advances may not depend on the technological culture – or, to put the issue the other way round, that the technological culture may be less likely than other options to bring about the progress we need. A telling example is the south Indian state of Kerala, to which several commentators have turned, first (perhaps) in some puzzlement and then in increasingly serious interest. Kerala is poor even by Indian standards: per capita income is $330 a year and must support a dense population. Yet Kerala enjoys a life expectancy comparable to that of the United States, a UN-certified 100 percent literacy rate, and a quality-of-life index higher than those of such 'miracles of development' as Taiwan and South Korea. These gains have been achieved not by western-style economic development – the most striking recent example of such development has been the destructive over-fishing of Keralan waters by an internationally financed fleet – but through land distribution attendant on a nineteenth-century religious revival. The basis of Kerala's progress has not been machines but care for justice.[12]

The resources for such development exist in western societies as well, especially among historical minorities. In *A Tradition That Has No Name*, Mary Field Belenky and her colleagues explore how social cohesion, psychological and intellectual liberation, and family stability are accomplished in minority communities (again) not by financial or technological means but by traditions of moral leadership and dialogue based in the family.[13] The structure of established moral 'bonds' – 'I love Your Majesty / According to my bond' (1.1.92–3) – seems to pose not a reactionary obstacle to progress in social equality and economic security but a frame in which progress can be made. Goneril's way, by contrast – 'the laws are mine, not thine' (5.3.161) – denies mutuality and makes personal bonds merely the tools of the isolated self. She will be autonomous, a rule to herself. But she forfeits her own ends, because not even the ends of the *libido dominandi* can be attained without community.

To enact the bond of love is to acknowledge one's dependence on people and circumstances one cannot control. Cordelia herself enacts this mostly in human terms; she never meets poor Tom or encounters what he has to say about unaccommodated nature. Yet her way, sketched out to Lear, affords the grounds of possible, imaginable action. Goneril goes straight for the dark. You cannot go in her way very long. Cordelia also dies, of course, but not without showing how others, in circumstances beyond the play's ending, may be able to reconstruct a liveable polity. It is an image of how a lifeworld, perhaps any lifeworld, perhaps ours, may survive the assaults of a practical culture inimical to it.

Notes

1   K. R. Monroe, *The Heart of Altruism: Perceptions of a Common Humanity* (Princeton: Princeton Univ. Press, 1996) p. 11.
2   J. D. Cox, *Shakespeare and the Dramaturgy of Power* (Princeton: Princeton Univ. Press, 1989) pp. 3–40.
3   J. Habermas, *The Philosophical Discourse of Modernity*, F. Lawrence (trans.) (Cambridge, Mass.: MIT Press, 1987) pp. 79, 118; F. Jameson, *Postmodernism, or The Cultural Logic of Late Capitalism* (Durham: Duke Univ. Press, 1991).
4   All quotations from the play are from D. Bevington (ed.), *The Complete Works of Shakespeare*, updated 4th ed. (New York: Longman, 1997) and are annotated parenthetically in the text. Bevington conflates Quarto and Folio texts; the disparities between them do not, I believe, challenge my argument materially.
5   J. Dollimore, *Radical Tragedy: Religion, Ideology and Power in the Drama of Shakespeare and His Contemporaries* (Brighton: Harvester Press, 1984) p. 197.
6   S. L. Goldberg, *An Essay on 'King Lear'* (Cambridge: Cambridge Univ. Press, 1974) p. 22.
7   R. Weimann, *Shakespeare and the Popular Tradition in the Theatre* (Baltimore: Johns Hopkins Univ. Press, 1978) pp. 73–85; M. Mooney, *Shakespeare's Dramatic Transactions* (Durham: Duke Univ. Press, 1990) pp. 129–49.
8   W. Carroll, '"The Base Shall Top Th'Legitimate": The Bedlam Beggar and the Role of Edgar in *King Lear*', *Shakespeare Quarterly*, 38 (1987) 433. The evidence concerning Elizabethan and Jacobean beggars is given and analysed by A. L. Beier, *Masterless Men: The Vagrancy Problem in England 1560–1640* (London: Methuen, 1985); P. Slack, *Poverty and Policy in Tudor and Stuart England* (London: Longman, 1988) pp. 91–112; and C. Hill, *The World Turned Upside Down: Radical Ideas During the English Revolution* (Baltimore: Penguin, 1975) pp. 39–56, 277–86. This evidence is applied to *Lear* by R. Selden, 'King Lear and True Need', *Shakespeare Studies*, 19 (1987) 143–69; M. Heinemann, '"Demystifying the Mystery of State": *King Lear* and the World Upside Down', *Shakespeare Survey*, 44 (1992) 75–83; and especially by W. Carroll, *Fat King, Lean Beggar: Representations of Poverty in Shakespeare's England* (Ithaca: Cornell Univ. Press, 1996).

 9 R. Strier sees the Servant as the play's clearest example of the 'paradox of service through resistance' (*Resistant Structures: Particularity, Radicalism, and Renaissance Texts* [Berkeley: Univ. of California Press, 1995]), p. 194.
10 G. C. Spivak, 'Can the Subaltern Speak?', in C. Nelson and L. Grossberg (eds), *Marxism and the Interpretation of Culture* (Urbana: Univ. of Illinois Press, 1988) pp. 271–313.
11 A. Sherbo (ed.), *Johnson on Shakespeare*, viii (New Haven: Yale Univ. Press, 1968) pp. 702–5.
12 For data and reflection on Kerala, see R. Franke, *Life Is a Little Better: Redistribution as a Development Strategy in Nadur Village, Kerala* (Boulder, Co.: Westview, 1992); B. McKibben, *Hope, Human and Wild: True Stories of Living Lightly On the Earth* (Boston: Little, Brown, 1995) pp. 119–69; *Whose Common Future? Reclaiming the Commons* (Philadelphia: New Society Publ., 1993) pp. 80–1, 182–3.
13 M. F. Belenky, L. A. Bond, and J. S. Weinstock, *A Tradition That Has No Name: Nurturing the Development of People, Families, and Communities* (New York: Basic Books, 1997).

3
Dostoevsky and the Prisoner

Paul J. Contino

Many times a week on a variety of American television shows such as *Law and Order*, *NYPD Blue*, and *Homicide*, viewers behold a dramatic portrayal of a suspected criminal being interrogated by a tough, savvy police detective. Having already witnessed a vicious crime, the viewer feels a visceral repulsion for the suspect by the time of the interrogation. We want the detective to elicit a confession through trickery, coercion, even force. But if we catch ourselves, we might remember that this suspect, guilty or not, is a person, not prey. As persons we are free and enact our freedom by taking responsibility for our actions. Televised images of interrogation and confession, however, usually don't culminate in a criminal taking responsibility for a crime. Neither do they suggest the possibility that the detective feels a responsibility to foster such an act. Praised for their verisimilitude, such scenes of interrogation reveal that despite the landmark *Miranda* v. *Arizona* (1966) decision, the act of police interrogation remains 'somewhat akin to that of a hunter stalking his game'.[1]

One such show, *Homicide*, takes place in a Baltimore precinct much like that depicted in *Homicide: A Year on the Killing Streets*, by David Simons, an experienced police beat reporter who spent a full year with unlimited access to Baltimore's homicide unit. Simons' observations and dour conclusions suggest why television crime-shows so rarely image anything like responsibility on the part of either criminal or cop:

> The majority of those who acknowledge their complicity in a killing must be baited by detectives with something more tempting than penitence. They must be made to believe that their crime is not really murder, that their excuse is both accepted and unique, that

they will, with the help of the detective, be judged less evil than they truly are. ... *Miranda* and its accompanying decisions established a uniform concept of a criminal defendant's rights and effectively ended the use of violence and the most blatant kind of physical intimidation in interrogations. That, of course, was a blessing. But if the further intent of the *Miranda* decision was, in fact, an attempt to 'dispel the compelling atmosphere' of an interrogation, then it failed miserably.

And thank God. Because by any standards of human discourse, a criminal confession can never truly be called voluntary. With rare exception, a confession is compelled, provoked and manipulated from a suspect by a detective who has been trained in a genuinely deceitful art. That is the essence of interrogation, and those who believe that a straightforward conversation between a cop and a criminal – devoid of any treachery – is going to solve a crime are somewhere beyond naïve. If the interrogation process is, from a moral standpoint, contemptible, it is nonetheless essential.[2]

At the risk of locating itself 'somewhere beyond naïve', this essay asks: must the process of interrogation by necessity be morally 'contemptible'? The literary and religious imagination of Fyodor Dostoevsky suggests not. Dostoevsky, who knew first-hand the experience of interrogation and incarceration, shows in his novels how the scene of interrogation *might* provide the occasion for moral accountability. In turning to Dostoevsky's images of the law's relation to the suspect and prisoner, I wish to suggest that the private experience of reading Dostoevsky's novels can be translated into public discourse – that, as Habermas suggests, the literary public sphere may be intertwined with the political public sphere.

One of Dostoevsky's most influential readers, the Russian thinker Mikhail Bakhtin, writes in 'Art and Answerability' that we are in fact *answerable* to the art and literature that we encounter: 'Art and life are not one, but they must become united in myself – in the unity of my answerability'.[3] And so, in his own formal analysis of the novels of Dostoevsky, Bakhtin discerns an ethical imperative: that we acknowledge and respect the mystery, complexity and freedom of other persons. As author, Dostoevsky portrays his characters as *unfinalisable*: he sees and hears them as free and indeterminable, ever capable of change or surprise. Indeed, Dostoevsky often depicts a character pleading that his personhood be recognised and respected by those who would reify him.

Two such scenes in *The Brothers Karamazov* centre upon Dmitri (or Mitya) Karamazov as he stands imprisoned before the law – first as suspect, later as convict. Such scenes depict the workings of an institution, so their implications extend beyond the ethical to the social and political. These political implications, however, emerge from the fact that the ground for social transformation lies in particular person-to-person encounters, out of which wider systemic changes may unfold. In his portrayal of Mitya's arrest, inquisition and agonised decision to escape, Dostoevsky suggests two things. First, to the extent that the law is concerned with reaching a suspect's conscience and moving him to be truthful, in interrogation its representatives must approach the suspect as a particular person, with *attention*, as that word is used by Simone Weil. Weil speaks of 'a way of looking [that] is first of all attentive. The soul empties itself of all its own contents in order to receive into itself the being it is looking at, just as he is, in all his truth'.[4] Such attentive looking renounces the urge to reduce the person to just another 'case' within the category 'suspect'. Second, to the extent that the law is concerned with restoring the corrupted soul of the convict, sentencing also requires attention, here in the form of classical casuistry, which stresses the need to attend to the particularity of person and situation. I believe that Dostoevsky's suggestions prove germane to current debates about the means of police interrogation,[5] or the extent to which judges may employ personal discretion when legislatures pass laws that insist 'three strikes and you're out'.

The need for the confessor

Early in *The Brothers Karamazov*, the monastic elder Zosima speaks of the regenerating influence the Church can have upon the criminal's conscience. After the criminal has been judged and sentenced by the state, the Church, 'like a tender loving mother, holds aloof from active chastisement herself ... [and] always keeps up relations with the criminal as a dear and still precious son'.[6] For Zosima, the intimate, homely relationship between mother and son best images that between Church and convict – a contemporary image of which can be seen in Sister Helen Prejean's relationship with Matthew Poncelet in Tim Robbins' film *Dead Man Walking*. More than any of his previous works, Dostoevsky's final novel embodies a theology of the ordinary, everyday and particular. The novel consistently recognises what David Tracy calls 'the extra-ordinariness of the ordinary': the myriad ways in which 'the gift of manifestation disclosed decisively in Jesus Christ ... [is] now disclosed everywhere, in each particular' and especially in 'the shocking, lovable, real otherness of all concrete others'.[7] *Karamazov* affirms a sacramental vision in its depiction of the graced, healing capacities of interpersonal encounter. Indeed, early in his own ministry, Zosima serves as confessor to Mikhail, his 'mysterious visitor', who has committed murder. Their confessional encounter culminates in Mikhail's public confession and his release from isolating, self-consuming guilt. Mikhail must translate his dream of public confession into an actual deed, enacted in the real situation of a particular time and place. To confess and thus restore his bond to his fellow townspeople would be to enact a deed of love. But, as Zosima stresses, 'love in action is a harsh and dreadful thing compared with love in dreams' (p. 49); 'it is won slowly by long labor' (p. 298); it is 'work', as Helen Prejean insists at the end of *Dead Man Walking*.

Zosima is a realist. His realism, and that of his student Alyosha Karamazov, can be understood as incarnational, grounded as it is in 'the gift of manifestation disclosed in Jesus Christ'. Zosima states this starkly: 'if it were not for the precious image of Christ before us, we should be undone and altogether lost' (p. 299). Further grounding Zosima's realism is his gritty understanding of the world Christ entered. Given the realities of human pride and self-absorption, active love of others and acceptance of their love requires, with grace, 'labor and fortitude' (p. 49). Indeed, Mikhail's deed of active love, his public confession, calls for the sacramental, mediating presence of another, Zosima. As Bakhtin suggests in his reflections upon images of confession in Dostoevsky: 'I cannot manage without another, I cannot become myself without another'.[8] Dostoevsky's characters recognise that they must take responsibility for their deeds, and must do so humbly, with the assistance of others. To accept one's need for someone else requires humility, and *humble* proves an apt synonym for *prosaic*, a concept which illuminates the way confessions can be efficacious.

By stressing the word *prosaic*, I employ and develop a concept which Gary Saul Morson and Caryl Emerson see as central to Bakhtin's work:

> Prosaics encompasses two related, but distinct, concepts. First, as opposed to 'poetics', prosaics designates a theory of literature that privileges prose in general and the novel in particular over the poetic genres. Prosaics in the second sense is far broader than theory of literature; it is a form of thinking that presumes the importance of the everyday, the ordinary, the 'prosaic'.[9]

Again, the emphasis here is on the 'extraordinariness of the ordinary'. But one might develop this notion of the prosaic further by employing two other Bakhtinian concepts. On the one hand, a person is called upon to recognise the *open* dimension of personhood: her 'unfinalisability', capacity to change, to develop in new, unpredictable ways. On the other hand, a person is called to balance this recognition with that of the *closed* dimension of personhood: that she must, finally, make a concrete choice and act, apply her 'signature' upon her deed before others and take responsibility for it. To manage this balance in everyday life is to forge what I call here a 'prosaic self'. Dostoevsky's characters forge such a self only through the loving mediation of others. Characters like Mikhail in *The Brothers Karamazov* and Raskolnikov in *Crime and Punishment*, isolated and consumed by guilt for their criminal deeds, need confessors like Zosima or Sonia whose attention to their spiritual situations penetrates and liberates.

Dostoevsky's work often suggests that one person can help transform another with a very small act of kindness or attention. In various chapters of Dostoevsky's *A Writer's Diary*, for example, Morson observes the vital though 'isolated cases' of familial closeness and ordinary kindness that, taken together, 'shape good lives'.[10] These stories of 'ordinary people living prosaic lives' stand in tension with the apocalyptic strain that runs through later chapters of *A Diary*. One such instance of the powerful effect of the small deed is in Dostoevsky's own recollection of 'the Peasant Marey'. Dostoevsky, incarcerated in Siberia for his politically subversive associations and acts, initially felt utter disgust toward his fellow prisoners. He describes this revulsion in his *Memoirs from the House of the Dead*, a work which itself 'unleashed a huge debate in the press about Russian justice and the system of imprisonment'.[11] Of his prison mates he writes: 'I closed my eyes and refused to look'.[12] One day, having felt especially intense loathing, he lay in his barracks and 'lost himself in reverie'. He recalled, as a boy, being stricken with fear that a wolf was near and fleeing into the arms of a nearby peasant, Marey. In prison, Dostoevsky remembers the gentle, 'maternal' way in which Marey reassured, held and blessed him.[13] With this vivid recollection of a kind person's care, 'this solitary encounter', the imprisoned Fyodor is able to turn to his fellow prisoners with a new heart and open eyes. As his biographer Joseph Frank points out, this moment of remembrance served to restore Dostoevsky's 'faith in the Russian common people as, in some sense, the human image of Christ'. Encompassing as this faith may be, indeed 'charged with an intense nationalistic animus'[14] in its emphasis upon the *Russian* peasant, it nevertheless nurtured in Dostoevsky a healing capacity to *look*, from face-to-singular-face, at his fellow prisoners:

> And so when I climbed down from my bunk and looked around, I remember I suddenly felt I could regard these unfortunates in an entirely different way and that suddenly, through some sort of miracle, the former hatred and anger in my heart had vanished. I went off, peering intently into the faces of those I met. This disgraced peasant, with shaven head and brands on his cheek, drunk and roaring out his hoarse, drunken song – why he might also be that very same Marey; I cannot peer into his heart, after all.[15]

Dostoevsky relinquished the labels he had applied to the prisoners and began to see them as persons – like Marey in their mystery and capacity for surprising, gracious charity.

Dostoevsky's understanding of the healing capacities of human encounter reaches its most mature embodiment in *The Brothers Karamazov*. Like such twentieth-century personalists as Emmanuel Mounier, Jacques Maritain, Gabriel Marcel and Nicholas Berdyaev, Dostoevsky stresses the spiritual reality, dignity, freedom and responsibility of each person in the face of institutions and systems of thought that would reduce and reify his or her personhood. Vyacheslav Ivanov writes that Dostoevsky's 'whole striving ... was to *penetrate* and *enter into the multitudes of life* around him; he does not need to fill himself up, but *to lose himself*. Living beings, access to whom was immediately opened up to him, are not things of the world, but people – human personalities; because they are of the same nature as he'. As an example, Ivanov suggests Dostoevsky's account of his own incarceration: 'The spirit, listening with strained attention to how the prisoner in the next room lives and moves about, demands of his neighbour but a few slight signals in order to divine the unexpressed, the unsaid'.[16] In *Memoirs from the House of the Dead*, Dostoevsky himself emphasises such attention: 'One need only remove the outer husk and scrutinise the grain within attentively, closely and without prejudice, to see things in the people of which he had never dreamed'.[17] And Bakhtin, influenced by Ivanov, stresses the way Dostoevsky rejects any 'degrading *reification* of a person's soul, a discounting of its freedom and unfinalisability'.[18] Dostoevsky's confessors – Zosima, Alyosha, Sonya, Myshkin, Tikhon – themselves reflect such personalism in their respect for the person to whom each attends, and in their work to assist that person toward accepting the everyday realities of personal freedom and responsibility.

Those guilty or even suspected of murder are not, however, usually so fortunate as to have such mediating figures as Sonia or Zosima (or Helen Prejean). For these, the more typical confessional situation – commonly imaged in the television shows mentioned earlier – is far closer to a Foucauldian scene of coercive, institutional power than a Buberian scene of interpersonal dialogue and I–Thou relation. In fact, Dostoevsky recognised and portrayed the legal system of his own time as similarly flawed. But he also saw that system as *necessary*, as it provided the primary realm of public confession and personal account-ability. For Raskolnikov and Mikhail, both guilty of murder, one-to-one confessional dialogue is only a crucial first step that precedes their second, vital step of public confession before appropriate authorities, and their concomitant willingness to accept punishment as a means of atonement.

The wolf and the hunters

Mitya Karamazov, though severely tempted, is not guilty of murdering his father Fyodor, and his long interrogation is a 'torment' in part because of this. He bears, however, other guilt. Hours earlier, he has struck down and left for dead the elderly Grigory, who for years served as his surrogate father. And Mitya has, to his deep shame, stolen the three thousand roubles which his betrothed, Katerina, had entrusted him to deliver and spent almost all of the money at two wild orgies at Mokroe, where he has followed Grushenka, whom he loves. He has brutally beaten his father and publicly abused the weak father of little Ilyushka. Driven by passions and impulse, Mitya has never taken responsibility for the real violence and pain he has inflicted on others.

Mitya's interrogators, however, only serve to corrode his sense of responsibility. They finalise him and refuse to enter into his situation. They see him as 'murderer' and that alone. At crucial moments, however, others – including one police officer – utter words that suggest attentiveness to Mitya and a corresponding recognition that he must sign for, must take responsibility for, past deeds. These utterances yield a firmer sense of self in Mitya and help him to recover what Bakhtin calls the 'deepest I', the prosaic self with which one meets the other in responsible confession.[19]

From the start of his interrogation, Mitya himself recognises the unequal situation that exists between him and his interrogators. He declares: 'I don't pretend to be on equal terms with you' (p. 434). Ippolit Kirillovich, the prosecutor, tells Mitya: 'you have a perfect right not to answer the questions put to you now, and we on our side have no right to extort an answer from you' (p. 442). But by virtue of their positions he and the district attorney, Nikolay Parfinovich, do attempt to extort a confession and coerce Mitya to speak; they have charged Mitya with murder and can carry him to prison when their questioning is over. Richard H. Weisberg notes that 'Continental pretrial procedures aim to elicit a confession; hence the inquisitor's curiosity legally extends to every aspect of a suspect's personal life'.[20] This creates a situation in which Mitya is, to use Aaron Fogel's phrase, 'circumstantially forced to speak'[21] – hardly the ideal confessional encounter. The relation of Ippolit Kirillovich and Nikolay Parfinovich to Mitya is *not* that of Zosima to Mikhail.

The question this essay asks is whether Mitya's interrogators might *approach* such a relation. Simone Weil, writing sixty years later (although not about this scene), suggests such a possibility. She envisions a 'supernatural virtue of justice' which 'consists of behaving exactly as though there were equality when one is the stronger in an unequal relationship. Exactly, in every respect, including the slightest details of accent and attitude, for a detail may be enough to place the weaker party in the condition of matter, which on this occasion naturally belongs to him; just as the slightest shock causes water that has remained liquid before freezing point to solidify'.[22] Weil goes on to describe the more typical situation, in which 'contempt ... the contrary of attention' defines the law's relation to the criminal: 'Everything combines, down to the smallest details, down even to the inflections of people's voices, to make him seem vile and outcast in all men's eyes including his own. The brutality and flippancy, the terms of scorn and the jokes, the way of speaking, the way of listening and of not listening, all these things are equally effective'.[23] Contempt toward the criminal or suspect reifies him, reduces his personhood to 'the condition of matter'. Attention, although it never denies the criminal's or suspect's responsibility for his actions, 'means giving ... attention to the victim of affliction as to a being and not a thing; it means wishing to preserve in him the faculty of free consent'.[24] In another essay, Weil describes the act of attention as a kind of *kenosis* or self-emptying: 'The soul empties itself of all its own contents in order to receive into itself the being it is looking at, just as he is, in all his truth'.[25] Christ, who in his Incarnation and Crucifixion 'emptied himself', is the exemplar of *kenosis*, and the kenotic spirituality receives great emphasis in the Orthodox tradition. Weil, like Zosima, believes that 'punishment cannot be humane unless it passes through Christ'.[26] Her words can be understood as prosaic to the degree that they are embodied in particular interactions between representatives of the law and the criminal suspect. Punishment becomes humane when 'the whole organization of penal justice … [is] directed toward obtaining from the magistrates and their assistants the attention and respect for the accused that is due from every man to any person who may be in his power'.[27]

At first Mitya seems eager to co-operate with his questioners, and seeks just such 'attention and respect' from them in return. He offers a forthright confession when, initially, he believes they have come to arrest him for the murder of Grigory. When they accuse him of the murder of Fyodor, he is just as forthright in his avowal of innocence in one crime and guilt in another: 'Not guilty. I am guilty of the blood of another man, but not of my father's' (p. 432). When he learns that Grigory is in fact alive, he declares that he 'feel[s] like a new man' and, while conscious of the 'horrible suspicion … hanging over [him]', he is eager to assist his questioners (p. 434). He expects that, throughout the questions, his human freedom will be respected. When he sees that they will minutely record his testimony, he responds first with surprise, then with 'consent' and direction:

> 'Well write it; I consent, I give my full consent, gentlemen, only … do you see. … Stay, stay, write this. Of disorderly conduct I am guilty, of violence on a poor old man I am guilty. And there is something else at the bottom of my heart, of which I am guilty, too – but that you need not write down' (he turned suddenly to the secretary) 'that's my personal life, gentlemen, that doesn't concern you, the bottom of my heart, that's to say. … But of the murder of my old father I'm not guilty.' (p. 434)

Mitya increasingly realises, however, that his questioners do not care about his 'consent' or what is at 'the bottom of [his] heart', or his desires that they share 'mutual confidence' and refrain from 'rummag[ing] in [his] soul' (p. 438). 'A man is not a drum,' he reminds them, but he progressively grows painfully conscious of the way they treat him as if he were a thing. He notices the prosecutor winking to the district attorney 'on the sly' (p. 436) and pleads with them to 'drop that conventional method of questioning' (p. 440) which aims to sneak up on the speaker. He compares his situation to that of a hunted beast: 'I'm a wolf and you're the hunters' (p. 445).

In part, Mitya shares the blame for his situation, due to his own flight from responsibility: he 'absolutely refuse[s] to answer' (p. 441) questions concerning his desperate need for three thousand roubles. He insists: 'Oh, gentlemen, you needn't go into details, how, when, and why, and why just so much money ... that's my private life, and I won't allow any intrusion into my private life' (pp. 440, 441). But his insistence denies the reality of his situation: revealing such private details is imperative if he wishes to be publicly exonerated. He justly asserts his unfinalisability – his right to be respected as a human being – but resists signing for his shameful theft from Katerina: 'that you need not write down ... that doesn't concern you' (p. 434).

Mitya falls short of a prosaic balance of openness and closure by his unwillingness to sign and 'close' his story with the details concerning Katerina. But his inquisitors fall far shorter in their utter insistence upon closure and unwavering resistance to opening themselves to Mitya's complex situation. They refuse to allow Mitya to surprise them; they have already made up their minds. Even when 'it was evident that [Mitya] was trying more than ever not to forget or miss a single detail of his story', as he describes himself outside his father's window, 'both attorneys listened ... with a sort of awful reserve [and] looked coldly at him' (p. 445). Mitya senses them laughing at him after he has 'softly' described the way 'the devil was conquered' at that moment (p. 446). He feels their refusal to take seriously his own deeply serious belief that grace had intervened. He becomes indignant: 'But, you see, I didn't murder him, you see my guardian angel saved me – that's what you have not taken into account. And that's why it's so base of you, so base!' (p. 449). Chilly, detached, they order Mitya to strip. Naked, Mitya 'was almost ready to believe himself that he was inferior to them, and that now they had a perfect right to despise him' (p. 456). Their cold closure toward him as a fellow human being halts him from explaining his relationship to Katerina: 'And you expect me to be open with such scoffers as you, who see nothing and believe in nothing ... and to tell you another nasty thing I've done, another disgrace, even if that would save me from your accusation! No, better Siberia!' (p. 459).

The prosecutor, who responds 'with the most frigid and composed air' to Mitya's righteous fury (p. 459), exhorts him 'to enter into our position' (p. 462), but refuses to enter into Mitya's, even when Mitya does, in fact, reveal his great disgrace. He casts a 'cold smile' upon

Mitya's 'vital difference' between thief and scoundrel and an amused smile at Mitya's anguished explanation of why he could not go to Katya for money (pp. 465, 467). Both prosecutor and district attorney laugh when Mitya tries to explain. By the end, Mitya has fully confessed, but hides his face in despair because his listeners receive and respond to his confession with, in Weil's words, 'the terms of scorn and … jokes'. It is as if Mitya has been reduced to 'the condition of matter': 'His face now expressed complete, hopeless despair, and he sat mute and passive as though hardly conscious of what was happening' (p. 470). Their dismissal of him as a 'closed case' incites him to foreclose his possibilities himself, to the point of again considering suicide (p. 471).

Mitya's words fail to open the hearts of his listeners: their cold words and response reduce him to despair. Other words, however – like those spoken earlier by Markel Makarovich – prove restorative. Only one representative of the law evinces a prosaic balance in his approach to Mitya: 'the good-natured police captain', Mikhail Makarovich, who allows himself to be surprised by Grushenka's 'gentle soul', renounces the labels – 'fury', 'harlot' (p. 431) – with which he had earlier branded her, and enters into her suffering (p. 437). His words have a forceful, beneficial impact upon Mitya. Akin to Zosima's earlier image of the Church's maternal relation to the convict, Makarovich's approach to the prisoner is paternal. His tearful 'look of warm, almost fatherly, feeling for the luckless prisoner', his confession that he 'was unfair' to Grushenka, and voicing of 'a great deal that was irregular' embody Weil's conception of 'the supernatural virtue of justice' in their own very natural way. Indeed, the captain's generous words elicit deep gratitude in Mitya and restore his resolve to speak: 'Mitya jumped up and rushed toward him. "Forgive me, gentlemen, oh, allow me, allow me!" he cried. "You've the heart of an angel, Mikhail Makarovich, I thank you for her. I will, I will be calm, cheerful, in fact"' (pp. 437–8). Mikhail Makarovich displays just the kind of attention and respect that Dostoevsky, drawing from his own experience, saw as vital to the treatment of suspects and prisoners:

> Every man, whoever he may be, and however low he may have fallen, requires, if only instinctively and unconsciously, that respect be given to his dignity as a human being. … I have met good and noble commandants. I have seen the effect they have produced on

these fallen ones. A few friendly words – and for the prisoners it was almost a moral resurrection. They rejoiced like children and like children they began to love.[28]

Grushenka's word and presence, however, play the most important role in leading Mitya to acceptance of responsibility. She avows her 'faith in [Mitya's] noble heart' (p. 477), which serves to heal him of the despair to which his interrogators have brought him and help him to recover a voice capable of taking public responsibility for his misdeeds. After Grushenka's avowal, Mitya articulates before the Mokroe towns-people his newly achieved sense of personal responsibility for others: 'We all make men weep, and mother, and babes at the breasts ... of all I am the lowest reptile!' And he admits his past misdeeds: 'I've sworn to amend every day of my life, beating my breast, and every day I've done the same filthy things'. His words offer an implicit response to his brother Ivan's rebellion in the face of human suffering. Mitya concurs with Ivan's position: human beings, by doing the 'same filthy things', cause others, including children, to suffer. Ivan's sole focus is that of children's suffering, and Mitya is himself responsible for such suffering: in his cruel abuse of Snegiryov before the eyes of the town and Snegiryov's own son, he is indirectly responsible for Ilyushka's subsequent torment, illness and death. Ivan's focus upon children's suffering has in part, however, kept him from considering the second part of Mitya's response: suffering itself can be beneficial. It can shock one away from persistent irresponsibility and, through expiation, assist one in acting responsibly. Mitya continues: 'I understand now that such men as I need a blow, a blow of destiny to catch them as with a noose, and bind them by a force from without. Never, never should I have risen of myself! But the thunderbolt has fallen. I accept the torment of accusation, and my public shame, I want to suffer and by suffering I shall be purified' (p. 481).

In *Crime and Punishment*, Dostoevsky had created an earlier image of the way that the law might approach a suspect with attention in the figure of Porfiry Petrovich, the police examiner (and literary model for TV's Columbo). Porfiry meets with Raskolnikov three times, and in the first two meetings, as Raskolnikov clearly perceives, Porfiry is 'after [him] like a pack of hounds'.[29] After both meetings Raskolnikov responds to Porfiry's ambushes with merely a resolve to fight, with a desire 'to squeeze [his interrogator] like a lemon' (p. 229). In their third meeting, however, Porfiry's manner changes, as does Raskolnikov's response. The examiner knows Raskolnikov is guilty, but no longer asserts his power.

Aware of the way he can impale another with a look, he 'lower[s] his eyes, as if he did not want to glance further to embarrass his former victim, ... as if he now scorned to use his earlier tricks and stratagems' (p. 379). Porfiry makes it clear to Raskolnikov that he will soon arrest him but nevertheless will 'leave [him] at liberty for a day or two longer' so that he might 'come forward with a confession' (p. 389). One may employ Weil's words: although he is 'the stronger' Porfiry here 'wish[es] to preserve in [Raskolnikov] the faculty of free consent'. Like Mikhail Makarovich, Porfiry embodies Weil's 'supernatural virtue of justice'. Weil insists that such a virtue must be mediated by God and, indeed, Porfiry's exhortation to Raskolnikov is infused with the language of faith: 'Don't let yourself loathe life. ... Perhaps it is through this that God seeks to bring you to Himself ... find your faith and you will live. ... Perhaps, also, suffering is a good thing. Suffer then. ... Perhaps you ought to thank God. ... Do what justice demands ... it is the sacred truth that life will sustain you. ... Think it over my dear chap, and pray' (pp. 388–9). Porfiry's image here evokes Helen Prejean more than Columbo. The day Raskolnikov hears his words he accepts Porfiry's invitation to confess.

Casuistry and punishment

In the judicial system, confession leads to punishment. In *The Brothers Karamazov* Mitya is guilty of much, but not of murder. What ought his punishment, his sentence, to be? The process by which Mitya and Alyosha discern an answer exemplifies the potential of *casuistry*, a practice increasingly denied judges today. Two months after his arrest, Mitya integrates and develops his nascent insights into personal responsibility and suffering in the 'Hymn' he proclaims to Alyosha:

> Even there, in the mines, underground, I may find a human heart in another convict and murderer by my side, and I may make friends with him, for even there one may live and love and suffer. One may resurrect and revive a frozen heart in that convict, one may wait upon him for years, and at last bring up from the dark depths a lofty soul, a feeling, suffering creature; one may bring forth an angel, resurrect a hero! There are so many of them, hundreds of them, and we are all responsible for them. ... It's for the babe I'm going. Because we are all responsible for all. For all the 'babes', for there are

big children as well as little children. All are 'babes'. I go for all, because someone must go for all. I didn't kill father, but I've got to go. I accept it. (p. 560)

For all its impassioned idealism, Mitya's hymn retains some measure of prosaic realism. Like the imprisoned Dostoevsky after his remembrance of Marey, Mitya fervently refuses to reduce any fellow prisoner to a category and embraces instead the dignity and potential of the person before him. The frozen-hearted, murderous convict cannot be simply dismissed. Through an attentive 'making friends' with that convict, one may assist in bringing forth 'a hero'. Further, Mitya affirms a situation of suffering, here 'in the mines, underground', a place of 'great sorrow' (p. 560), as a productive setting for him to enact his work of responsible, active love.

But Mitya's vision also lacks realism, a prosaic awareness of his own possibilities and limits. He as yet believes that Siberia is the only and necessary place where he can enact such work, and believes that he will 'lose God' (p. 557) if he chooses to escape with Grushenka to America. Mitya has still to embrace further prosaic wisdom: lessons of proportion and readiness. Though guilty of much, Mitya is innocent of the murder of his father. Twenty years in Siberia, bereft of Grushenka, would be a disproportionate punishment and, given his character, an intolerable burden for him to shoulder. In his fledgling desire to serve, he is unready for such a burden. He needs to retain that desire, but needs also to discern within the contours of his own particular situation the best and most just means of enacting it.

The process of discernment is hard work, tormentingly so at times, and work which usually requires the assistance of another. In the legal sphere, judges are called upon to do such work after listening to the arguments of advocate and prosecutor. Mitya looks to Alyosha, whom he 'love[s] ... more than anyone' (p. 556), to serve as his judge: 'You will be my judge in it. ... It's your decision that will decide it. ... You shall decide my fate' (pp. 562–4). Alyosha, as an attentive, *kenotic* confessor, relinquishes any such hierarchical stance of authority; his words are not imposed from above. Unlike Ivan, who exhibits his kinship to the Grand Inquisitor – '[Ivan] doesn't ask me, but orders me to escape' (p. 564) – Alyosha descends to a position alongside Mitya. He attentively wishes *with* his brother, but will not decide *for* him: 'After the trial you'll decide by yourself. Then you'll find that new man in yourself and he will decide' (p. 565). As he typically does, Alyosha responds to the person facing a decision with words that draw upon and reaffirm the person's own: he reflects back to Mitya the crucial phrase, 'new man', that he has uttered. Alyosha uncovers and affirms his brother's 'deepest I', his capacity to wish, decide and act.

The benefits of Alyosha's intervention emerge four days after the trial, when he visits Mitya again. Mitya has come to his decision. Although he does not yet rest easily with his choice, he no longer speaks of escape as necessarily 'losing God': 'I shall escape, that was settled apart from you; could Mitya Karamazov do anything but run away? But I shall condemn myself, and I will pray for my sin forever' (p. 724). His intention to pray for his sin forever, to continue speaking with God, suggests that he no longer sees the choice as either Siberia and God or America and loss of God. Just before uttering these words, Mitya has shown that he has discerned and accepted the limits of his particular capacities: 'I am not ready! ... I wanted to sing a "hymn"; but if a guard speaks to me, I have not the strength to bear it, for Grusha I would bear anything ... anything except blows, that is. ... But she won't be allowed to come *there*' (p. 723).

Alyosha's response affirms Mitya's own insights:

'Listen, brother, once for all', he said. 'This is what I think about it. And you know I would not tell you a lie. Listen: you are not ready, and such a cross is not for you. What's more, you don't need such a martyr's cross when you are not ready for it. If you had murdered our father, it would grieve me that you should reject your cross. But you are innocent, and such a cross is too much for you. You wanted to make yourself another man by suffering. I say, only remember that other man always, all your life and wherever you escape to; and that will be enough for you. Your refusal of that great cross will only serve to make you feel all your life an even greater duty, and that constant feeling will do more to make you a new man, perhaps, than if you went *there*'. (p. 723)

In his role as confessor, Alyosha opens himself to Mitya's situation. He affirms Mitya's insight into his lack of readiness rather than imposing his own from above. Again Alyosha reflects back to his brother the ideas and images he has used himself: 'not ready', 'such a cross', 'another man', '*there*'. The last sentence quoted suggests the prosaic balance of open and closed: Alyosha professes Mitya's potential to become the 'new man' in America, even as he stresses that an attentiveness to his 'duty' will be his brother's means to such a state.

Throughout this dialogue, Alyosha reveals another prosaic quality – a capacity for casuistry. In the course of their discussion, Mitya observes that they are talking like the Jesuits, and Alyosha smilingly assents, much to Mitya's joy: '"I love you for always telling the whole truth and never hiding anything", cried Mitya, with a joyful laugh. "So I've caught my Alyosha being Jesuitical. I must kiss you for that"' (p. 724). This chapter is entitled, appropriately, 'The Lie Becomes the Truth', and the title refers not only to the passionate reunion of Mitya and Katerina but also to casuistry, as Dostoevsky here embraces as truth a Jesuit practice he has earlier rejected as a lie when practised by such figures as Smerdyakov and Fetyukovich, the defence attorney. However, Smerdyakov's justification of apostasy in an earlier scene – like Fetyukovich's defence of patricide – does not represent true casuistry. Both comprise sophistical attempts to be clever, motivated by a narcissistic desire for approval and praise. Smerdyakov seeks Ivan's praise (p. 117); Fetyukovich seeks the crowd's. Further, Smerdyakov is motivated by a resentful desire to hurt Grigory, his pious foster father. Rather than attending to the real contours of the situation, both seek to call attention to themselves. As a result, both distort the situation at hand and commit travesty upon the Scripture they cite. Alyosha *is* being 'Jesuitical' and 'casuistical' in the root and best senses of the words. John W. O'Malley elucidates these senses in *The First Jesuits* when he turns to the study of 'cases of conscience':

> The need the Jesuits felt to study such cases grew out of the complex nature of the confessor's task. If the confessor was a judge, then he had to assess the morality of the penitent's actions and assign a suitable penance; if a doctor of the soul, he needed solid information for the instruction of the penitent's conscience. As had long been assumed in law and ethics, circumstances differ from instance to instance, and they influence questions of culpability and morality. ... The study of cases was meant, therefore, to facilitate the application of general norms like the Decalogue to different sets of circumstances according to consistent principles. Is what I am doing good or bad in *these* circumstances, and may I, or must I, continue to do it?
>
> Confession was the sacrament in which the priest's role could most easily devolve into an exercise in manipulation and control. Casuistry, it is often charged, expressed and promoted the devolution. The charge is not implausible, but the basic impulse behind

casuistry was the desire to clarify complicated moral issues, to sort out claims of seemingly conflicting moral absolutes down from the high heavens of abstraction to the more lowly human reality of 'time, places, and circumstances.'[30]

Alyosha attends closely to Mitya's particular circumstance: the crucial fact of Mitya's innocence in the murder of Fyodor, Mitya's impulsive character and deep love for Grushenka, the fact that others will not be endangered by the bribery of the soldiers. He refuses to impose a universal rule that one must never bribe. But he does not thereby exemplify a 'situationalist ethic' *à la* Joseph Fletcher, who distinguishes his 'neocasuistry' from Dostoevsky's 'classical casuistry': 'Like classical casuistry, [neocasuistry] is case focused and concrete, concerned to bring Christian imperatives into practical operation. But unlike classical casuistry, this neocasuistry repudiates any attempt to anticipate or prescribe real-life decisions in their existential particularity'.[31]

Alyosha, on the other hand, *does* apply the constant principle of personal responsibility (that his mentor Zosima has continually stressed) to the situations he encounters. In this sense he does anticipate real-life decisions. He embraces his brother's decision to escape as the best, most *responsible* course Mitya can take in his situation. As such, Alyosha locates and affirms Mitya's deepest desire: that he be responsible. Responsibility cannot be discovered through the automatic application of a universal rule. Alyosha assists Mitya in discerning amidst moral ambiguities. He accepts the open avenue of Mitya's escape, even as he fosters Mitya's desire to embrace closure through duty, prayer and penitence. And he 'smil[es] gently' when his brother teases him for 'being Jesuitical' (p. 724). He thus images for Mitya the foundational virtue of prosaic selfhood: humility.

Dead Man Walking

In his depiction of Mitya Karamazov as prisoner – first as suspect, later as convict – Dostoevsky suggests the necessity of seeing the prisoner as a person, not reductively as a case within a category – 'suspect', 'convict', 'criminal' – that contemptuously reifies. He shows the despair to which such reification can lead, and the possibility that its opposite, attention, might be offered to the suspect, and to the convict in the form of casuistry. Attention may prove restorative and supportive of the prisoner's conscience and responsibility. Attention, however, itself entails an embrace of personal responsibility for the prisoner on the part of the interrogator or judge. We recall Zosima's claim that we are each responsible for everyone. Lee Griffith suggests that such responsibility is central to the Biblical understanding of justice:

> To speak of biblical justice is to speak of the Hebrew concept of *tsedeka*, a word that has connotations of both 'justice' and 'righteousness'. ... Moses Maimonides summarized the spirit of *tsedeka* when he said that to accuse someone of a crime was to enter into a commitment with that person, to take responsibility for that person, to become that person's sister or brother.[32]

By citing the Biblical tradition as an alternative path for our system of justice, do we necessarily embrace the 'eschatological utopia' of Zosima? No – for the prosaic vision of *The Brothers Karamazov* suggests not apocalyptic transformation but the process of slow change, through the particular encounters of particular people. Such encounters, marked by attention to the afflicted, may lead to particular transformations of those involved. Small transformations, successively forged, may prove cumulative, may slowly create institutional, social and political change. A contemporary exemplar of such labour, and the spirit of *tsedeka*, can be found in Sister Helen Prejean, C. S. J., author of *Dead Man Walking*. Prejean's work began with slowly forged relationships with particular death-row inmates – and the families of their victims – to whom she became spiritual advisor and confessor. Out of such one-to-one work, her understanding deepened; she organised others to transform systems that inflict pain in people's lives, most especially to abolish the death penalty. Dostoevsky makes a single appearance in Prejean's book when her colleague cites him when appearing before the Pardon Board: 'He ends with a quote from Dostoevsky, that famous quote about how a society is judged not by how it treats its upstanding citizens, but by how it treats its criminals'.[33] Dostoevsky was, of course, passionately opposed to the death penalty, and most forcefully enunciates this opposition through the character of Prince Myshkin in *The Idiot*. Prejean's book – largely personal narrative – is like a polyphonic novel in its willingness to represent many voices, including those who passionately disagree with her. Her story assists the reader in seeing prisoners who have committed the most abhorrent deeds as persons. Number one on the paperback bestseller list – the inspiration for a highly regarded film – Prejean's book has been a catalyst in the continuing public debate over capital punishment, even amidst the avatars of the culture industry. When Prejean attended the

1996 Academy Awards, she explained: 'My whole thing about going ... is, a billion people look at the Academy Awards and "Dead Man's" gonna come up four times. Jesus said to get on the housetops. So this is a real, real, real big housetop. It's a billion people!'[34] Her presence at such an event along with her story has fostered an authentic climate of public opinion and perhaps consequent change.

Prejean would insist that the actual experience of meeting and attending to prisoners and the poor is vital: 'That's the soil out of which everything else comes. Out of that you begin to see people as persons, you see their suffering and passion is born. And when passion is born, commitment is born, and when commitment is born, then the Gospel can really be lived'.[35] I would suggest, though – along with Habermas, Bakhtin and others – that such transformations may *commence* in attentive reading. Novels as rich as *The Brothers Karamazov* and our conversations with others about them may – to extend Prejean's metaphor – plant the seeds from which springs commitment to social change. 'We've become better people since we read *The Karamazovs*', Dostoevsky's readers told him.[36] In the story of Mitya's imprisonment, we may begin to see our own suspects and prisoners differently. Much as Dostoevsky, in recollecting the protective image of Marey, recognised the personhood of his fellow prisoners, so might we – and the police, prosecutors and judges among us – through an attentive reading of the stories and images offered by Dostoevsky.[37]

Notes

1 From the first edition of Inbau and Reid's 1953 primer in criminal investigation, cited in Y. Kamisar, *Police Interrogation and Confessions: Essays in Law and Policy* (Ann Arbor: Univ. of Michigan Press, 1980) p. 226, n. 11.

2 Cited in Y. Kasimar, W. R. LaFave, and J. H. Israel, *Modern Criminal Procedure*, 8th ed. (St. Paul: West, 1994) pp. 605–6.

3 M. Bakhtin, 'Art and Answerability', in *Art and Answerability: Early Philosophical Essays*, M. Holquist and V. Liapunov (eds), V. Liapunov (trans.) (Austin: Univ. of Texas Press, 1990) p. 2.

4 S. Weil, *Waiting for God*, E. Craufurd (trans.) (New York: Harper, 1951) p. 115.

5 See, for example, J. D. Grano's recent *Confessions, Truth, and the Law* (Ann Arbor: Univ. of Michigan Press, 1994) which sees the *Miranda* v. *Arizona* decision as hindering law enforcement and argues for its overturning. In several recent cases in California judges have insisted upon using such discretion.

6 F. Dostoevsky, *The Brothers Karamazov*, R. Matlaw (ed.), C. Garnett (trans.) (New York: Norton, 1981) p. 56. All subsequent references are to this edition and will be cited parenthetically in the text.

7 D. Tracy, *The Analogical Imagination: Christian Theology and the Culture of Pluralism* (New York: Crossroad, 1991) pp. 381–2.

8 M. Bakhtin, *Problems of Dostoevsky's Poetics*, C. Emerson (ed. and trans.) (Minneapolis: Univ. of Minnesota Press, 1984) p. 287.

9 G. S. Morson and C. Emerson, *Mikhail Bakhtin: Creation of a Prosaics* (Stanford: Stanford Univ. Press, 1990) p. 15.

10 G. S. Morson, 'Introductory Study', in F. Dostoevsky, *A Writer's Diary. Volume One, 1873–76*, K. Lantz (trans.) (Evanston: Northwestern Univ. Press, 1993) pp. 16, 17.

11 J. Frank, *Dostoevsky: The Stir of Liberation* (Princeton: Princeton Univ. Press, 1986) p. 215.

12 F. Dostoevsky, *Memoirs from the House of the Dead*, R. Hingley (trans.) (Oxford: Oxford Univ. Press, 1983) p. 236.

13 F. Dostoevsky, *A Writer's Diary*, p. 355.

14 J. Frank, *Dostoevsky: The Years of Ordeal: 1850–1859* (Princeton: Princeton Univ. Press, 1985) p. 125.

15 F. Dostoevsky, *A Writer's Diary*, p. 355. This passage is also cited by Frank, who, working with Boris Brasol's version, translates the second sentence as: 'I walked around, looking *attentively* at the faces that I met' (*Years of Ordeal*, p. 123, italics added).

16 From Ivanov's essay 'Dostoevsky and the Novel-Tragedy' (1911), unavailable in English but translated by R. L. Jackson, *Dialogues with Dostoevsky* (Stanford: Stanford Univ. Press, 1993) pp. 258–9.

17 F. Dostoevsky, *Memoirs*, p. 184.

18 M. Bakhtin, *Problems of Dostoevsky's Poetics*, p. 61, his emphasis.

19 Ibid., p. 294.

20 R. H. Weisberg, *The Failure of the Word: The Lawyer as Protagonist in Modern Fiction* (New Haven: Yale Univ. Press, 1984) p. 47.

21 A. Fogel, *Coercion to Speak: Conrad's Poetics of Dialogue* (Cambridge: Harvard Univ. Press, 1985) pp. 225–6.

22 S. Weil, op. cit., p. 143.

23 Ibid., p. 154.

24 Ibid., p. 153.

25 Ibid., p. 115.

26 Ibid., p. 155.

27 Ibid.

28 F. Dostoevsky, *Memoirs*, p. 134.

29 *Crime and Punishment*, 3rd ed., G. Gibian (ed), J. Coulson (trans.) (New York: Norton, 1989) p. 215. Subsequent references are to this edition and will be cited parenthetically in the text.

30 J. W. O'Malley, S. J., *The First Jesuits* (Cambridge: Harvard Univ. Press, 1993) p. 144, his emphasis.

31 J. Fletcher, *Situation Ethics: The New Morality* (Philadelphia: Westminster, 1966) p. 29.

32 L. Griffith, The *Fall of the Prison: Biblical Perspectives on Prison Abolition* (Grand Rapids: Eerdmans, 1993) p. 95.

33 H. Prejean, C. S. J., *Dead Man Walking: An Eyewitness Account of the Death Penalty in the United States* (New York: Vintage, 1993) p. 165.

34 H. Prejean, C. S. J., 'Live Nun Talking'. Int. with P. Zapor, *The Tablet*, 30 March 1996, p. 15.
35 Ibid.
36 R. F. Miller, *The Brothers Karamazov: Worlds of the Novel* (Boston: Twayne, 1992) p. 7.
37 My gratitude to Bruce Berner, Thomas Werge, David Morgan, Janet Larson and Marie Mullins for helpful reading and editorial suggestions.

4
Unmasking the Idol of the Market in 'Bartleby'

Clarence Walhout

In 1857, when Herman Melville was casting about for lecture topics to take on the Lyceum road, he sardonically suggested the following topic to George Curtis, editor of *Putnam's Magazine*: 'Daily progress of man toward a state of intellectual and moral perfection, as evidenced in the history of 5th Avenue & 5 points'.[1] Since Fifth Avenue and Five Points was a location that 'epitomised the unbridgeable gap between the rich and the poor', Melville's irony reflects his sensitivity to the social problems of mid-century America and especially to the social stresses brought about by a young and unshackled capitalist economy. In her recent biography of Melville, Robertson-Lorant describes some of these problems: bank failures and panic in Wall Street; New York bankruptcies, bread lines, and protest gatherings; widespread unemployment and homelessness in northern cities; class differences and political anger; increased street crime.[2]

While social criticism is not as overt in Melville's writing as it is in the essays of his contemporaries Emerson and Thoreau, his fiction moves steadily from adventure narrative toward the development of social, ethical and philosophical themes. Robertson-Lorant describes Melville's social attitudes at the time he turned to short fiction in the early 1850s: 'For Melville ... writing *was* a political career, because he confronted the social and political issues of the day in his stories and sketches. Although he relied on writing for psychological survival, deep down he still believed art had the capacity to change the way Americans perceived reality, and he still imagined he could influence the course of history with his pen'.[3] The stories written for magazine publication and later collected in *Piazza Tales* (1856) were 'quietly showing how individuals were crippled by the economic and social order'.[4] 'Bartleby the Scrivener', first published in *Putnam's*, a magazine that appealed to a well-educated, politically liberal audience, raises profound questions about ethics and the role of religion in the public sphere.

Melville's social critique

Bartleby, an inscrutable man who has come to work as a copyist for a lawyer (the first-person narrator of 'Bartleby the Scrivener'), remains one of the most enigmatic personalities in American fiction.[5] At first Bartleby does a commendable job of copying manuscripts, but within a few days he suddenly and mysteriously refuses to do any work at all. The lawyer tolerates Bartleby's presence in his office for a time, but when Bartleby's strange behaviour begins to draw critical attention the lawyer abandons him. Eventually the homeless and impoverished copyist is consigned to a New York prison where he dies of self-imposed starvation. The final words of the story – 'Ah, Bartleby. Ah, humanity' – indicate that Melville is interested in seeing what is deeply representative about Bartleby and not merely what is socially and psychologically strange. The structure and symbolism of the story focus our attention on the tragedy and irony of Bartleby's situation, not simply on his personal oddities. In his isolation and passivity, Bartleby is Melville's emblem of the human condition.

The descriptive details that indicate Bartleby's human condition can be summarised briefly. First, the lawyer's offices face an adjacent tall building on Wall Street, and hence the light through the windows comes down 'from far above, between two lofty buildings, as from a very small opening in a dome'.[6] At one end of the main corridor a window faces a 'white wall'; at the other end the window faces a wall made 'black by age and everlasting shade'. Bartleby is assigned to work in a space which is enclosed by a 'high green folding screen' and which looks out through a window at a 'dead wall' three feet away (pp. 41, 46). Eventually he spends much of his time staring at this blank wall. All of these images of light and dark, of enclosures, of staring and gazing, are recurrent image clusters in Melville's work and indicate symbolically the loneliness and isolation of human beings in an inscrutable universe. At times Melville's characters strike out aggressively, like Captain Ahab in *Moby-Dick*, against the walls that limit their vision and understanding ('To me, the white whale is that wall, shoved near to me'). At other times they are passive, like Bartleby, or reflective, like Captain Vere in *Billy Budd* ('he would absently gaze off at the blank sea'). But in every case the symbols indicate the desire to escape an existing set of social norms and circumstances and to penetrate to the ultimate and real conditions of existence. Using William Lynch's terms in *Christ and Prometheus*, we may say that such symbols represent the human desire for unconditionality on the part of those who are socially conditioned.[7]

At the end of the story Bartleby's death in a foetal position, 'his knees drawn up, and lying on his side, his head touching the cold stones' of the prison wall, suggests that from birth to death his life was symbolically one of facing walls (p. 73). The forehead/wall image in Melville's work symbolises the inability of the human mind to comprehend the mysterious universe that lies beyond the wall. The comparison of the prison to the pyramids of Egypt indicates that Bartleby's condition as prisoner is the ancient and universal condition of humanity. The spot of green grass in the prison courtyard offers by its colour a link to the green partition in the lawyer's office, making it clear that the office, too, is a kind of prison with only a patch of green to symbolise hope. Living as prisoners in an inscrutable universe is the inescapable fate of human beings in Melville's fiction.

Other descriptive images indicate that Bartleby's human condition is depicted in social as well as metaphysical terms. He is like those dead letters he once sorted in his job in the post office: he is sent to the lawyer, who, when he cannot 'read' Bartleby, moves to a new address, as if to say that the letter is not sent to him. Bartleby ends in the dead-letter office of society, the prison, as a person of no apparent social value. Yet the lawyer murmurs at his death that he now lives 'with kings and counselors' (p. 73). This allusion to the book of Job suggests that Bartleby has status in the courts of heaven even if he had none in the courts of earth. Finally, Bartleby's refusal of food is a symbolic refusal of the sustenance which society provides. Food images and eating form another recurrent pattern of imagery throughout Melville's work; the ways in which characters eat, and the kinds of food they eat or refuse to eat, indicate their ways of appropriating or rejecting the values of their societies. Bartleby's refusal of food is not so much an act of passive resistance against society as it is a symbolic token of the inability of society to provide for his deepest needs.

During the course of his narrative, the lawyer attempts to understand Bartleby by reviewing all their encounters. He explains how Bartleby created in him a turmoil of conflicting emotions and attitudes, and he admits that all his attempts to help Bartleby ended in failure. The lawyer's narrative of frustration and failure reveals his generous and patient temperament, but it also reveals his limitations. Although the lawyer is a kind and intelligent interpreter of human motives and although he weighs all the explanations for Bartleby's behaviour that a good and decent man could think of, he is a person who cannot see beyond social norms. If Bartleby represents the human condition, the lawyer represents the typical social response to others. His limitations are the limitations of his society. Through the lawyer's generous but limited perspective, Melville reveals the inability of nineteenth-century American society to comprehend the humanity of a person like Bartleby.

A cursory account demonstrates the charitable lengths to which the lawyer goes in an attempt to deal with Bartleby. After several attempts to reason with the inscrutable scrivener, the lawyer simply decides to tolerate Bartleby's presence: 'Yes, Bartleby, stay behind your screen, thought I; I shall persecute you no more. … At last I see it, I feel it; I penetrate to the predestinated purpose of my life. I am content. Others may have loftier parts to enact, but my mission in this world, Bartleby, is to furnish you with office-room for such period as you may see fit to remain' (p. 65). When the lawyer feels that his own reputation is being threatened, he decides that he must get rid of Bartleby but, rather than calling the police, the lawyer packs up his entire office and moves to new premises, leaving Bartleby behind. When the tenants of his former building descend upon him in complaint about Bartleby's 'haunting' of the building, the lawyer offers to find Bartleby other employment and even offers to take him into his own home, but Bartleby still 'prefer[s] not to make any change at all' (pp. 68, 69).

The lawyer is an extremely charitable man, but in the end he places a limit on his charity. His limitations are seen most clearly in his reason for abandoning Bartleby; he is unwilling to keep Bartleby in his office when Bartleby's presence begins to damage his professional image: 'At last I was made aware that all through the circle of my professional acquaintance, a whisper of wonder was running round, having reference to the strange creature I kept at my office' (p. 65). After moving his office, the lawyer intercedes again on Bartleby's behalf out of fear 'of being exposed in the papers' (p. 68). The lawyer's limitations are also evident in his summary of his lifelong personal philosophy: 'the easiest way of life is the best' (p. 40). This is not a philosophy of laziness, for the narrator is a hard-working lawyer. Rather, the 'easy way' means living in tune with the expectations and norms of society, gleaning what society offers in exchange for ordinary participation in it. The narrator's profession as lawyer indicates his allegiance to the laws of his society and its modes of living. He is a thoroughly socialised man. The fact that this good man is unable to comprehend Bartleby indicates that the social and psychological explanations that society makes available to him do not touch the core of Bartleby's need.

As readers we can see better than the lawyer himself what is implied in his final words, 'Ah, Bartleby. Ah, humanity'. This utterance can be illuminated by one of the lawyer's many attempts to deal with Bartleby before he is taken to prison. One day the lawyer tells Bartleby that he must leave the premises; the lawyer says that he will assume that when he returns on Monday morning Bartleby will be gone. The narrator says, 'It was truly a beautiful thought to have assumed Bartleby's departure; but, after all, that assumption was simply my own, and none of Bartleby's. The great point was, not whether I had assumed that he would quit me, but whether he would prefer to do so. He was more a man of preferences than assumptions' (p. 61). The lawyer is a man of assumptions; Bartleby is a man of preferences.

What does it mean to be a man of assumptions? Whenever anyone makes an assertion, he or she is also making certain assumptions which are implied by the assertion. In addition, whenever anyone performs an action, that person is implicitly making certain assumptions about the value of that action. To assert and to act imply assumptions of one kind or another. The lawyer is a man of assumptions because in all his assertions and actions he implicitly accepts the values of his society. Bartleby, however, is a man of preferences, not assumptions. This implies ultimately that Bartleby finds no assumptions on which meaningful assertions or actions can be based. In the end he cannot speak or act; his philosophy of preferences when pushed to the extreme provides no basis for any assertions or actions whatsoever. He dies as the emblem of total passivity in a world in which he can find no basis for meaningful assertions or actions.

We need not assume that Bartleby was consciously living out a philosophy of preferences; there is no indication that he is capable of understanding his situation. Yet his enigmatic life is an example of the practice of such a philosophy. Nor does the lawyer understand such a philosophy. As far as he can see, Bartleby's preferences or lack of them are simply social choices. As readers, however, we can see from the story as a whole that Bartleby acts out the implications of existing in a world about which no final or absolute assumptions can be made and in which social accommodation provides no answers to the meaning of life. If we cannot understand the world in which we live or find any basis for values in it, why act? Indeed, why prefer anything? To prefer one thing over another is in itself to affirm value. And so Bartleby can only say 'I prefer not to'.

Since Melville sees the world as indeterminate, to respond as Bartleby does is no less logical or human than to respond as the lawyer does. Indeed, Bartleby's negative preferences more deeply evoke an agonised uncertainty about life than do the lawyer's conventional social assumptions. Bartleby is not Melville's model human being, for living does require some set of assumptions, but Bartleby represents at an elemental level our deep human need for value and understanding. For Bartleby the quest for meaning is totally without fulfilment or direction, but it is in the profoundest sense a human quest. Melville's imagination thus rescues the humanity of Bartleby from the inability of conventional society to understand him.

With this understanding of Bartleby's humanity in mind, we can also see the ultimate ethical dimension of the story. The moral problem for the lawyer is essentially this: what responsibility for Bartleby do I have? The lawyer did not seek responsibility; it came to him unexpectedly. Even so, he does not shun it. Indeed, his charity goes far beyond what ordinary economic or business practices would demand. Nevertheless, he does place a limit on his responsibility. He says in effect that he will exercise responsibility up to the point at which he himself is being hurt. In his and in his society's system of values, self ultimately takes precedence over others. There are, in other words, conditions placed on the responsibility he is willing to exercise. In the story Melville offers no solution to this ethical problem, but he focuses it as sharply as any author has. Is human worth predicated on social productivity, or do human beings have inherent worth even if they are as unproductive, enigmatic and unresponsive as Bartleby?

The society of which the lawyer is an exemplary citizen is nineteenth-century capitalistic America. The story of Bartleby is subtitled 'A Story of Wall-Street', and the lawyer's obsequious references to John Jacob Astor, together with his complacent acceptance of a financially secure life, indicate that moneyed interests and bourgeois comfort are all that the lawyer desires. The lawyer's ethical limitations can thus be seen as Melville's critique of American capitalism and its inability to understand those who do not embrace its economic assumptions. It is a critique of a society that claims the moral values of tolerance, charity and philanthropy but that undercuts these values by placing even greater value on the individualism of the market economy, as evidenced by the final triumph of self-interest over charity on the part of the lawyer. Bartleby is a victim of a society in which economic structures and individualism take precedence over charity and real personal worth.

In the years preceding the writing of 'Bartleby', Melville had been reading Emerson, America's leading spokesman for the gospel of individualism. Emerson's individualism had a philosophical rather than an economic focus, but even so Melville read Emerson with some scepticism from the start, and later he came to believe that Emerson's ideas were too 'disconnected from social concerns and devoid of compassion'.[8] Emerson's doctrine of self-reliance assumes that a common or universal humanity provides a basis for individual confidence and self-assertion. In 'Self-Reliance' he writes: 'Nothing can bring you peace but yourself. Nothing can bring you peace but the triumph of principles'.[9] To discover oneself is for Emerson also to discover the universal human values holding individuals together in social unity. Emerson's call to individualism is grounded in his view of the ultimate unity of all things. He writes that 'greater self-reliance' grows out of a new respect for the divinity in man and that individualism is balanced by 'the resolution of all into the ever-blessed ONE'.[10] Emersonian individualism and American social democracy, thus, ultimately go hand in hand. For Emerson, social harmony is, in theory at least, the natural counterpart of genuine individualism.

Melville's individuals, in contrast, are questers who do not discover within themselves a universal source for human solidarity but who discover others in a world of difference and diversity. Ishmael, the narrator in *Moby-Dick*, is representative. Periodically he discovers 'a damp, drizzly November' in his soul and is driven by his inner uncertainties to seek contact with others in a world of action and interaction. Far from being nourished by an inner sense of a universal humanity that resolves differences, he is energised by a variety of engagements with a range of diverse individuals aboard the *Pequod*. Ishmael's ability to recognise and accept individual differences without either surrendering to or dominating others is what justifies his survival at the end of the novel. With Queequeg he forges a bond of friendship, but neither he nor Queequeg sacrifices personal identity for the sake of the other; their personal and cultural identities are maintained even as they find mutual understanding and affection in their shared activities. Melville's characters do not find the peace that Emerson associates with self-trust and self-assertion; at best they discover a contingent peace that comes from acceptance of others in a distressful world. As a group, they reflect, in a phrase taken from Emmanuel Levinas, 'a pluralism that does not merge into unity'.[11]

The lawyer's preoccupation with Bartleby, his distress (and perhaps sense of guilt) at Bartleby's death and his need to tell Bartleby's story reveal not only a concern with Bartleby but also a crisis in self-understanding. The lawyer's sense of identity is inseparable from the ethical relationship that entered his life with Bartleby's appearance. Though he is tolerant of others, as in the case of Turkey and Nippers, the lawyer is not fully empathetic. His understanding of self and the other is defined by his society. Though he tries to see Bartleby without prejudice, in the end he cannot fathom the scrivener because Bartleby's kind of otherness does not fit within his social world. Melville's implicit critique of Emersonian individualism comes from his profound sense of the differences among individuals and the need to bridge those differences if a democratic society is also to be a moral society. Because of his sense that differences preclude unity at a deep psychic or ontological level, Melville does not echo Emerson's call to radical individualism. Because Melville's characters are unable to answer ultimate questions about the meaning of life, they must find their identities through relationships with one another. But societies also lack the power to answer ultimate questions and can do no more than establish functional systems and formal structures to regulate and direct human behaviour. Melville's work thus sounds a strong note of social realism and scepticism. No society fully comprehends or resolves the problems of self-understanding and social responsibility and therefore the moral claims of people upon one another reach beyond the value systems that societies adopt as their working models.

Melville's characters, thus, are typically individuals without a strong sense of communal identity; they simply adapt in a variety of ways to their social environments. Many become lonely questers on the voyage of life, *isolatoes*, as Melville calls them in *Moby-Dick*. Some become domineering or scheming individuals who manipulate others; some become conformists and defenders of the *status quo*. Melville seems to have a special feeling for the social nonconformists who suffer from uncertainty about themselves and become victims of accident or exploitation. Their loneliness is made poignant by our realisation that society cannot fill the vacuum that remains when metaphysical confidences are lost. The innocence and helplessness of these isolated selves is expressed in the words the lawyer uses about Bartleby: 'But he seemed alone, absolutely alone in the universe. A bit of wreck in the mid-Atlantic' (p. 60). The Romantic confidence in the self that Emerson proclaims is not in Melville's view borne out by experience. Lacking transcendental assurances, Melville's isolatoes experience the Romantic agony of doubt and uncertainty and depend for their identities on their relations with other human beings.

Perhaps Bartleby's initial interest in the scrivener's position and his reluctance to quit the lawyer's office stem from an unconscious recognition of this need. Certainly the more conventional lawyer's self-understanding becomes dependent on his relationship with Bartleby, as his difficulty in leaving Bartleby behind reveals: 'then – strange to say – I tore myself from him whom I had so longed to be rid of' (p. 67). Social relationships are all that Melville's characters have to lead them out of the agony of the isolated self. That is why Bartleby's fate, for Melville, is the paradigmatic tragedy. The possibilities offered by American capitalism and individualism are not sufficient for Bartleby. Whatever the specific reasons for his behaviour may be – and the reasons remain baffling – he cannot find his human worth within his social world.

Readers often respond to Bartleby in one of two ways. Some suggest that Bartleby needs psychological counselling to help him accept the gracious offers of the lawyer. The difficulty with this suggestion is that counselling efforts are attempts to bring patients into an existing system; they are means generated by the system to sustain its own structures. But the system is what Melville is challenging. A second suggestion is that, if Bartleby refuses all offers of help, he deserves his fate; nothing can be done. But this is exactly the dilemma Melville is raising. Bartleby doesn't respond to the lawyer, and yet he is depicted as having human worth. Thus, these two common responses do not address the deep ethical question of the story, namely, how to deal with a person who does not contribute to the system or participate in it and yet has human worth. It is perhaps the deepest ethical question any society faces.

Social assessment

Melville's story does not offer solutions to the lawyer's dilemma, and in the end Bartleby dies a victim of a system that can construct no other alternative. But is it possible for us as interpreters to see the issues more clearly than the lawyer? Using Habermas' model, we may say that what is wrong with the society of 'Bartleby' is that it has no public sphere to which the lawyer can turn or find direction. The lawyer's moral concern for Bartleby's welfare is formed by the existing economic system and the ideology that supports it. Society, at least as it is represented in the story, provides no public means for inquiring into moral issues or for creating alternative measures for dealing with people like Bartleby. In the story the lawyer thinks and acts on his own. He hears and rejects the harsh recommendations of his other employees, but there is no evidence that he discusses the case with anyone else. Melville is not pinning the blame on the lawyer for failing to consult others; rather, he is exposing the calcified institutions of the lawyer's society, institutions that establish the routines of the lawyer's life but do not give him the answers he is looking for or the means for pursuing them. We have noted that the economic institutions – the business practices and the legal institutions that support them – simply view Bartleby as an undesirable intruder. But the whole of society is riddled with the consequences of wealth and economic success. At one point, the lawyer recalls 'the bright silks and sparkling faces I had seen that day, in gala trim, swan-like sailing down the Mississippi of Broadway' and observes how a person like Bartleby gets lost 'among uncaring strangers' who deem that 'the world is gay' and that 'misery there is none'. As his conscience is more and more disturbed by Bartleby's presence, the lawyer recognises the total absence of a social identity for the likes of Bartleby: 'The [possibility of there being a] bond of a common humanity now drew me irresistibly to gloom' (p. 55).

Religion, too, proves indifferent or impervious to the lawyer's concerns. As the lawyer is on his way to Trinity Church one Sunday morning, he stops at his office only to discover that Bartleby has been living there around the clock. Distraught by Bartleby's apparent misery and loneliness, he reflects on how '[o]f a Sunday, Wall-Street is deserted as Petra' and that the place where Bartleby spends his nights and weekends is friendless and 'all through Sunday is forlorn' (p. 55). The lawyer does not continue on to the church services because 'the things I had seen disqualified me for the time from church-going' (p. 56). The church apparently is not the place to go for the kind of moral guidance for which the lawyer is looking. Even the high-sounding biblical theme – 'A new commandment give I unto you, that ye love one another' – is reduced to a platitudinous and self-justifying formula. The lawyer quotes this text to himself when he is tempted to get angry with Bartleby and perhaps commit 'a diabolical murder' like that of Colt's murder of Adams. The religious teaching is turned into a pragmatic principle: 'Aside from higher considerations', the lawyer ponders, 'charity often operates as a vastly wise and prudent principle – A great safeguard to its possessor. ... Mere self-interest, then, if no better motive can be enlisted, should, especially with high-tempered men, prompt all beings to charity and philanthropy' (p. 64). Later the narrator thinks 'that these troubles of mine, touching the scribner, had been all predestinated from eternity, and Bartleby was billeted upon me for some mysterious purpose of an all-wise Providence', but nothing from religious traditions or institutions gives him satisfying answers or solutions (pp. 64–5). When he moves his office, the lawyer leaves Bartleby with these inconclusive words: 'good-bye, and God some way bless you' (p. 67). For the lawyer, religion over-arches the world of human desperation and uncertainty but remains exterior to the real social needs of human beings. It fails to act as a sensor for the economic system or to alert it to the crises of people like Bartleby. As an association, religion has become subject to self-interest, to economic principles.

Judicial and penal institutions are no better equipped to deal with Bartleby. After Bartleby has been confined to 'the Tombs, or, to speak more properly, the Halls of Justice', the lawyer assures the officer in charge 'that Bartleby was a perfectly honest man, and greatly to be compassionated' (pp. 70–1). But this innocent man is nevertheless imprisoned in this hopeless place. In the course of the lawyer's narrative we see that there are public institutions and practices – social, economic, legal, judicial, religious, philanthropic – that shape his thinking but that none of these institutions offers a solution to the lawyer's dilemma. Public institutional life has rigidified in ways that deprive Bartleby (as a representative outsider) of his human identity and fulfilment. In this sense, we can say that in the society depicted in 'Bartleby the Scrivener' there are no vibrant civil associations or social movements, and hence there is no functional public sphere to assist in bridging the differences between Bartleby and the narrator. Institutions and practices become truly democratic in a public way only when the concerns of all individuals are incorporated justly into the public life of the society. The goal of a democratic public sphere is to listen to and respond to all the fundamental rights and needs of all its members.

An alternative

Is it possible for us as contemporary readers to move from Melville's critique to a constructive alternative for dealing with Bartleby? Perhaps we can, if we consider the possibility that religion might have not only a reproductive social function but also a prophetic, utopian function. As Paul Ricoeur explains, the positive social function of religion is to envision a future, a possible utopia, that aims to improve society and to offer alternatives to the ills of the past and present. In its authentic forms, religion can function as a critique of ideology rather than as a type of ideology. Ideology and religion (in its non-ideological forms) can then serve as dialogic contestants, if not partners, in the quest for social justice and freedom. In our day, when ideologies tend to abandon their integrative role and to serve political ends, or when, in Habermas' words, they are colonised by the marketplace, science, and technology, the utopian and integrative power of religion 'may help to unmask the idol of the market'.[12]

How can this view of the social function of religion serve to illuminate 'Bartleby the Scrivener'? Although the lawyer experiences a great range of emotions and proposes a great range of possibilities for dealing with Bartleby, none of them are successful because they arise from within the system and exhibit nothing of what Ricoeur calls the 'utopian imagination'. The religious imagination of Christianity, however, envisions a society that looks beyond the capitalist and individualistic values of the lawyer's society. It is a social ideal that is modelled on the life of Jesus. In this model the only conditions placed on moral responsibility are those of love and concern for other human beings. This concern is not earned or deserved by those who benefit from it; it is given freely simply because those others are human. Although human practice has often turned the Christian vision into a self-centred concern, the 'new commandment' of Christianity has always been 'that ye love one another'. On the surface, the lawyer in 'Bartleby' seems to exhibit Christian virtues, going the second mile and offering help beyond what most other employers would offer. But in a profound sense he represents the opposite of the Christian norm, as his self-centred application of the new commandment reveals. His relationship with Bartleby is ultimately determined by the employer/employee relationship established by American capitalism. The example of Jesus, on the other hand, is one that refuses to place economic limits on one's responsibility for others; it displaces the employer/employee relationship with a much deeper level of ethical responsibility. The religious model of Christianity is one in which the complete sacrifice of self is freely made for the well-being of others. Since this norm is not an option in the lawyer's socially-formed value system, religion serves as a critique of the ideology of the lawyer's society.

A Christian perspective on the lawyer's dilemma offers no concrete solution or immediate course of action for dealing with Bartleby. But this lack of specificity is not a failure of religion nor does it serve as the basis for its indictment. Concrete public solutions for deep social problems demand a coalition of religious, political, economic, ethical, psychological and other concerns, not the separate and independent contributions of these various institutions. Yet the absence or rejection of religious voices in public life and discourse may increase public tolerance for the neglect of the poor and destitute. This possibility is clarified by Yitzchok Alderstein. In Jewish traditions, he writes, the integration of religion, ethics and law in public life is the source of social concern, a concern that would reach out to people such as Bartleby: 'Because Jewish law has a religious basis, and answers to a higher authority than the state, it can easily intertwine the ethical with the purely legal. Feeding the poor, visiting the sick, helping a neighbour are not just admirable acts; they are demanded by statute, and become part of the fabric of daily life'.[13] America's failure to find political solutions to the problems of homelessness and poverty is evidence as clear as any that religion does not fully capture the ears of those who hold power in the public sphere. Religion itself may have become too ideological in its public utterances, but the public sphere has also been too impervious to the constructive and imaginative expressions of religious awareness.

If religion has often failed in its public role, the failure is not entirely that of religion itself, for religion is often absorbed by and assimilated into the secularised economic and political success story of America, as 'Bartleby' demonstrates. The only religious sentiments that are tolerated in Melville's story are ones that endorse the economic/political establishment. But this commodified American public religion only exposes the danger that threatens healthy self-critique and social reform. The danger appears most clearly in an indifferent or callused attitude toward those who suffer because of the system. When a society assigns to all who suffer the responsibility for their own suffering, it fails to recognise its social role and responsibility in the lives of its members. The cases at the fringe of society – the Bartlebys, the homeless, the poverty-stricken, the destitute elderly, the disabled – most clearly expose the lack of sufficient self-critique in a society and the need for a revitalised public sphere. Traditionally, religion more than any other social institution has viewed these 'fringe' populations as the focus of its concern. To exclude religion from the public sphere or to demean its influence is both a failure to admit into the public dialogue an institutional voice that has traditionally expressed concern for oppressed populations and a failure to understand the public social role of religion.

Of course, religion – and theology as its conceptual articulation – needs, as Linell Cady argues in *Religion, Theology, and American Public Life,* to respond to changes in modern life and thought before it can rightfully claim a public voice.[14] Perhaps religion can reclaim that right by following Ricoeur's model for utopian integration. If religion can see prophetically beyond its own preserve and speak with a utopian imagination, it may contribute to an understanding of the values and goals of a society. If it is to do so, it needs to refrain from dogmatically dictating political solutions and unilaterally insisting on specific social/economic programmes, for people with the same religious beliefs can interpret the social implications of their beliefs very differently. The utopian vision is a vision of possibilities, not a single-minded remedy for concrete political actions. But the utopian vision is not just pie-in-the-sky sentimentality either; it does not simply seek some idealised and unreachable goals for social life. It is concerned with the concrete goals and purposes of the particular society within which it functions; it engages in an imaginative search for the ethical values which a moral society ought to pursue.

Notes

1 L. Robertson-Lorant, *Melville: A Biography* (New York: Clarkson Potter, 1996) p. 404.
2 Ibid., pp. 404–5.
3 Ibid., p. 348.
4 Ibid., p. 336.
5 The MLA database shows over 200 articles on 'Bartleby the Scrivener' since 1960. This 'Bartleby Industry' is sardonically and amusingly reviewed in D. McCall, *The Silence of Bartleby* (Ithaca: Cornell Univ. Press, 1989).
6 H. Melville, 'Bartleby, the Scrivener: A Story of Wall-Street', in W. Berthoff (ed.), *Great Short Works of Herman Melville* (New York: Harper & Row, 1969) p. 46. Subsequent references are to this edition and are noted parenthetically.
7 W. F. Lynch, *Christ and Prometheus: A New Image of the Secular* (Notre Dame: Univ. of Notre Dame Press, 1970).
8 McCall, *The Silence of Bartleby,* p. 6; Robertson-Lorant, *Melville,* p. 446.
9 R. W. Emerson, 'Self-Reliance', in B. Atkinson (ed.), *The Selected Writings of Ralph Waldo Emerson* (New York: Modern Library, 1950) p. 169.
10 Ibid., p. 159.

11 E. Levinas, *Time and the Other* (Pittsburgh: Duquesne Univ. Press, 1987) p. 42.
12 P. Ricoeur, *Lectures on Ideology and Utopia*, G. H. Taylor (ed.) (New York: Columbia Univ. Press, 1986) p. 231.
13 Y. Alderstein, 'When Words Kill', *First Things*, June–July, 1996, p. 16.
14 L. E. Cady, *Religion, Theology, and American Public Life* (Albany: State Univ. of New York Press, 1993) pp. 21–9.

5
Constructing Female Public Identity: Gaskell on Brontë

Pamela Corpron Parker

Margaret Oliphant, the late Victorian novelist and biographer, was twenty-nine when Elizabeth Gaskell's *The Life of Charlotte Brontë* first appeared in 1857. She later recalled its impact on the reading public's idea of women writers: Mrs. Gaskell 'originated in her bewilderment a new kind of biography. ... The *Times* blew a trumpet of dismay; the book was a revolution as well as revelation. ... That cry shattered indeed altogether the "delicacy" which was supposed to be the most exquisite characteristic of womankind. The softening veil is blown away when such exhibitions of feeling are given to the world'.[1] Oliphant's response notes Gaskell's 'revelation' of the private details of Brontë's life, but more significantly she acknowledges her 'revolution' in writing 'a new kind of biography', an account of the life of a woman writer. In *The Life of Charlotte Brontë*, Gaskell reconstructs the Romantic myth of the solitary (male) genius struggling against society, offering instead a portrait of a woman artist enmeshed in gender-specific constraints and reaping few of the benefits of literary fame. In a literary marketplace dominated by biographies of 'great men' and their 'great works', Gaskell adapts biographical conventions to a female subject to contest the predominant nineteenth-century view of literary history that recorded only masculine public achievement. Her *Life* was, as Oliphant argued, 'a plea for every woman dropped out of sight',[2] an alternative history in a culture accustomed to thinking of itself as divided into public and private, male and female, professional achievement and domestic sacrifice.

As a prolific and reform-minded writer, Elizabeth Gaskell strained the limits of women's culturally-prescribed roles and frequently opposed male-controlled public discourses in her many social-problem novels such as *Mary Barton* (1848), *Ruth* (1853) and *North and South* (1854). Her works consistently explore cultural constructions of femininity, examine female public appearance[3] and contest the bourgeois ideal of feminine privacy and domesticity. Gaskell thus both epitomises and articulates the discursive conflicts surrounding nineteenth-century conceptions of 'woman' and 'writer'. All her writings dramatise the interdependence of social and domestic concerns and expose the public and political nature of private life. Gaskell often appropriated political, religious and literary discourse to promote women's entry into the public sphere and to justify her own anomalous position as a woman writer. *The Life of Charlotte Brontë* both reflects the Victorian preoccupation with literary personalities and offers an innovative model of female literary subjectivity. In doing so, Gaskell reappropriates the dominant narrative of the public man of letters and produces one of the first successful literary biographies of a woman by a woman.[4] *The Life of Charlotte Brontë* constitutes what Rita Felski calls a 'female counter public sphere',[5] which normalises women's contributions to literary culture even as Gaskell urges the reader to a more sympathetic understanding of the particular struggles, eccentricities and gifts of one of Britain's most enigmatic literary figures.

Biography and the public woman

By the mid-nineteenth century, the massive expansion of the popular press generated an unprecedented supply of information on public figures. The reading public clamoured for details on various public personalities, particularly literary figures. As Mary Jean Corbett argues, the celebrated name, whether male or female, became a marketable commodity which translated itself into numerous biographies, autobiographies and memoirs.[6] As a result, the divisions between private and public life became increasingly difficult to decipher. Until mid-century, the female biographical tradition had been largely hagiographic and usually came in the form of family memoirs, bio- graphical sketches or collective biographies of exemplary women. These memoirs are often introduced with the rhetoric of sacred duty, as an obligatory response to requests to memorialise someone recently deceased. Most were published posthumously within five to ten years of the subject's death. The memoir was a more acceptable vehicle for women writers than the biography and autobiography because it was a less 'selfcentered' narrative which 'legitimated the telling of their own lives without demanding that they commit full disclosure'.[7] Through- out the eighteenth and nineteenth centuries, numerous women wrote hagiographic memoirs of female relatives and friends. Similarly, at the end of the nineteenth century, Eliza Lynn Linton and Anne Thackeray Ritchie wrote well-received memoirs of their families' noteworthy literary circles. Gaskell adapts this memorialising quality but also engages in a broader debate regarding women's vocation and public identity.

In creating a narrative of the woman artist, Gaskell had few models available to her, so she borrowed from the masculine biographical and autobiographical traditions of Plutarch, Johnson and Wordsworth. From Plutarch, she took the classical concept that biographies should be morally edifying, from Johnson the practice of using private letters and familial anecdotes to give insight into the public man, and from Wordsworth the Romantic model of the solitary genius in conflict with a larger society. Gaskell also adapted the narrative conventions and higher moral tone of domestic fiction which, as Nancy Armstrong argues, 'helped produce a subject who understood herself in psychological terms'.[8] Gaskell used the patterns of her own fiction, 'with its suffering daughters, profligate son and stern father, and its emphasis on upbringing and environment, female endurance and courage'[9] to give subjectivity to Charlotte Brontë, her real-life domestic heroine. In addition, Barrett Browning's *Aurora Leigh*, a novel-length poem depicting the life of a woman writer, provided another important model. The epigraph on the *Life*'s title-page suggests Gaskell's familiarity with *Aurora Leigh* and presages Gaskell's desire to make the often hidden narratives of women's lives – in this case, the life of Charlotte Brontë – part of the public discourse:

> ... Oh my God,
> Thou has knowledge, only Thou,
> How dreary 'tis for women to sit still
> On winter nights by solitary fires
> And hear the nations praising them far off.

As Corbett argues, *Aurora Leigh* 'contests the separation of spheres by producing a new subject that united both public and private, poetic and personal experience'.[10] For literary women such as Gaskell and Brontë, the contradictions and confusions of publicity and privacy were not only their lived experience but also a consistent topic of exploration in their writing. Perhaps more than any other nineteenth-century text, *The Life of Charlotte Brontë* demonstrates what Nancy K. Miller calls the 'problem of imagining public female identities'.[11]

Gaskell's contributions to the construction of a public female identity can be understood more clearly by placing the *Life* within the context of other contemporary biographies. In Andrea Kershaw's comparison of Samuel Smiles' biographies of great industrialists and other 'self-made men' to Gaskell's *The Life of Charlotte Brontë*, she notes that Smiles' *Life of George Stephenson* (also published in 1857) implies that men are not shaped or limited by the social conditions of their lives, but are able to rise above them through such virtues as hard work, tenacity and thrift.[12] In the opening to the *Life*, however, Gaskell specifically foregrounds the importance of her subject's historical, social and gender contexts: 'For a right understanding of the life of my dear friend, Charlotte Brontë, it appears to be more necessary in her case than in most others, that the reader should be acquainted with the peculiar forms of population and society amidst which her earliest years passed, and from which both her own and her sisters' first impressions of human life must have been received'.[13] In this passage, Gaskell emphasises the importance of understanding a subject's specific familial and communal context, but she also implies that in Brontë's 'case' it is even 'more necessary' to acquaint the reader with this personal history. In part, Gaskell wants to prove that Brontë's 'peculiar' upbringing is responsible for her unusual artistic vision, but she also tacitly suggests that 'most other' biographical subjects are male. Clearly, the masculine paradigm of 'self-made men' and great 'men of letters' is insufficient to explain either Brontë's literary success or her habitual isolation. Unlike other nineteenth-century biographical subjects, such as Matthew Arnold or Sir Walter Scott, Brontë's public achievements prompted her to retreat into further obscurity. Her literary popularity brought her neither public approbation nor greater personal freedom; no amount of hard work, tenacity or thrift could free her from the notoriety created by the rigid gender constraints and harsh critical double standards of her reading public. While revealing these painful disjunctions between Brontë's personal and professional life, Gaskell examines her own developing sense of professional identity, a process which is bolstered by her interpretation of her friend's life and career.

Shortly after Brontë's death in the spring of 1855, Gaskell wrote to George Smith, Brontë's publisher: 'Sometime, it may be years hence – but if I live long enough, and no one is living whom such a publication would hurt, I will publish what I know of her, and make the world (if I am but strong enough in expression) honour the woman as much as they have admired the writer'.[14] This statement, with its qualifying phrases and parenthetical self-deprecation, exemplifies well the subtle and complex negotiations often required by women writers to gain access to the literary marketplace. Gaskell's earliest letters to Smith reveal her desire to write of Brontë's life, though she had originally envisioned a smaller project more in keeping with the family memoir tradition: 'my children, who loved her, would like to have what I could write about her; and the time may come when her wild sad life, and the beautiful character that grew out of it may be made public. I thought that I would simply write down my own personal recollections of her'.[15] This plan domesticated Gaskell's ambitions as well as her subject's 'wild sad life'. Her tentative language demonstrates both her desire to avoid appearing too eager to capitalise on Brontë's death and the necessary rhetorical deference she adapted to negotiate her way through a male-controlled publishing industry.

Despite these preliminary negotiations for the role as Brontë's biographer, Gaskell insisted that it came upon her 'most unexpectedly'.[16] When Patrick Brontë asked her to be his daughter's biographer less than three months after Charlotte's death, Gaskell promptly wrote to Smith, enclosing Mr. Brontë's letter as proof of his official paternal sanction. In her accompanying letter, she tells Smith of her determination to take on the project: 'I have consented to write it, *as well as I can.* Of course it becomes a more serious task than the one which, as you know, I was proposing to myself. ... Still I am very anxious to perform this grave duty laid upon me well and fully'.[17] In underscoring her self-doubt, Gaskell frames her task in the rhetoric of sacred duty. Her role as the author of one of England's most hotly-anticipated biographies becomes a compulsory burden; it is 'laid upon' her. She must 'perform this grave duty ... well and fully' not only for Brontë's sake, but for her family, her literary colleagues and the wider reading public. Though she assures Smith that she had 'taken some time to consider the request',[18] she had been quick to seize the opportunity offered her. By the time she began negotiating her fee with her publisher, her 'Memoir' had become the 'Biography', indicating her increasing sense of professionalism. As a writer, then, Gaskell had already claimed a place as a public woman for herself.

Reinterpreting Charlotte Brontë

Gaskell took her responsibility as a biographer seriously, sifting through hundreds of letters, interviewing Brontë's family and friends, and travelling to the places where she had lived and worked, including

Brussels. Like most biographers, she selected and transformed the random details and events of Charlotte Brontë's life into a coherent pattern, establishing both a theme and an explanation for her subject.[19] Her detailed rendition of Brontë's private life makes visible what is usually invisible: the intricate and often conflicting web of relationships and domestic duties that were at the heart of most nineteenth-century women's lives. Brontë's 'peculiar' historical and domestic circumstances serve as both explanation and theme of Brontë's life and letters.

To refute earlier accounts of Brontë's 'coarseness' and 'unwomanliness', Gaskell promoted the private, conventional Charlotte Brontë over that elusive, more controversial public persona, Currer Bell. In a letter to Ellen Nussey, Brontë's lifelong friend and correspondent, Gaskell explains her strategy: 'I am sure the more fully *she* – Charlotte Brontë – the *friend*, the *daughter*, the *sister*, the *wife*, is known, ... the more highly will she be appreciated'.[20] Gaskell explicitly establishes in the *Life* a gendered division between the two personas: 'Charlotte Brontë's existence becomes divided into two parallel currents – her life as Currer Bell, the author; [and] her life as Charlotte Brontë, the woman. There were separate duties belonging to each character – not opposing each other; not impossible, but difficult to be reconciled' (p. 334). In presenting Brontë as divided between her duties as 'woman' and 'author', Gaskell suggests that neither category is natural nor exclusive; both are the result of evolving and shifting cultural constructions in need of revision. Gaskell argues that these duties – these spheres – often conflict and may appear separate, but are not irreconcilable.

Gaskell's ambivalence about contemporary notions of women as selfless and domestically circumscribed creatures undergirds the entire biography. As Kershaw argues, the rhetoric of 'manliness' so prominent in the biographies of 'self-made men' is transformed by a rhetoric of 'womanliness' when applied to Brontë.[21] For this defence of Brontë's 'womanliness', Gaskell martialled hundreds of letters, domestic details and personal testimonies to attest to Brontë's good breeding, innate feminine delicacy and adherence to feminine duties. In her 'personal descriptions of Miss Brontë', Gaskell emphasises her 'daintiness' and her 'slight, frail body'. She waxes eloquent over Brontë's 'delicate long fingers ... [whose] peculiar fineness of sensation ... [made] her handiwork, of whatever kind – writing, sewing, knitting ... clear in its minuteness' (p. 124). She details Brontë's tasteful selection of clothing, her sensible management of her father's house and her tender nursing of her sisters and their ageing housekeeper, Tabby. Gaskell even includes the testimony of a 'gentleman' who was so 'singularly attracted by [Brontë's] ... pleasant countenance, sweet voice, and gentle timid manners ...' that he 'conquer[ed] a dislike he had previously entertained in her works' (p. 501). She insists Reverend Nicholls was attracted to Charlotte Brontë not for her 'literary fame [which would] I imagine repel him when he saw it in the possession of a woman. He had seen her as a daughter, a sister, a mistress, and a friend ... the love of such a man – a daily spectator of her manner of life for years – is a great testimony to her character as a woman' (p. 490). Gaskell's 'great testimony to [Brontë's] character as a woman' governs her interpretation throughout the biography.

Yet Gaskell's praise of her friend's feminine nature and domestic prowess is simultaneously undercut by her graphic depiction of female suffering. As she recounts Branwell Brontë's ill-used educational advantages, Patrick Brontë's demanding eccentricities and Arthur Nicholls' wish that his wife discontinue writing after their marriage, an impression of male privilege and female suppression emerges. Brontë's quintessentially feminine death in complications related to pregnancy emphasises Gaskell's portrait of gender-specific victimisation as does the self-effacing epitaph on Brontë's tombstone (which Gaskell replicates at the opening of the biography):

> Charlotte, Wife of the Rev. Arthur Bell Nicholls, A.B., and Daughter of the Rev. P. Brontë, A.B., Incumbent. She Died March 31st, 1855, in the 39th Year of her Age. (p. 59)

Despite her literary prominence, Brontë's virtual disappearance under the weight of her domestic relationships and her husband's and father's professional titles establishes her common experience of subordination with all women.

Gaskell's rhetoric of 'womanliness' and womanly subjection is further supported by Brontë's aversion to publicity. To protect her sisters' privacy as well as her own, Brontë maintained her masculine pseudonym even after the publication of her second novel, *Shirley* (1849). During this time, the identity of Currer Bell was a subject of tremendous speculation. Gaskell contrasts the Brontë sisters' quiet domestic peace with the unruly public discussion of 'the much vexed question of sex' (p. 326). As Gaskell phrases it, 'while the existence of Currer Bell, the author, was like a piece of a dream to the quiet inhabitants of Haworth Parsonage, who went on with their uniform household life, ... the whole reading world of England was in a ferment to discover the unknown author' (p. 326). The encroaching public 'ferment' threatened Brontë's private peace and serves as one of Gaskell's chief antagonists. Gaskell's portrait presents a Brontë who peremptorily dismissed all who speculated that she was 'publishing'. The following letter to Ellen Nussey, reprinted by Gaskell, indicates Brontë's vehement desire to maintain her privacy:

> I have given *no one* the right either to affirm, or to hint, in the most distant manner, that I was 'publishing' – (humbug!). ... Though twenty books were ascribed to me, I should own none. I scout the idea utterly. Whoever, after I have distinctly rejected the charge, urges it upon me, will do an unkind and an ill-bred thing. The most profound obscurity is infinitely preferable to vulgar notoriety: and that notoriety I neither seek nor will have. (p. 343)

Brontë's preference for 'profound obscurity' over 'vulgar notoriety' partly explains her isolated existence and serves as further evidence that she was no 'coarse', publicity-seeking woman, despite her place as one of Britain's most popular novelists. Gaskell acknowledges Brontë's shy pleasure in the local people's pride in her literary fame, but she notes that it was Mr Brontë's reflected glory that pleased Charlotte most. Thus, Brontë's public notoriety is presented as undesirable and burdensome, the result of a greedy public's insatiable appetite for scandal and private detail.

None the less, in describing Brontë's feminine delicacy, her aversion to publicity and her private suffering, Gaskell's project of 'making known' the 'woman' Charlotte Brontë was, ironically, one of feminine publicity – that is, of publishing the private and capitalising on the same public curiosity that both Gaskell and Brontë professed to abhor. For it was Brontë's anomalous position as an 'authoress' that placed her in the glare of public attention, made the identity of Currer Bell an object of continuous speculation and prompted the sale of thousands of copies of the *Life*. Similarly, Gaskell was asked to write Brontë's biography because Patrick Brontë considered her 'an established Author'.[22] As Miriam Allott notes, '[Gaskell's] own literary "prestige" helped make the *Life* popular, but the fame of the Brontës helped still more'.[23] Though both Brontë's father and her husband disliked the publicity accompanying Brontë's literary career, they hoped to counteract the number of unauthorised biographies that were circulating by sanctioning Gaskell's project. Entrusting the biography to Gaskell, an 'established Author', woman and friend of Brontë, ostensibly guaranteed that the book would be both professionally competent and femininely 'delicate'. Once again the established divisions of public and private become obscured with respect to a woman writer.

Despite the common biographical expectation that she would comment on both the life and the letters of her subject, and despite Mr. Brontë's explicit request that Gaskell 'make some remarks on her works',[24] Gaskell avoids direct literary assessment of Brontë's novels. Instead, Gaskell makes several noncommittal statements such as, 'Everyone has a right to form his own conclusion respecting the merits and demerits of a book' (p. 359). Perhaps this reticence is due to her own ambivalence regarding Brontë's work, which is well documented in her letters.[25] The *Life* relies rather on the reader's supposed familiarity with the novels, supplying critical assessments by reprinting the London critics' reviews, both positive and negative.

Though Gaskell exercises an uncharacteristic reticence regarding her opinion of Brontë's books, she does not hold back against Brontë's critics. Early speculation over Currer Bell's identity had preoccupied the London press, and reviews often varied in their praise or condemnation according to the critic's perception of the author's sex.[26] Critics such as George Lewes voiced a discomfort with what he deemed an 'over-masculine vigour' in Brontë's writing (p. 155). Elizabeth Rigby's anonymous 1847 review of *Jane Eyre* concluded that, if Currer Bell was a woman, she was 'one who has, for some sufficient reason, long forfeited the society of her own sex'; and James Lorimer of the *North British Review* surmised that the author of *Jane Eyre* was 'a woman pretty nearly unsexed' (pp. 360, 149). Where reviewers were concerned, Gaskell's favourite defence was a good offence. Her resentment regarding the critical double standard applied to women writers becomes an explicit topic in the *Life*. She launches into numerous tirades against 'thoughtless critics' for their 'want of Christian charity', complains about the 'gossiping conjectures' of the reading public and condemns the reviewers' 'stabbing cruelty of judgment'. Her most virulent attacks were directed towards the anonymous critics who tried to expose Brontë. For instance, Elizabeth Rigby is indicted for her 'conjectures as to the authorship of *Jane Eyre*' as well as her 'cowardly insolence', 'failed logic' and 'misuse of prepositions' (pp. 334, 360). Gaskell bolsters her own authority by quoting the 'good and noble Southey': 'In reviewing anonymous works myself, when I have known the authors I have never mentioned them, taking it for granted they had sufficient reasons for avoiding the publicity' (p. 360). In short, Gaskell turned the burden of unwanted criticism and publicity back on the reviewers. The reader must either embrace Gaskell's condemnation or join the ranks of the nosy public. Not surprisingly, Gaskell's attempts to discipline Brontë's critics did not spare her from their barbed attacks after the publication of the biography.

Constructing an authorial self and an audience

Gaskell's reinterpretation of Charlotte Brontë as paradoxically both private and public was intricately involved in her own self-construction as a woman writer and public figure. In constructing a public female identity for Brontë, Gaskell strongly identifies with her subject, but as a literary rival she must also distance herself. Deirdre d'Albertis argues that Gaskell's biography 'displays a disguised form of literary competition with Brontë, a desire to "novelize" – however lovingly – her rival's life and to subordinate the other woman as the subject of her text'.[27] Gaskell well understood that both Brontë's life and work, as well as her own, would be interpreted through the narrow lens of traditional femininity. Much of the biography is couched in the rhetoric of feminine duty and sentimental friendship, but Gaskell's position as Brontë's interpreter offered her an undeniable opportunity for self-assertion. As Brontë's hand-picked biographer, Gaskell confirmed her own place in literary history. In other words, Gaskell participated in a process which necessarily publicised herself as well as her subject.

Throughout the *Life*, Gaskell positions herself not only as narrator but also as a character. She plays the role of intimate confidante and mourning friend as well as literary colleague and biographical researcher. The text is peppered with narrative intrusions not only as the conventional first-person narrator ('I believe', 'I fancy', 'I imagine'), but also as a witness and participant in private events: 'I was with Miss Brontë when she received Mr Cuthbert Southey's note' and 'I remember Miss Brontë's shiver' (pp. 173, 356). While this more informal, intimate style of narration is typical of much Victorian literature, Gaskell inserts and asserts herself into the text more than was characteristic of her previous fiction. As both narrator and subject, she frequently appears in particular scenes, including her first meeting with Brontë in the Lake District and her first visit to Haworth. She quotes directly from her own letters to friends and privileges her first impressions of Brontë. Most significantly, she includes letters that emphasise their relationship to one another as literary peers. One passage begins: 'I had given Miss Brontë, in one of my letters, an outline of the story on which I was then engaged' and continues with Brontë's detailed commentary on *Ruth*, including her protest at the heroine's death at the conclusion (p. 74). Later, after a long letter detailing the arrangements of a visit, Gaskell says, 'I received a letter from which I am tempted to take an extract, as it shows both her conception of what fictitious writing ought to be, and her always kindly interest in what I was doing' (p. 504). Gaskell's inclusion of their professional collaboration establishes her as a literary peer.

Thus, like many biographies, *The Life of Charlotte Brontë* reveals as much about the author as it does about her subject, particularly her feelings regarding female authorship and public roles. While the *Life* defends Brontë, it also defends the right of all women of 'talents' to use their 'gifts'. If, as Winifred Gerin argues, Gaskell serves as an apologist for Brontë's literary career,[28] she also defends her own. The *Life* reveals Gaskell's oscillation between her culturally prescribed roles as friend, wife and mother and those of biographer, novelist and literary rival. In numerous passages, Gaskell directly addresses these conflicting roles, establishing the right – and the duty – for women with God-given 'talents' to exercise them, even if it meant venturing into traditionally masculine spheres.

The *Life*, simply by its place as a biography of a woman written by another literary woman, refutes Robert Southey's injunction to Charlotte Brontë that 'Literature cannot be the business of a woman's life, and ought not to be' (p. 173). The following often-quoted passage is Gaskell's most compelling response to critics such as Southey:

When a man becomes an author, it is probably merely a change of employment to him. ... But no other can take up the quiet, regular duties of the daughter, the wife, or the mother, as well as she whom God had appointed to fill that particular place: a woman's principal work in life is hardly left to her own choice; nor can she drop the domestic charges devolving on her as an individual, for the exercise of the most splendid talents that were ever bestowed. And yet she must not shrink from the extra responsibility implied by the very fact of her possessing such talents. She must not hide her gift in a napkin; it was meant for the use and service of others. In humble and faithful spirit must she labour to do what is not impossible, or God would not have set her to it. (p. 334)

In this passage, Gaskell is speaking not only of Charlotte Brontë but also of herself. Though she emphasises the pre-eminence of the 'regular' domestic duties allocated to women, Gaskell also asserts the compelling moral responsibilities of women with 'talents'. A talented woman 'must not hide her gift'; she has a moral duty – an 'extra responsibility' – to use it for 'the use and service of others'. In Gaskell's feminist interpretation, Christ's injunction to let one's light shine (Luke 8:16–18) applies to both men and women. By extension, writing literature can be a sacred calling that not only justifies but necessitates women's entry into the literary marketplace. *The Life of Charlotte Brontë* provides a necessary corrective, not only for the specific place of one woman writer, but for all women writers whose God-given talents could transform a corrupt and needy public. As d'Albertis argues, this passage articulates Gaskell's understanding of a writer's duty, the discourse that serves as the source of her literary authority. In her words, Gaskell views 'all work, domestic and literary, as being less a matter of choice – or of an exclusive literary vocation – than a charge from God to write for the use and service of others'.[29] As a Unitarian minister's wife, social reformer and writer, Gaskell had considerable ideological investment in constructing an alternative culture through her writing. Hence, she justifies her own vocation by putting her literary talents at the service of the larger community.

Like Gaskell's previous novels, *The Life of Charlotte Brontë* attempts to alter public opinion through literary narrative.[30] While her fiction tackles the problems of industrialism, domestic squalor and fallen women, *The Life of Charlotte Brontë* examines the problem of female publicity, attempting to transform the reading public into more sympathetic interpreters of women as literary figures. Gaskell represents Charlotte Brontë as a tragic domestic heroine and revises the conventions of masculine biography to suit a feminine subject, but she also attempts to discipline her readers into what she calls a 'larger and more solemn public' (p. 526). Through editorial passages and exemplary anecdotes she demonstrates the right and wrong way to 'read' Charlotte Brontë. She fictionalises the character of Charlotte Brontë in order to teach her audience how to correctly interpret her. As Gaskell states in her concluding paragraphs, her biography seeks to reform a reading public she perceived as being 'critical, unsympathetic, – inclined to judge harshly because they have only seen superficially and not thought deeply' into one which 'knows how to look with tender humility at faults and errors; how to admire generously extraordinary genius, and how to reverence with warm, full hearts all noble virtue' (p. 526). The application of these feminised, Christian values of mercy, sympathy and tenderness discipline the harsh (masculine) judgement that followed Charlotte Brontë during her lifetime and after her death. As Gabriele Helms explains, Gaskell's frequent use of indirect address and the inclusive 'we' 'seem to impute certain attitudes to the readers and direct their attitudes and actions'.[31] Gaskell's suggested alliance between herself as a narrator and the fictive readers flatters them and imposes a standard of greater tolerance towards Charlotte Brontë and, by extension, all women writers.

Ostensibly, *The Life of Charlotte Brontë* provides a portrait of a female artist whose public persona needs remediation, but in the process Gaskell contests the universalising logic of the nineteenth-century reading public which muted or trivialised women's literary con-tributions. She uses a rhetoric of Christian mercy which builds on her identity as a Christian subject and appeals to the reader's shared sense of justice, tolerance and empathy. *The Life of Charlotte Brontë* seeks to convince the reading public of the feminist claim that women's duties include putting their talents to work for the greater good of society. In other words, Gaskell argues that women writers have a moral responsibility to realise their full artistic potential, because their work also has the potential to hasten the Kingdom of God.[32]

The Life of Charlotte Brontë moves beyond a politics of resentment to claim women's power to renew public life, particularly through their writing. Gaskell's ambivalent narrative mixture of privacy and publicity, tragedy and triumph, personal identification and professional disassocia-tion reveals her own ambitions, conflicts and convictions. In reinventing Charlotte Brontë, Elizabeth Gaskell reinvents herself. She proves to herself and her reading public that literature *can* and *should* be the business of a woman's life.

Notes

1 M. Oliphant, *Women Novelists of Queen Victoria's Reign: A Book of Appreciations* (London: Folcroft Press, 1897) pp. 25–6.
2 Ibid., p. 26.
3 This term was originated by B. L. Harman, whose book, *The Feminine Political Novel in Victorian England* (Charlottesville: Univ. Press of Virginia, 1998), particularly the chapter on Gaskell's *North and South*, provides an insightful consideration of the conflicted role of female public figures in Victorian literature.
4 I. B. Nadel, *Biography: Fiction, Fact, and Form* (London: Macmillan, 1984) p. 125.

5   R. Felski, *Beyond Feminist Aesthetics: Feminist Literature and Social Change* (Cambridge: Harvard Univ. Press, 1989) p. 9.

6   M. J. Corbett, *Representing Femininity: Middle-Class Subjectivity in Victorian and Edwardian Autobiographies* (New York: Oxford Univ. Press, 1992) p. 101.

7   Ibid., p. 100.

8   N. Armstrong, *Desire and Domestic Fiction: A Political History of the Novel* (New York: Oxford Univ. Press, 1987) p. 23.

9   J. Uglow, *Elizabeth Gaskell: A Habit of Stories* (New York: Farrar, 1993) p. 399.

10 Corbett, *Representing Femininity*, pp. 68–9.

11 N. K. Miller, *Subject to Change* (New York: Columbia Univ. Press, 1988) p. 60.

12 A. Kershaw, 'The Business of a Woman's Life: Elizabeth Gaskell's *Life of Charlotte Brontë*', *Brontë Society Transactions*, 20 (1990) 11–24.

13 E. Gaskell, *The Life of Charlotte Brontë*, Alan Shelston (ed.) (New York: Penguin, 1980) p. 60. Subsequent references are to this edition and are noted parenthetically in the text.

14 J. A. V. Chapple and A. Pollard (eds), *The Letters of Mrs. Gaskell* (Cambridge: Harvard Univ. Press, 1967) p. 241.

15 Ibid., p. 242.

16 Ibid.

17 Ibid., p. 247, emphasis hers.

18 Ibid.

19 Nadel, *Biography*, p. 6.

20 *Letters*, p. 267, emphasis hers.

21 Kershaw, 'The Business of a Woman's Life', p. 18.

22 P. Brontë's letter to E. Gaskell as quoted in *A Man of Sorrow: the Life, Letters, and Times of the Reverend Patrick Brontë*, J. Lock and W. T. Dixon (eds) (London: Nelson, 1965) p. 493.

23 M. Allott, *The Brontës: The Critical Heritage* (Boston: Routledge, 1974) p. 128.

24 Ibid.

25 About *Jane Eyre*, she writes: 'it is an uncommon book. I don't know if I like or dislike it' (*Letters*, p. 25). Regarding *Shirley*, she says, 'I think I told you that I disliked a good deal in the plot ... but the expression of her own thoughts in it is so true and brave, that I greatly admire her' (*Letters*, p. 72). She is more enthusiastic about *Villette*, calling it 'wonderfully clever ... it reveals depth in her mind, aye, and in her *heart* too which I doubt if ever any one has fathomed' (*Letters*, p. 154).

26 For helpful summaries of the critical reception of Brontë's novels, see Allot, *The Brontës*, T. Winnifreth, *The Brontës and Their Background* (London: Macmillan, 1973), and R. Gounelas, 'Charlotte Brontë and the Critics: Attitudes to the Female Qualities of Her Writing', *Journal of the Australasian Universities Language and Literature Association*, 62 (1984) 151–70.

27 D. d'Albertis, *Dissembling Fictions: Elizabeth Gaskell and the Victorian Social Text* (New York: St. Martin's, 1997) p. 20.

28 W. Gerin, *Elizabeth Gaskell: A Biography* (Oxford: Oxford Univ. Press, 1980) pp. 164, 194.

29 d'Albertis, *Dissembling Fictions*, p. 20.

30 See my article entitled 'Fictional Philanthropy in Elizabeth Gaskell's *Mary Barton* and *North and South*', *Victorian Literature and Culture*, 25 (1997) 321–331, for a discussion of Gaskell's belief in the reformative effects of her fiction.
31 G. Helms, 'The Coincidence of Biography and Autobiography: Elizabeth Gaskell's *The Life of Charlotte Brontë*', *Biography,* 18 (1995) 347.
32 d'Albertis, *Dissembling Fictions*, p. 30.

6
Auden and the Dream of Public Poetry

Alan Jacobs

> Stop all the clocks, cut off the telephone,
> Prevent the dog from barking with a juicy bone,
> Silence the pianos and with muffled drum
> Bring out the coffin, let the mourners come.
>
> Let aeroplanes circle moaning overhead
> Scribbling on the sky the message He is Dead,
> Put crêpe bows round the white necks of the public doves,
> Let the traffic policemen wear black cotton gloves.
>
> He was my North, my South, my East and West,
> My working week and my Sunday rest,
> My noon, my midnight, my talk, my song;
> I thought that love would last for ever: I was wrong.
>
> The stars are not wanted now; put out every one,
> Pack up the moon and dismantle the sun,
> Pour away the ocean and sweep up the wood;
> For nothing now can ever come to any good.[1]

This poem, written by W. H. Auden in 1936 and never considered one of his major works, found new and unexpected life in 1994 when it was featured in the movie *Four Weddings and a Funeral*. A young man asked to speak at the funeral of his beloved finds that the words of 'another splendid bugger' speak for him, and reads the poem, in a cracking voice, to the assembled mourners.

Much of the credit for the strong response to this poem must go to John Hannah, the actor who plays the bereaved lover and whose recitation of the poem is indeed affecting. Moreover, one should not discount the appeal of the film's portrayal of a devoted gay couple whose relationship is the envy of all their straight friends, but clearly Auden's poem itself struck something of a chord in many viewers. Within months of the film's release one could purchase a recording of Hannah reading 'Funeral Blues' – as Auden called the poem in his 1940 collection *Another Time* – along with several other Auden poems. Within a year a chapbook of Auden's love poems as well as a substantial collection of his songs and occasional poems were released, both of which prominently featured 'Funeral Blues'.

Those of us who love and celebrate poetry, especially modern poetry, must of course be gratified by this unexpected burst of attention. But we may also ask ourselves why it happened to this particular poem, especially since it is not one of Auden's acknowledged masterpieces. I do not know of an anthology in which it appears, and Edward Mendelson did not include it among the hundred poems he chose for the second edition of Auden's *Selected Poems* (though Auden himself selected it for the first edition). And one does not have to read the poem very closely before noting that it is in some ways peculiar: for instance, the way it juxtaposes distinctive and even bizarre metaphors with shamelessly deployed clichés. The 'black cotton gloves' of the traffic policemen seem faintly comic for a funeral lament. Still more dubious is the skywritten news bulletin, 'He is dead', instead of, say, 'Eat at Joe's'. But even if the reader feels the dissonance in these metaphors, they are at least *new*, something which cannot be said for a line such as 'I thought that love would last for ever: I was wrong'. The poem seems to hover uneasily among sentimentality, parody and (especially in the final stanza) deep pathos.

A New Critical reading of 'Funeral Blues' (the kind of reading I have just sketched) discovers features of the poem that by the criteria of that theory can only be called faults. Close readers tend to value irony and paradox, but not tonal inconsistency, and they cannot abide the use of cliché. But these 'faults' are identifiable as faults primarily because close reading is just that – a way of *reading* – and this poem was not, at least at first, made to be read. Auden makes it clear that 'Funeral Blues' is primarily a song, intended for public and aural, rather than private and visual, consumption. The first version of what was to become 'Funeral Blues' appeared in *The Ascent of F6*, a play that Auden and Christopher Isherwood wrote for the Group Theatre in 1936. Sung by two characters named Lord Stagmantle and Lady Isabel Welwyn over the body of one James Ransom, the song included the first two stanzas we have now, along with three additional stanzas of virtually unrelieved irony. In 1938 a revised version that follows our current text was published in an anthology called *Poems for To-day* (Third Series) under the title 'Blues'. But Auden continued to think of the poem as a song. In the 1958 *Selected Poems* he calls it one of 'Two Songs for Hedli Anderson'; Anderson was an actress Auden met when they were both working with the Group Theatre in the thirties. And in the last edition of the *Collected Poems* that he oversaw, Auden placed the poem in a group of 'Twelve Songs'.[2]

In light of this complicated textual history one could argue that *Four Weddings and a Funeral* has rescued 'Funeral Blues' from a context – that of a private, solitary reading – essentially foreign to its purposes, and placed it within a more congenial environment, thereby releasing its power and making evident its virtues. The cinema is in no sense identical to the stage – as we will have cause to reflect – but approximates it more closely than does the printed word. When read aloud or sung, 'Funeral Blues' *works* in a way that it may not on the page. The human voice, as John Hannah has demonstrated, gives resonance to the assortment of strange tropes and flat clichés; the *utterance* of the poem knits up these heterogeneous linguistic threads into a tightly woven garment of grief. We understand, hearing the poem, that clichés and strained metaphors alike are resources called upon in the disarray of bereavement.

Or so I contend, by way of explaining the poem's sudden popularity. But why would Auden write such a song only to have it disappear into the great jumble of his *Collected Poems*? The immediate origins of this phenomenon lie, not in Auden's work, but in a brief and relatively little-known essay by T. S. Eliot. For the early Auden inherits from Eliot a great dream, one in which both poetry and English society are restored to some imagined earlier state of wholeness and integration. 'Stop all the clocks', in each of its forms, is a tentative but hopeful step toward the realisation of that dream, but the story I want to tell describes the dream's abandonment.

Eliot's dramatic dream

Consider: Auden is known to students of literature almost exclusively through the poems he wrote for the page, while his dramatic poetry – though it fills approximately a thousand pages in the edition of his *Complete Works* which Mendelson is in the process of editing – remains almost completely unknown. The case of Eliot is quite similar in this respect: critics often speak of *Four Quartets* as Eliot's 'farewell to poetry' even though he wrote verse plays for another two decades, and the fame of *The Waste Land* could never console Eliot for his failure to complete what he often considered his most important project, *Sweeney Agonistes*.

What is particularly ironic about these case studies in poetic reputation is that for Auden and Eliot dramatic poetry was absolutely central to a vision they (with many other modern artists) shared: the vision of a culture of unified sensibility. That term, of course, derives from Eliot's famous historical thesis about a European 'dissociation of sensibility' that 'set in' in the seventeenth century, and 'from which we have never recovered'.[3] As Eliot's thoughts on this subject developed, it became more and more clear to him that individual sensibilities could only be unified and integrated if civil society were reunified and reintegrated. In short, Eliot increasingly came to believe that only a fully functioning public sphere could rescue Western culture from its long agony, and to hope that a 'reconstruction' or 'restoration' of the English tradition of poetic drama could serve in the building of that public sphere.

Eliot's first significant, if tentative, move to articulate these hopes comes in an essay published in 1919 called 'The Possibility of a Poetic Drama'. He claims, 'The Elizabethan Age in England was able to absorb a great quantity of new thoughts and new images, almost dispensing with tradition, because it had this great form of its own [i.e., the drama] which imposed itself on everything that came to it. Consequently, the blank verse of their plays accomplished a subtlety and consciousness, even an intellectual power, that no blank verse since has developed or even repeated; elsewhere this age is crude, pedantic, or loutish in comparison'.[4] Eliot here attributes to Elizabethan society something very like what he attributes to certain individual writers in his articulation of the difference between a unified and dissociated sensibility: 'The poets of the seventeenth century, the successors of the dramatists of the sixteenth, possessed a mechanism of sensibility which could devour any kind of experience'.[5] But note that in the first passage social integration is the *consequence* of the dramatic poets' own integrated minds. Eliot admits that 'the drama is only one among several poetic forms', but contends that it 'is capable of greater variation and of expressing more varied types of society, than any other', and further claims that 'when one day it was discovered lifeless, subsequent forms which had enjoyed a transitory life were dead too'.[6] And not just literary forms, but also, presumably, social forms of life were lost with the demise of poetic drama.

This social integration, according to Eliot, was not the achievement of heroic figures like Marlowe or Shakespeare: rather, such poets were the beneficiaries of a general development. When he makes this point Eliot fairly drools with envy: 'To have, given into one's hands, a crude form, capable of indefinite refinement, and to be the person to see the possibilities – Shakespeare was very fortunate. And it is perhaps the craving for some such *donnée* which draws us on to the present mirage of poetic drama'.[7] If we were to understand just how much is given to the dramatic poet in such an age 'we should see then just how little each poet had to do; only so much as would make a play his, only what was really essential to make it different from anyone else's. When there is this economy of effort it is possible to have several, even many good poets at once. The great ages did not perhaps *produce* much more talent than ours; but less talent was wasted'.[8]

Eliot's account suggests that an age that lacks such a pre-existing dramatic form will be not just artistically but politically impoverished. But Eliot's cultural history offers no hope that a single poet, or even a collection of gifted poets, will be able simply to *create* the needful form if it is missing. So he looks again at his contemporary scene: is anything appropriate 'given' to us? In the last paragraph, as an apparent afterthought, Eliot tosses out a suggestion: 'The Elizabethan drama was aimed at a public which wanted *entertainment* of a crude sort, but would *stand* a good deal of poetry; our problem should be to take a form of entertainment, and subject it to the process which would leave it a form of art. Perhaps the music-hall comedian is the best material. I am aware that this is a dangerous suggestion to make'.[9] Then follow three ambiguous sentences that distinguish, in a vague way, treating art seriously, treating it solemnly and treating it as a joke. End of essay.

But, having fled unceremoniously from his own notion, Eliot found himself unable to ignore it, and when Marie Lloyd died in 1922 he discovered an occasion to return to the idea. Lloyd was, for Eliot as for many others, the greatest of the music-hall entertainers. And what made her great, says Eliot, was her ability to use her art to forge a temporary but powerful union with her audiences. While other performers could

> amuse their audiences as much [as] and sometimes more than Marie Lloyd, no other comedian succeeded so well in giving expression to the life of that audience, in raising it to a kind of art. ... The working man who went to the music-hall and saw Marie Lloyd and joined in the chorus was himself performing part of

the act; he was engaged in that collaboration of the audience with the artist which is necessary in all art and most obviously in dramatic art.[10]

Throughout this brief eulogy Eliot hints at, though he never specifically mentions, ancient Athenian drama. In the sentence just quoted one might think of the ending of Aeschylus' *Eumenides*, when the audience quite literally 'joins in the chorus' and marches with the actors out of the theatre of Dionysus to celebrate the past, present and future of Athens. And when Eliot says that Marie Lloyd's audiences were 'not so much hilarious as happy' he seems to be invoking that complex Greek word commonly if inadequately translated as 'happiness' – *eudaimonia* – which for the citizens of Athens was the ultimate goal of drama.

But if Marie Lloyd's music hall is the closest equivalent in post-war London to the theatre of Dionysus, the parallel is not after all as close as Eliot would like. For the music hall is a class-specific phenomenon – it is, in Habermasian terms, a 'partial' rather than a 'universal' public sphere. Marie Lloyd, says Eliot, is 'the expressive figure of the lower classes'. In her music and comedy, working people 'find the expression and dignity of their own lives'. Such a gift is not available either to the aristocracy, who 'are subordinate to the middle class, which is gradually absorbing and destroying them', or to the middle classes (Eliot shifts to the plural here) themselves, who 'have no such idol' as Marie Lloyd because they 'are morally corrupt'. And even the lower classes, who have tragically just lost their 'idol' and 'expressive figure', may not last much longer, since their representative dramatic form is being replaced by the 'cheap and rapid-breeding cinema' which threatens to reduce the lower classes to 'the same state of protoplasm as the bourgeoisie'.[11]

This is strong language for the Eliot of 1922, though it would become characteristic of him when another dozen years had passed. His frustration was no doubt intensified by the fact that he was not and could never be a member of the lower classes; Athenian drama was in its own way a class-specific phenomenon too, but it was at least the product of a class with whom Eliot could identify. What is needed, one may clearly infer from the essays I have been citing, is a modern form that in some way combines the energies and resources of the music hall with the energies and resources of Athenian drama. This combination is represented in the very title of Eliot's great theatrical project, which he started working on soon after the completion of *The Waste*

Land and only a few months after the death of Marie Lloyd: *Sweeney Agonistes*. But he never finished the play. Perhaps his theory of the sociological origins and development of great dramatic traditions, or rather of their failure to originate and develop, found empirical confirmation in his own work.

Auden's inheritance

For Auden and the other Left writers of the thirties – that is, almost every writer in England among that 'second generation', the younger siblings as it were of Eliot, Pound, Woolf, Yeats and Joyce – participation in the public and political was not laboriously pursued, it was simply given. From the start of Auden's career the drama offered itself as a genre in which public dreams could be realised: his first collection, *Poems* (1930), begins with his dramatic 'charade' *Paid on Both Sides*, and his criticism in the thirties frequently returns to the question of a meaningful public role for poetry. Thus the avowedly Leftist Auden, and the Eliot who deemed himself 'classicist in literature, royalist in politics, and Anglo-Catholic in religion', alike focused a remarkable amount of their time and energy in the thirties on the construction of a poetic drama and theory oriented toward the reconstitution of the public sphere. In one of the most interestingly condensed ironies of modern literary history, when the Group Theatre inaugurated its first public season in the autumn of 1935, it featured a double bill: Auden's medievalist masque *The Dance of Death* and Eliot's still fragmentary *Sweeney Agonistes*.

To understand how odd this juxtaposition is, one needs to compare, however briefly and inadequately, Eliot's argument about the European 'dissociation of sensibility' with Habermas' account of *The Structural Transformation of the Public Sphere*. The two arguments have the same form, in that they describe how cultural and historical circumstances first enabled and then disabled a vibrant public sphere, but the differences are enormous. For Eliot, the European mind began to disintegrate in the seventeenth century, just about the time at which Habermas sees the 'bourgeois public sphere' beginning to assemble. Moreover, Eliot's understanding of 'unified sensibility' depends upon a certain valorisation of poetry, especially dramatic poetry, while for Habermas the literary genre that played the greatest role in establishing the 'literary public sphere' is the novel. Eliot has nothing to say about the novel, but one can readily infer that for him it is a debased genre. It is only a slight over-simplification to say that Habermas' understanding of a workable public sphere is social–democratic, Eliot's aristocratic.

While Habermas thinks that 'a robust civil society can develop only in the context of a liberal political culture', Eliot would surely reply that in such a culture a robust civil society is impossible. (Indeed, he makes such a case explicitly in his suppressed 1934 volume *After Strange Gods* and, in a different way, in *The Idea of a Christian Society*.) This contrast is worth noting because Auden, whose politics were much closer to Habermas' than Eliot's, had only one strong model of literary 'publicness' available, which meant that he had to engage in a long process of revising Eliot's understanding of the potential public role of poetic drama.

Thus, as the young Auden worked through his understanding of what drama and poetry should be, Eliot could provide, if not a model for dramatic composition, a (contestable) model for dramatic theory; and indeed Auden often responds, usually covertly, to Eliot's pronouncements. In a 1934 review, for instance, though he never mentions Eliot's name he extends and meditates upon Eliot's suggestion about the music hall as a potential model for modern drama: 'If the would-be poetic dramatist demands extremely high-brow music and unfamiliar traditions of dancing, he will, of course, fail; but if he is willing to be humble and sympathetic, to accept what he finds to his hand and develop its latent possibilities, he may be agreeably surprised to find that after all the public will stand, nay even enjoy, a good deal of poetry'.[12] A year later, in writing a kind of manifesto for the Group Theatre, Auden seems to adapt ideas from Eliot's essay on Marie Lloyd: 'Drama began as the act of a whole community. Ideally there would be no spectators. In practice every member of the audience should feel like an understudy' (p. 273).

Eliot seems to have provided Auden with certain co-ordinates to help him fix his proper artistic tasks. But in what may be an example of the anxiety of influence, Auden seems to have gone out of his way to avoid the literary models that Eliot tended to favour. If Auden was influenced by Athenian or Elizabethan tragedy, he preferred not to acknowledge it. In the thirties he was determined to find medieval models. He told a friend that for anyone wanting to understand *Paid on Both Sides* – the title of which is taken from a line in *Beowulf* – 'literary knowledge of the Mummers' play with its Old–New year symbolism is necessary'.[13] Similarly, his *Dance of Death* is an adaptation of both the medieval *danse macabre* and English mystery plays – one of which, *The Deluge* from the Chester cycle, was, at Auden's bidding, coupled with *The Dance of Death* in two private performances by the Group Theatre in 1934. If Eliot fixed on the last years of Elizabeth I as his Golden Age, Auden usually looked further back. And above all what he found in that earlier time was a significant public role for poets. It was largely in hopes of restoring or recovering such a role for poets that he wrote plays and served as 'secretary of ideas' for the Group Theatre.[14]

None the less, Auden was aware of the temptations of nostalgia and understood that it could quickly render inauthentic any would-be appropriation of the poetic or cultural past. From the start of his career he had been determined to write poetry of the world he actually lived in, and his propensity for including industrial equipment, power stations, aeroplanes and (especially) pylons in his verse was so immediately noticeable that it quickly became a focus for parody. All his plays have contemporary settings. For Auden, medieval drama exemplified a public poetry rooted in its lifeworld, but for that very reason its protocols and techniques could not simply be transferred to another, radically different time. The role of the medieval dramatists had to be followed, rather than their productions. And Auden devoted a great deal of his poetic energies in the thirties to following that example, especially in the plays he wrote with Isherwood.

Even as Auden worked so hard in and for the theatre (as theorist, as manifesto writer, as 'secretary of ideas', as solitary and collaborative playwright), he was simultaneously working at the development of another kind of public poetry – as though he were preparing for the possible failure of his dramatic projects. Throughout the thirties, Auden also sought to develop a public poetry that did not require the apparatus of the theatre. Almost from the beginning of his career, he understood that public poetry comes in more than one variety. In a journal entry from 1929, he asked: 'Do I want poetry in a play, or is Cocteau right: "There is a poetry of the theatre, but not in it"?' (p. 301). The different versions of 'Stop all the clocks' indicate that several years later Auden had not decided whether his poetry should live inside or outside the theatre, that he was seeking to maintain a double poetic presence, patrolling a boundary that demarcated genres and social institutions alike. 'Stop all the clocks' stands at the juncture of these two related but different attempts to reassociate the poetic sensibility and reinvigorate the public sphere.

Creating community

The Modernist emphasis on the dramatic as the impersonal – Pound's personae, Yeats' masks, Joyce's *deus absconditus* paring his fingernails – is well known. What is less well known is the history of the transformation of that emphasis in the next generation of British writers, especially in Auden. The dramatic is important to Auden not because it is impersonal and hence a repudiation of the Romantic cult of personality; instead, for Auden the drama represents the public and the communal. In this respect Eliot, as his comments on poetic drama and the music hall indicate, serves as a kind of bridge between the two generations, which, following the example of Paul Fussell, I will call the Modernists and the Moderns.[15]

Both generations wrote plays. But when they employed other poetic genres in which there is the possibility of retaining at least some of the characteristics of drama they made very different choices. As Carol Christ has so effectively argued, the Modernists prove themselves to be true heirs – not, after all, the enemies – of the Victorian poets by making the dramatic monologue their normative genre.[16] This supports their anti-Romanticism, because it allows for the creation of a poetic persona clearly marked as different from that of the author. But Auden – who was followed in this practice by others – wrote almost no dramatic monologues: instead he wrote songs.

The speaker, or rather the singer, of a song is not necessarily, and in some cases demonstrably not, the poet. The singer-songwriter is a creation of the 1960s and as a cultural standard owes almost everything to Bob Dylan, who had inherited it from bluesmen like Robert Johnson and folk singers like Woody Guthrie. But the pre-1960s popular song invested very little energy in creating a distinctive personality for its singer: the character expressed in a song lyric is attenuated and stylised, typical rather than idiosyncratic. 'Stop all the clocks' features a bereaved lover, not J. Alfred Prufrock or Hugh Selwyn Mauberly, thus showing its origins in the songs of the music hall or cabaret.

This heritage is nicely limned in Richard Hoggart's account of working-class life in early twentieth-century England, *The Uses of Literacy*. In the sections devoted to music, he describes the semi-professional singers who performed at working-men's clubs, clubs that retained the characteristics of an 'older environment', that of the music halls. Hoggart contrasts the singing style favoured in such clubs with the more idiosyncratic approach of American 'crooners':

> The manner of singing is traditional and has fixed characteristics. It is meant to embody intense personal feeling, but is much less egocentrically personal and soft-in-the-middle than the crooning styles; it aims to suggest a deeply felt emotion (for the treachery of a loved one, for example), but the emotion has not the ingrown

quality shown by the crooners. With the crooners, ... one is in the world of the private nightmare; here [in the clubs], it is still assumed that deep emotions about personal experiences are something all experience and in a certain sense share.[17]

Moreover, when Hoggart notes the unpopularity in England of certain well-known American songs, he attributes that failure to 'the lack of sufficiently generalised emotion': one might say too much like the dramatic monologue.[18] Few of us are inclined to sing along with 'The Love Song of J. Alfred Prufrock'. But in 'Stop all the clocks' the rich profusion of tropes makes the simply direct last line exceptionally potent. Calling attention to itself by the measured tread of its six stresses ('For nothing now can ever come to any good'), it can be readily echoed by bereaved lovers, or lovers who can imagine bereavement. Its emotion is 'sufficiently generalised'.

Hoggart's description of the musical preferences of the working-class English is relevant to Auden's songs in another way. Earlier I mentioned how 'Stop all the clocks' seems to hover between pathos and parody, as do many of Auden's songs. In the 1958 *Selected Poems*, for instance, the second of the 'Two Songs for Hedli Anderson' also combines the banal and the innovative in a way that can almost make a reader queasy:

> O the valley in the summer where I and my John
> Beside the deep river would walk on and on
> While the flowers at our feet and the birds up above
> Argued so sweetly on reciprocal love,
> And I leaned on his shoulder; 'O Johnny, let's play':
> But he frowned like thunder and he went away.

That's the familiar first stanza; by the last, the effect is surreal:

> O last night I dreamed of you, Johnny, my lover,
> You'd the sun on one arm and the moon on the other,
> The sea it was blue and the grass it was green,
> Every star rattled a round tambourine;
> Ten thousand miles deep in a pit there I lay:
> But frowned like thunder and you went away.[19]

Hoggart makes it clear that the working-class people who listened raptly to sentimental songs knew perfectly well that the songs were sentimental, and that some kind of corrective was occasionally called for, perhaps in the form of parody. 'But', he goes on, 'the limits of this are intuitively defined: I once heard a young man deliver his own mocking version of a popular sentimental song, and not only fail to make the company laugh, but raise in them the strong, though unexpressed, sense that he had been guilty of a lapse of taste. He ... had not so much laughed affectionately at the emotions as destroyed them'.[20] What is remarkable and disorienting about Auden's practice is that he combines the direct expression of emotion and its parody in a single song in such a way that it becomes hard to distinguish affectionate laughter from destructive contempt.

This technique places a great responsibility on readers, who must find their way through this maze of passions or accept being lost in it. For the actual listener of the song the problem can be (though it is not always) simplified by the music written for the poet's words. In the case of 'Stop all the clocks', Benjamin Britten decided to play it straight in the tune he wrote for its *Ascent of F6* version, for, though those lyrics are still stranger and apparently more parodic than the ones that appear in Auden's collections, listeners seem to have been deeply moved by the song: Isherwood refers to it as an 'overwhelming funeral dirge' while Sidnell calls it a 'magnificent blues number'.[21]

Without the music, judgements about Auden's songs can be diverse indeed. For instance, 'Miss Gee', one of the ballads Auden was so fond of writing in this period, describes the illness and death, from cancer, of a repressed spinster. To me, and to a number of other critics, this is a sober and sobering poem; but Valentine Cunningham refers to it as one of Auden's 'savagely jaunty sick-joke lyrics', and when Isherwood found out that Auden wanted to write a ballad about Isherwood and his boyfriend Heinz, he 'objected absolutely' to having his experiences depicted in the 'heartless comic style' of 'Miss Gee'.[22]

One can imagine several motives for this ambiguous kind of song. For Sidnell – describing similar tendencies in Auden's plays – 'in such verse Auden seems to be working both sides of the stylistic street. If it was taken at face value as the language of poetic tragedy (as it often was), well and good; if not, the bolt hole of burlesque had been prepared'.[23] There is probably something to this view; Auden was not above playing games with his audience (especially in political matters, about which, throughout the thirties, he was more ambivalent than he felt he could acknowledge). But whatever he was up to in his plays, it may well be that in his songs Auden was taking the public and dialogical dimensions of such verse seriously – seriously enough to encourage the reader/listener to become a co-maker with him, a participant in the establishment and elaboration of poetic meaning. In the absence of the complex context of the theatre, Auden in poems like 'Stop all the clocks' may have been violating the singularity typically associated with the lyric voice in order to build a kind of community of voices: song becomes the means by which a partial and quite temporary public sphere is established.

In 'Stop all the clocks' a number of voices may be discerned. We have, of course, the modern inventive poet with his original tropes (e.g. the white public doves whose necks bear funereal bows); but there is also, especially in the third stanza, the exaggeration conventional to popular love poems and poetic elegies alike; and the methodical deconstruction of the cosmos depicted in the final stanza reads like a parodic inversion of creation myths or nursery rhymes. Are these competing or complementary ways of representing loss? If one understands the lyric voice to be essentially singular, the song stands guilty of vocal incoherence. But this is to neglect an ancient tradition of lyric poetry, one that despite its great lineage is so little understood that it has no agreed-upon name. Nietzsche, who is responsible more than anyone else for calling this tradition to the modern attention (in *The Birth of Tragedy*), uses its old Greek name and names it the 'dithyrambic'; W. R. Johnson in his admirable *The Idea of Lyric* seeks a somewhat broader designation and calls it the 'choral'.

Johnson, who mentions Auden but rarely, seems to be invoking the Auden we have been investigating when he writes that 'if the name of choral has almost disappeared from our literary vocabulary, the choral imagination and the choral act have, so far from disappearing, made an extraordinary comeback in modern times'. The choral lyric is necessary, contends Johnson, because 'Humans beings have, after all, not only private emotions and selves but also public emotions and selves'. The role of the 'solo lyric' may be, in part, to 'clarify the limits and the nature of the private self'; but

> [the] choral poet imagines those emotions which lead us to want to understand both the possibility of our communion with each other and the possibility of our communion with the world. ... [T]he modern choralists, in their different ways, attempt to countervail [the characteristically modern] process of alienation by reaffirming our kinship with each other and with the world that begets us and nourishes us.[24]

This is the specifically *literary* tradition on which Auden draws as he writes his songs and ballads of the Thirties. It dovetails neatly, I think, with the popular music tradition discussed earlier, especially in its need for a properly typical and stylised representation of emotion: the energies of 'Stop all the clocks' derive from Pindar and Marie Lloyd alike. Such emotive representation draws explicitly on readily identifiable artistic models in order to emphasise its continuity with other utterances, other people, a continuity which yields at least a momentary sense of community.

But is this sense of community in any way authentic? Can the solitary reader of a poem ever experience what Hoggart's (perhaps idealised) participants in the culture of the working-men's clubs knew? Can the reader ever feel what the audience at *The Ascent of F6* felt? These are questions that take on ever greater significance as the music halls, and the working-class culture described by Hoggart, retire further into the recesses of the past; and as Faber allows *The Ascent of F6* to go out of print while collections and selections of Auden's poems succeed one another with impressive regularity. The community in the reader's mind may be the only one that poets today can hope to cultivate.

A loss of faith

I have said that Auden resisted nostalgia. But as the thirties drew to a close, along with his theatrical partnership with Isherwood, and as the doubts I have enumerated grew stronger in his mind, the nostalgic note began to creep into his critical writings. As it did, the Eliotic influence that Auden had earlier tried to suppress found its outlet.

The great project of the Group Theatre was failing. Its hope to become a place of meeting and reconciliation for the classes of Britain was never realised. Though it repeatedly announced its solidarity with working people, the reality was rather different, as Cunningham explains (citing a 1935 article in the *New Statesman*):

> Group's handful of Sunday nighters were scarcely the masses: 'small Sabbatical assemblies' of bourgeois Lefties in 'juvenile beards, dark-blue shirts, and horn-rimmed spectacles, which are not the representative insignia of the working class,' was how Ivor Brown saw them. ... Brown couldn't 'see much point' in audiences who 'either see the point of the propaganda already or see the point of nothing but their own importance.' The amateurism of the Group's acting was often criticised; more damagingly, [Stephen] Spender found Auden

and Isherwood's plays 'undergraduate smoker' (he meant Oxford and Cambridge) stuff. Group was run, in fact, very like an undergraduate society, with its programme cards, bottle parties, and its intimate revues before invited audiences. A comparison Auden cannot have found welcome.[25]

The comparison would certainly have been unwelcome: Auden had hoped that the Group Theatre, and English poetic drama more generally, would bring him and people like him out of the narrow intellectual world and into the society from which they had been exiled not only by the persistence of the British class system but also by the advent of Romantic aesthetic isolationism. Auden had no interest in a *very* partial public sphere that deceived itself into believing that it was universal. As it became clear that his theatrical work was not succeeding in its integrating mission, Auden turned more and more to the choral or dithyrambic traditions, but he could not see these traditions as offering the social salvation that he had earlier hoped to find in the theatre.

In 1938 Auden edited *The Oxford Book of Light Verse* and his editorial comments illuminate the questions with which this essay is occupied. In Auden's utterly idiosyncratic definition, light verse is written 'when the things in which the poet is interested, the things which he sees about him, are much the same as those of his audience, and that audience is a fairly general one'. In such a case the poet 'will not be conscious of himself as an unusual person, and his language will be straightforward and close to ordinary speech' (p. 363). Auden is at pains to insist that 'light verse can be serious', and that it is only because we still live 'under the social conditions which produced' Romanticism that we fail to understand this. Since the Romantics, 'it has been only in trivial matters that poets have felt in sufficient intimacy with their audience to be able to forget themselves and their singing-robes' (p. 364). Auden then explicitly invokes what Raymond Williams calls the myth of the 'organic community of Old England': 'As the old social community broke up, artists were driven to the examination of their own feelings and to the company of other artists. They became introspective, obscure, and highbrow' (p. 365). The 'interests and perceptions' of the post-Romantic poet 'are not readily acceptable to his society'; he is, therefore, 'acutely aware of himself as the poet, and his method of expression may depart very widely from the normal social language' (p. 363). As it happens, this is a pretty good description of Auden's early lyric poetry, so famous for its obscurity, but it is just what he sought to avoid in his plays.

One might infer from these statements that Auden, like Eliot, longs for an unselfconscious absorption in the rituals and practices of an organic community, but this is not quite so. Auden continues, 'The more homogeneous a society, the closer the artist is to the everyday life of his time, the easier it is for him to communicate what he perceives, but the harder for him to see honestly and truthfully, unbiased by the conventional responses of his time. The more unstable a society, and the more detached from it the artist, the clearer he can see, but the harder it is for him to convey it to others' (p. 364). Either extreme, absorption or detachment, disables the artist from productive engagement with society. What is called for, Auden posits, is a productive tension, in which the poet is 'still sufficiently rooted in the life of his age to feel in common with his audience', but the society as a whole is 'in a sufficient state of flux for the age-long beliefs and attitudes to be no longer compulsive on the artist's vision' (p. 364). Was there a time in the history of English literature when this balance was best achieved, when the tension was most productive? Yes: it was the Elizabethan age.

Here the young lion of English poetry unexpectedly rejoins Old Possum; the hero of the intellectual Left meets the voice of classicism, royalism, Anglo-Catholicism. But let us also note that Auden's picture of Elizabethan society requires less unanimity than Eliot's; it is actually closer to the Habermasian claim that 'a lifeworld in which cultural traditions are open to criticism' is the medium in which civil society can best flourish. Moreover, at the end of this odd introduction Auden seeks once more to keep Eliot at arm's length. He does so by reminding himself of the larger socio-political context in which nostalgia is unacceptable:

> The old pre-industrial community and culture are gone and cannot be brought back. Nor is it desirable that they should be. They were too unjust, too squalid, and too custom-bound. Virtues which were once nursed unconsciously by the forces of nature must now be recovered and fostered by a deliberate effort of the will and the intelligence. In the future, societies will not grow of themselves. They will be either made consciously or decay. (p. 368)

Or, as Eliot had written twenty years earlier, 'Tradition ... cannot be inherited, and if you want it you must obtain it by great labour'.[26] Auden, however, is arguing for neither royalism nor aristocracy, but 'a democracy in which each citizen is as fully conscious and capable of making a rational choice as in the past has been possible only for the wealthier few'. Only 'in such a society will it be possible for the poet, without sacrificing any of his subtleties of sensibility or his integrity', to write what Auden calls light verse: 'For poetry which is at the same time light and adult can only be written in a society which is both integrated and free' (p. 368).

This is indeed a compelling vision, as far as it goes. But on the obvious question of how such a society may be achieved, Auden is silent. There is no hint from him that the drama, or any other form of art, could contribute to the formation of a genuine public sphere. In this sense he repudiates Eliot's dream and seems covertly to employ the Marxist distinction between base and superstructure: the whole introduction implies that art, as a superstructural phenomenon, is utterly dependent for its health and its character on the health and character of the economic base. Socio-political conditions determine poetry, not the other way round; and the social conditions which produced Romanticism may not be reversible. By the end of the thirties Auden was wondering if anyone could write truly choral or dithyrambic poetry, and, if so, whether it would make any difference. Less than a year after writing the introduction to *The Oxford Book of Light Verse,* Auden sounded a note for which he would later become notorious. This is from the defence counsel's speech in 'The Public v. the Late Mr. William Butler Yeats':

> Art is a product of history, not a cause. Unlike some other products, technical inventions for example, it does not re-enter history as an effective agent, so that the question whether art should or should not be propaganda is unreal. The case for the prosecution rests on the fallacious belief that art ever makes anything happen, whereas the honest truth, gentlemen, is that, if not a poem had been written, not a picture painted, nor a bar of music composed, the history of man would be materially unchanged. (p. 393)

Many experiences led Auden to this disillusionment about the public role of art – not least the history of the Group Theatre – but one, perhaps, was crucial. Like many European and American artists he had gone to Spain during the Civil War and tried to serve the Republican side, but he was frustrated not only by his own inability to make a difference but also by his discovery that the Spanish war was not as morally unambiguous as the artistic partisans of the Republicans were leading everyone to think. Among the many atrocities committed by Republican supporters, one in particular stood out for Auden in a way that, at the time, he could not understand:

> On arriving in Barcelona [in January 1937], I found as I walked through the city that all the churches were closed and there was not a priest to be seen. To my astonishment, this discovery left me profoundly shocked and disturbed. The feeling was far too intense to be the result of a mere liberal dislike of intolerance, the notion that it is wrong to stop people from doing what they like, even if it is something silly like going to church. I could not escape acknowledging that, however I had consciously ignored and rejected the Church for sixteen years, the existence of churches and what went on in them had all the time been very important to me. If that was the case, what then?[27]

Thus, even as Auden was writing what many thought the great poetic anthem of the Spanish Civil War, 'Spain', he knew he was telling only a small portion of what he knew to be true and was therefore for all practical purposes lying. This explains why 'Spain' and political poems like it – most notably the famous 'September 1, 1939' – were later renounced by Auden and excluded from his *Collected Poems*.

When Auden came to America, he retained his interest in and commitment to poetic drama, but he had shed the political imperatives that had shaped his earlier projects. His first poetic drama in America was a collaboration with Benjamin Britten on the operetta *Paul Bunyan* – a distinctively American subject to match Auden's new country, a subject indebted to the folk sources of American culture, but a work with no pretence whatever to political relevance or social leadership. Auden then went on, with Chester Kallmann, to the rarefied air of opera proper. It is not likely that the masses would have much interest in a libretto about the hubris of a modern artist (*Elegy for Young Lovers*) or an adaptation of a play by Euripides (*The Bassarids*), especially when the words are accompanied by the dissonant tonalities and strange orchestrations of Hans Werner Henze. Just as Auden's quest for a theatre of social integration metamorphosed into a desire to write words in service of music, his dithyrambic or choral songs were replaced by a fascination with occasional poetry and a virtual compulsion to dedicate poems to friends. Auden became a proponent of local culture – the chief locality being the page on which a poem is printed. The poet as liberator became the poet as servant, the poet as friend. As Lucy McDiarmid has argued, much of

Auden's later poetry takes the form of an oft-repeated act of penitence for his former and long-standing poetic arrogance.[28] Auden's loss of faith not just in the politically transformative power of art but in any social role for art had led him to search for another faith – the one represented by the closed and shuttered churches of Barcelona.

Because he had become a Christian, Auden was free to pursue more private and local projects. One of his closest friends and deepest influences in his first years in America was Reinhold Niebuhr, the great theologian of the public realm, who never for a moment would have taken seriously any claims by poetry to orient and give structure to society. That is theology's job. If God had saved the world, the artist didn't have to. Poetry (whether private or public, dramatic or lyric) is utterly irrelevant to the reconstitution of the public sphere, which is why Auden makes this request in one of his greatest poems, 'At the Grave of Henry James':

> All will be judged. Master of nuance and scruple,
> Pray for me and for all writers living or dead;
>   Because there are many whose works
> Are in better taste than their lives; because there is no end
> To the vanity of our calling: make intercession
>   For the treason of all clerks.[29]

In Auden's Christian understanding such a restriction of ambition represents moral and spiritual progress, but those with a higher view of the potential social value of art have not always been so complimentary.[30]

In some respects it is clear why things fell out this way for Auden. He, like Eliot, did not have a particular gift for dramatic composition. Auden never admitted this limitation directly, but acknowledged it by recruiting collaborators – Isherwood in the thirties and Kallmann after his move to America – who could provide him with narrational and structural forms upon which he could poetically elaborate. The critical consensus is that neither Auden nor Eliot ever wrote a wholly success-ful play. It is conceivable that larger cultural forces are at work here, that, for instance, as literacy and the habit of literary reading increased, people became less comfortable with, or felt less need for, the public experience of going to the theatre; or (more likely) that they ceased to think of the theatre as a place where their more refined tastes could find satisfaction. Middlebrow drama – from J. M. Barrie and Arthur Pinero to J. B. Priestly and Terence Rattigan – dominated the London stage in the first half century, but surely this is the usual state of affairs wherever the drama flourishes. Even acknowledged masters of their craft like Brecht, Pirandello and Beckett are perennially unlikely candidates for boffo box-office; what then can the less practised and accomplished highbrow dramatist hope for?

To take a still longer and broader perspective, we have Sidnell's sobering contention, in his excellent history of the Group Theatre, that attempts to reclaim legitimate public space by means of the theatre will inevitably fail:

> The attempt to create a theatre in which actors, dancers, singers, musicians, designers, poets, and a 'participating audience' would engage in collaborative creation informed the European theatre at its very beginnings and has eluded it ever since. If such a 'total theatre' is impossible to achieve it may be because – as theorists from Aristotle to Brecht have explained – the consuming reality of ritual actions is incompatible with a thoroughly self-conscious art.[31]

If, as some of the Romantics dreamed, the fall into self-consciousness can be reversed, this incompatibility is not eternal; there is hope for reconciliation of dramatic art and the community. But in any case the 'total theatre' must happen, it cannot be willed into existence; a viable public culture will create the 'total theatre', not the other way round.

This seems to be, as I have argued, the conclusion reached not just by Auden but also by Eliot; and it is hard not to think that Christianity had a great deal to do with their reaching this conclusion. In Eliot's case the conversion to Christianity came first, and scepticism about the cultural power of art developed gradually. But Auden's experience was differently ordered: because he lacked religious faith he struggled mightily for several years to maintain faith in art. When his experiments in poetic drama failed and his choral songs were absorbed by the silent world of printed verse, he left his native England for an America where he hoped to start from zero. It didn't work out that way: the Old World followed him to the New. But the nightmarish persistence of the Old World that he fled was, ironically, instrumental in his reclamation of Christian faith and practice and in the solidification of his conviction that 'poetry makes nothing happen'.

In November of 1939, less than two months after the Nazis completed their staggeringly rapid conquest of Poland, their own cinematic record of the victory (called *Sieg im Polen*) was being shown in a theatre in

Yorkville, a neighbourhood in Manhattan then predominantly German. Not surprisingly, especially since the United States was not yet involved in the war, the movie-goers were quite sympathetic to the Nazi cause; they knew what Hitler had done to restore German pride and economic and cultural stability; many of them had come to the US during the economic crises that debilitated Germany in the 1920s.

But Auden, when he saw *Sieg im Polen*, was not prepared for the extremity of the viewers' reactions to this film. Whenever the Poles appeared on the screen – always as prisoners, of course, in the hands of the Wehrmacht – the audience would shout, 'Kill them! Kill them!' Auden was stunned. 'There was no hypocrisy', he recalled many years later: these people were unashamed of their feelings and attempted to put no 'civilized' face upon them. 'I wondered, then, why I reacted as I did against this denial of every humanistic value'.[32] On what grounds did he have a right to demand, or even a reason to expect, a more humane response? The kind of culture that supports poetry was not even able to sustain or defend *itself* before those who preferred evil and brutality, much less shape the public sphere. Late in his life Auden often said, as he did in this interview, that his inability to account for, much less justify, his own horror 'brought [him] back to the Church'.

Notes

1   W. H. Auden, *The English Auden*, E. Mendelson (ed.) (London: Faber, 1977) p. 163. Subsequent references to this collection will be cited parenthetically in the text.

2   The different versions of 'Funeral Blues' can be found in Auden, *Collected Poems*, rev. ed., E. Mendelson (ed.) (London: Faber, 1991) pp. 116–21; Auden, *Selected Poems* (New York: Random, 1958) pp. 31–3; Auden, *Complete Works, Volume I: Plays and Other Dramatic Writings, 1928–1938*, ed. E. Mendelson (Princeton: Princeton Univ. Press, 1988) pp. 350–1.

3   T. S. Eliot, *Selected Essays* (New York: Harcourt, 1951) p. 247.

4   T. S. Eliot, *The Sacred Wood: Essays on Poetry and Criticism*, 2nd ed. (London: Methuen, 1928) p. 62.

5   Eliot, *Selected Essays*, p. 247.

6   Eliot, *The Sacred Wood*, p. 61.

7   Ibid., p. 63.

8   Ibid., p. 64.

9   Ibid., p. 70.

10   Eliot, *Selected Essays*, pp. 406, 407.

11   Ibid., p. 407. The easy and potentially infinite reproducibility of a film is for Eliot part of the problem. This line of thinking resembles the common contrast in modern British thought described by Raymond Williams between the 'organic' and the 'mechanical' in a given culture. The music

hall represents the former, the cinema the latter. See *Culture and Society: 1780–1950* (New York: Columbia Univ. Press, 1983) p. 138.

12   Auden, *Complete Works, Volume I*, p. xxii.

13   Ibid., p. xvi.

14   So Rupert Doone, the artistic director of the Group, called him. See M. Sidnell, *Dances of Death: the Group Theatre of London in the Thirties* (London: Faber, 1984) p. 24.

15   P. Fussell, 'Modernism, Adversary Culture, and Edmund Blunden', in *Thank God for the Atom Bomb and Other Essays* (New York: Ballantine, 1988) p. 211.

16   C. T. Christ, *Victorian and Modern Poetics* (Chicago: Univ. of Chicago Press, 1984).

17   R. Hoggart, *The Uses of Literacy* (New Brunswick, NJ: Transaction, 1992) p. 113.

18   Ibid., p. 118.

19   Auden, *Selected Poems*, p. 32.

20   Hoggart, *The Uses of Literacy*, p. 123.

21   C. Isherwood, *Christopher and His Kind* (New York: Farrar, 1976) p. 268; Sidnell, *Dances of Death*, p. 197.

22   V. Cunningham, *British Writers of the Thirties* (Oxford: Oxford Univ. Press, 1989) p. 97; Isherwood, *Christopher and His Kind*, p. 288.

23   Sidnell, *Dances of Death*, p. 204.

24   W. R. Johnson, *The Idea of Lyric: Lyric Modes in Ancient and Modern Poetry* (Berkeley: Univ. of California Press, 1982) p. 177.

25   Cunningham, *British Writers*, p. 323.

26   Eliot, *Selected Essays*, p. 4.

27   J. A. Pike (ed.), *Modern Canterbury Pilgrims* (London: Mowbray, 1956) p. 41.

28   L. McDiarmid, *Auden's Apologies for Poetry* (Princeton: Princeton Univ. Press, 1990) *passim*.

29   Auden, *Collected Poems*, p. 312.

30   I have discussed some of these issues at length in Chapter 4 of my book, *What Became of Wystan: Change and Continuity in Auden's Poetry* (Fayetteville: Univ. of Arkansas Press, 1998).

31   Sidnell, *Dances of Death*, p. 257.

32   A. Levy, 'On Audenstrasse: In the Autumn of the Age of Anxiety', *The New York Times Magazine*, 8 August 1971, pp. 10–12, 42.

7
Narrative Labour in Raymond Carver

Michael Vander Weele

Raymond Carver's narrators, almost all drawn from the middle and working classes, describe a world in which 'the hard substance of the daily job fuses to the haze of the daydream'. The phrase is from Studs Terkel's *Working*, which remains one of our great registers of the meaning of work in America. In the introduction to his famous collection of interviews with American workers, Terkel warns about the 'specter that most haunts working men and women: the planned obsolescence of people that is of a piece with the planned obsolescence of the things they make. Or sell'. He continues, 'It is perhaps this fear of no longer being needed in a world of needless things that most clearly spells out the unnaturalness, the surreality of much that is called work today'.[1] The same sense of unnaturalness or surreality impinges on the narrative labour of Carver's storytellers.

With a few changes, Terkel's interviews could easily be the narratives of one of Carver's storytellers. Take this passage from spot welder Phil Stallings, working on a Ford assembly line on the Far South side of Chicago:

I stand in one spot, about [a] two- or three-feet area, all night. The only time a person stops is when the line stops. We do about thirty-two jobs per car, per unit. Forty-eight units an hour, eight hours a day. Thirty-two times forty-eight times eight. Figure it out. That's how many times I push that button. ...

You got some guys that are uptight, and they're not sociable. It's too rough. You pretty much stay to yourself. You get involved with yourself. You dream, you think of things you've done. ...

It don't stop. It just goes and goes and goes. I bet there's men who have lived and died out there, never seen the end of that line. And they never will – because it's endless. It's like a serpent. It's just all body, no tail. It can do things to you … (Laughs.)[2]

The curt, stoical account given in the face of an overwhelming yet anonymous process, the paring down of almost all connectives and the use of quick repetitions, the combination of boredom and dream, the ellipses, even the metaphor and its elaboration recall the style of Carver's short stories. Like Terkel's interviews, Carver's tales afford workers like Phil Stallings a public forum.

The failure of understanding

Any account of Carver's importance to our public life must begin with the remarkable influence of his style and his choice of subjects on the development of the short story. After the publication of *What We Talk About When We Talk About Love* (1980) it became popular to refer to Carver's spare style as 'minimalist', a term which referred, according to Kim Herzinger, to an 'equanimity of surface, "ordinary" subjects, recalcitrant narrators and deadpan narratives, slightness of story, and characters who don't think out loud'.[3] As applied to Carver, the term sometimes pertained to the pessimistic view of life reflected in this collection as well as to the strict formal restraints he imposed on himself. His minimalist style was quickly imitated in both the literary and the general magazines in which the stories first appeared. Perhaps it was inevitable. The severe restraints of Carver's colloquial style, its dark humour, quick repetitions, refusal of connectives – a language pared down almost to gesture – were too challenging to resist.

Here is a signature opening from the 1980 collection:

> That morning she pours Teacher's over my belly and licks it off.
> That afternoon she tries to jump out the window.
> I go, 'Holly, this can't continue. This has got to stop'.[4]

Even as Carver's narrator insists on the presence of past events through his deictic opening – '*That* morning *she* pours Teacher's over *my* belly' – the slick, dark humour distances us from these events.[5] The connective between ecstasy and death is limited to a temporal order ('That morning'/'That afternoon') and report of the attempted suicide issues into a comedic one-liner with its colloquial 'go' and 'stop' and the logical redundancy of 'this can't continue'. This clipped working-class vernacular, the use of abundant white space to elicit the reader's speculation about what goes unspoken, even the limiting of attributions to 'he said' and 'she said' became characteristic of much short fiction of the eighties and early nineties. While it may be too early to decide if this minimalist impulse was a passing fad or an effective historical change, for the last two decades it has seemed an important and persuasive way of translating private experience – in this case, the experience of loneliness – into the public sphere.

Carver also changed the course of the short story through his choice of subjects. With few exceptions, his stories comprise 'a long line of low-rent tragedies' ('One More Thing') featuring cannery workers, waitresses, motel keepers, high school teachers, the unemployed. Carver may not have been the first, and certainly was not the only, short-story writer to choose such down-to-earth subjects from urban (and occasionally rural) settings. But he gave expression to characters belonging to a lifeworld very different from that of the mythical 'silent majority' celebrated in the political discourse of the early 1970s. Carver once referred to his characters as the 'submerged population', insisting that short-story writers had always been writing about such people. 'Chekhov was writing about a submerged population a hundred years ago,' Carver pointed out. 'He wrote about doctors and businessmen and teachers sometimes, but he also gave voice to people who were not so articulate. He found a means of letting those people have their say as well.'[6] The British saw this affinity with Chekhov more quickly than the Americans did: the day after Carver died, the *London Times* referred to him as 'the American Chekhov'.[7]

As in Chekhov, we usually do not see Carver's subjects in action. If occasionally we see the action of Carver's stories unroll before our eyes, more often we hear it being recollected by a lower-middle-class character at some neutral site, whether a train station or airport bar or city park or detox centre or mall bench. We have been chosen by whatever happenstance to hear, and even help, these storytellers give an account, shape a testimony, begin a recovery. With a magical combination of intimacy and anonymity, the storytelling sets forth. It is as if we had taken the place of Studs Terkel sitting behind the tape recorder, or, better, poring over the transcriptions. Terkel's emphasis on speech and self-understanding in his subtitle, *People Talk about What They Do All Day and How They Feel about What They Do*, seems to find its match in the title of Carver's 1980 volume, *What We Talk about When We Talk about Love*. We hear in Carver's transcription-like stories, too, the workers' concerns and language, their lifeworld.

And we find ourselves sharing the same uneasiness of conscience to which Terkel confesses when he catches himself arranging the interviews and consuming the stories without giving their tellers further attention. In fact, Carver's narrators give us more responsibility to help create sense out of their world than the workers gave to Terkel. Once Carver slips us into the role of auditor, we experience the demand to make sense of, not only to collect, a pivotal moment in another's life story.

Just as *Working* gives us labourers who accepted Studs Terkel's invitation to enter a public sphere to sort out the meaning of work with him, so Carver's fiction gives us characters throwing out a narrative bridge to an auditor outside their personal sphere of influence who might help them understand the reasons for change in it. There are several characteristics that Carver's fictive narrators share with Terkel's workers in their attempts to enter or re-create a public sphere. First, they speak to an anonymous rather than a familiar auditor. This auditor is placed in the public position of judge or interpreter, as in Eudora Welty's 'Why I Live at the P.O.'. But unlike Welty's narrator, who tries to draw us from our public position into her private sphere, Carver's narrators are more interested in self-understanding than in self-justification. Theirs is a chastened prose that insists upon our public standing and the discipline of giving a public account. Second, the concerns of these narrators include the public as well as private significance of marriage, work, family, death. These characters have difficulty articulating, but none the less feel on their pulses, the anonymous social forces that shape them beyond their understanding. Whatever else these stories are about, they are about the difficulty of creating a forum for understanding the public conditioning of private events. Third, these stories can be described as an uneasy explosion of speech from a usually stoical narrator, almost like a verbal flare that seeks contact before it burns itself out. The intensity, combined with the puzzlement, of the narrator suggests an almost desperate desire for contact. The narrator seems to hope that together we can find the language necessary to move from event to significance.

Carver's compositional strategies lead the reader to experience first-hand the difficulty of establishing meaningful communication, of creating a discourse that navigates between personal experience and anonymous steering systems. His stories regularly situate the reader as silent partner to a narrator who tries (and usually fails) to establish a meaningful association with his or her auditor. That association seems a necessary precondition for understanding. The stories, increasingly told from a first-person point of view, are most often cast as tales, complete with teller, listener and inferable situation. They set up expectations of counsel and interpretation. That is, they seem to implicate us, asking about our responsibility for the broken testimony, the socially impoverished lifeworld, revealed in the strange but not quite unreal discourse of the teller's tale. Even titles such as *What We Talk About When We Talk About Love* and *Will You Please Be Quiet, Please?* show the complicity between speaker and auditor.

These elements are seen most clearly in the opening to 'Sacks': 'I want to pass along to you a story my father told me when I stopped over in Sacramento last year'.[8] The son is now passing on his father's story and storytelling situation to us. In the son's telling of his father's story of adultery, we are given the same role by him as he had been given by his father: 'You're an educated man, Les', his father had said. 'You'll be the one to figure it out'.[9] His father's sexual betrayal was bad enough, to be sure. But the tragedy lies in not being able to figure out how things like this happen, how the life one had lived suddenly sustains one no longer. 'You see what I'm saying?' the father had said. 'A man can go along obeying all the rules and then it don't matter a damn anymore. His luck just goes, you know?'[10] But the father wonders how such a transitory rush could have overcome him. That's what he had hoped talking to his son would help him figure out: What had happened to the beliefs, thoughts, structures he had lived by, that they could so easily be overthrown?

We can infer from the son's story that he hadn't recognised or hadn't admitted his father's request for help in interpreting. He had wondered, instead, about the plot of the story – whether the husband of the Stanley Products woman had caught his father when he went crashing through their window. Earlier, the son had similarly seen only a sack and the candy it held rather than his father's attempt to give him a gift for his wife and children. The story ends with a comparable interpretive puzzle for the auditor. The son tells us that he had forgotten the sack on the bar at the airport. 'Just as well', he tells his auditor. 'Mary didn't need candy, Almond Roca or anything else'. The story ends with the one-line paragraph, 'That was last year. She needs it now even less'.[11] We may ask why the son is telling us this story he had shown every sign of not wanting to hear. Are we really supposed to confirm that his wife needs the sack with his father's gifts even less now than she did a year ago? Has the son followed in his father's footsteps – or perhaps preceded them? And what about us? Are we similarly unable to make the storyteller's offering effective? Do we also require the counsel this tale would try to construct? By cornering the reader in such a way, these low-rent tragedies bring into sharp relief the plight of middle- or lower-middle-class narrators who have forgotten, if they once knew how, to exercise membership in a public sphere. The narrators try to reconstruct such a sphere for reflection with the auditor to whom they tell their tales. We assume that auditor's role as we read the stories and, stymied by story's end, we experience first-hand the difficulty of creating and sustaining a public sphere for rational discourse.

Our implication as audience in the storytelling situation can also be seen in the ending of 'Feathers'. Jack and Fran have been invited to dinner at the country home of Jack's co-worker Bud and his wife Olla. The tone of the evening is set by the raucous, if beautiful, peacock that flaps down just in front of the car as Jack and Fran come up the drive. An even more bizarre sight greets them in the living room:

> Fran nudged me and nodded in the direction of the TV. 'Look up on top', she whispered. 'Do you see what I see?' I looked at where she was looking. There was a slender red vase into which somebody had stuck a few garden daisies. Next to the vase, on the doily, sat an old plaster-of-Paris cast of the most crooked, jaggedy teeth in the world. There were no lips to the awful-looking thing, and no jaw either, just these old plaster teeth packed into something that resembled thick yellow gums. (p. 341)

Despite Fran's initial misgivings and uneasiness, after dinner she tries to make friends with Bud and Olla's ugly baby, Howard. She's attracted to, even as she disbelieves, the baby's and peacock's display of affection. After Jack has finished narrating the events of the evening, telling how Howard, with his pop eyes and stubby fingers, teamed up with the pet peacock strutting across the kitchen table, he acknowledges the importance to him of speech: 'That evening at Bud and Olla's was special. I knew it was special. That evening I felt good about almost everything in my life. I couldn't wait to be alone with Fran to talk to her about what I was feeling' (p. 354). But after the first flush of excitement disappears, we replace Fran as auditor in Jack's effort to understand what has happened to their life.

When Jack says, 'But I remember that night', we listen – in hope or perhaps only out of curiosity – to see what significance Jack has discovered in it (p. 355). The story ends, however, not with the significance Jack has wrested from experience but with a paratactic assemblage of the different elements he remembers. His final attempt at generalisation reveals the large gap between Jack's recognition that there's something more at stake and his inability to express it:

> I recall the way the peacock picked up its gray feet and inched around the table. And then my friend and his wife saying goodnight to us on the porch. Olla giving Fran some peacock feathers to take home. I remember all of us shaking hands, hugging each other, saying things. In the car, Fran sat close to me as we drove away. She kept her hand on my leg. We drove home like that from my friend's house. (p. 355)

This is not a duplicitous narrator but one who wants to speak to us to get things straight. His inability to do so stymies him. We are stymied, too. The individual initiative that had led Jack to narrate his experience doesn't become useful to him or to us, as his projected auditors. As Carver's readers, of course, this failure leads us to question what would be necessary to make such an initiative meaningful.

When Carver's narrators don't turn to us, puzzled, as if to say, 'You take it from here', it is usually because they are too discouraged and their stories too bleak to invite our efforts. One of the bleakest is 'Vitamins'. The story begins with work: 'I had a job and Patti didn't. I worked a few hours a night for the hospital. It was a nothing job. I did some work, signed the card for eight hours, went drinking with the nurses. After a while, Patti wanted a job. She said she needed a job for her self-respect. So she started selling multiple vitamins door to door' (p. 245). The vitamin business does very well at first, but by mid-winter nobody was buying vitamins. Patti's husband (who tells us the story) and Patti are drinking Scotch and, like most of Carver's characters, dreaming about a different life, in this case 'about how we'd be better off if we moved to Arizona, someplace like that'. The ending of this story, which is mostly about the husband's seeking refuge from tedious work, doesn't turn to the reader for help negotiating its meaning. The narrator tells us of coming home late from a bungled rendezvous with Patti's friend and co-worker. Patti is in bed with her clothes on, having a nightmare about work, screaming at her husband for letting her oversleep. He's rummaging around in the bathroom. His story ends, 'I knocked some stuff out of the medicine chest. Things rolled into the sink. "Where's the aspirin?" I said. I knocked down some more things. I didn't care. Things kept falling' (p. 263).

Significance and social interaction

A few of Carver's stories conclude more hopefully than the more typical quizzical endings associated with his name. These hopeful endings are productive; social intercourse gets established in them. With the publication of *Cathedral* in 1982, readers noticed a move away from the 'minimalist' style toward a more relaxed style and, at least sometimes, more hopeful stories. In 'A Small, Good Thing', for example, Carver revised an earlier story called 'The Bath', more than doubling its length and giving it a more optimistic ending. In a 1983 interview with Mona Simpson, Carver remarked that the stories in *Cathedral* were 'different than the stories that had come before'. He said that he experienced 'an opening up' when he wrote them.[12] In some of these stories the narrator's initiative begins to issue into general usefulness, both in the action represented by the story and in the narrative proper. When these narrators negotiate the move from event to significance, we can see what Carver imagines the requirements for such negotiation to be.

'Cathedral' and 'A Small, Good Thing' show us the requirements for social interaction and for the movement from event to significance. In 'Cathedral' a blind man named Robert, who is a friend and former employer of the narrator's wife, has come from Seattle to visit his dead wife's relatives in Connecticut. The wife has invited him to stay at their house for a few days. Late in the evening Robert and the narrator are sitting in the living room watching a programme on European cathedrals. Their social interaction begins with a confession and a request: 'If you want the truth', Robert says, 'that's about all I know [about cathedrals]. What I just said. What I heard him say. But maybe you could describe one to me? I wish you'd do it. I'd like that. If you want to know, I really don't have a good idea' (p. 371). The narrator stares hard at the cathedral on TV before deciding to take up the challenge. But he wonders if he's up to the task: 'How could I even begin to describe it? But say my life depended on it. Say my life was being threatened by an insane guy who said I had to do it or else' (p. 371). So the narrator begins by describing the cathedral's size; its buttresses, which he unhelpfully compares to the supports for viaducts; the sculpted figures carved into the cathedral's front. Next he talks about the building materials, and finally, in desperation, about the motives for building such a construction in the first place. Then he stops, admitting that he's not up to the task. His explanation again puts the focus on motivation: 'The truth is, cathedrals don't mean anything special to me. Nothing. Cathedrals. They're something to look at on late-night TV. That's all they are' (p. 372).

After Robert absolves the narrator of responsibility for their failed communication, he makes a more difficult request: '"Hey, listen to me. Will you do me a favor? I got an idea. Why don't you find us some heavy paper? And a pen. We'll do something. We'll draw one together. Get us a pen and some heavy paper. Go on, bub, get the stuff," he said' (pp. 372–3). The retrieval of the tools; the apprenticeship character of the work, with the blind man's hand riding the narrator's as it directs the pen; Robert's instructive encouragements – all are described in sufficient detail to emphasise the work involved in this strange drawing. The communal effort is rewarding for Robert. His job is in equal measure tactile observation and encouragement to keep the narrator going ('You got it, bub. I can tell. You didn't think you could. But you can, can't you? You're cooking with gas now. You know what I'm saying? We're going to really have us something here in a minute. How's the old arm?'). The encouragement, like that of a coach, soon turns to direction: 'Put some people in there now. What's a cathedral without people?' (p. 374). The reward for the narrator seems more ambiguous. 'It's really something', he says when Robert asks him what he thinks of their picture (p. 375).

Significantly, the narrator refers to his house both at the beginning and at the end of his description of the drawing process. When he first tells us about the drawing he tries to explain its relationship to his house: 'So I began. First I drew a box that looked like a house. It could have been the house I lived in. Then I put a roof on it. At either end of the roof, I drew spires. Crazy' (p. 373). Near the end of his account he describes the bizarre event in terms of his house once again: 'My eyes were still closed. I was in my house. I knew that. But I didn't feel like I was inside anything' (p. 375). This experience is consistent with Carver's sense of enclosures in the rest of his writing – that social enclosures aren't escaped but expanded – but it also contrasts with the narrator's early prejudice against the blind man. In the story's opening paragraph the narrator admits that 'his being blind bothered me. My idea of blindness came from the movies. In the movies, the blind moved slowly and never laughed. Sometimes they were led by seeing-eye dogs. A blind man in my house was not something I looked forward to' (p. 356). But the performance or action of the story makes clear that the reversal of this prejudice opens his house, lets it take on the airiness, the larger enclosure, of a cathedral. This kind of work has made his initiative meaningful, has led this 'homeless' worker toward more responsible citizenship.

'A Small, Good Thing' is written in third-person narration and therefore does not follow the tale structure of 'Cathedral' or Carver's other first-person narrations. But we see in the action a similar move from event to significance. On Saturday, Ann Weiss orders a birthday cake decorated with a spaceship and launching pad for her son, Scotty, who is about to turn eight years old. Monday morning her son is hit by a car when he steps off a curb on his way to school. Ann and Howard, her husband, keep vigil at his hospital bed. When they finally take turns going home for a bath and nap, each receives a phone call from a man who asks, without identifying himself, if they've forgotten about Scotty. When they return from the hospital for the last time, together, after Scotty's death, the same caller calls again. This time Ann recognises the noises in the background as those of the bakery. The bereaved parents confront the baker, who had wondered why no one had picked up his three-day-old cake. The baker confesses, '"I'm not an evil man, I don't think. Not evil, like you said on the phone. You got to understand what it comes down to is I don't know how to act anymore, it would seem. Please," the man said, "let me ask you if you can find it in your hearts to forgive me?"' (p. 404). Ann and Howard can make this shift from rage to forgiveness only because earlier they had been pulled out of themselves toward each other ('For the first time, she felt they were together in it, this trouble. She realized with a start that, until now, it had only been happening to her and to Scotty' [p. 384]) and toward others ('Ann saw the lips [of the African-American mother] moving silently, making words. She had an urge to ask what those words were. She wanted to talk more with these people who were in the same kind of waiting she was in. She was afraid, and they were afraid. They had that in common' [p. 391]).

Yet nothing has prepared them for the baker's turn from the work of confession to the work of communion: 'He found cups and poured coffee from an electric coffee-maker. He put a carton of cream on the table, and a bowl of sugar ... "You probably need to eat something", the baker said. "I hope you'll eat some of my hot rolls. You have to eat and keep going. Eating is a small, good thing in a time like this", he said' (p. 404). After they eat the rolls and drink the coffee, the baker begins to speak. 'They listened carefully. Although they were tired and in anguish, they listened to what the baker had to say. They nodded when the baker began to speak of loneliness, and of the sense of doubt and limitation that had come to him in his middle years. He told them what it was like to be childless all these years. To repeat the days with the ovens endlessly full and endlessly empty' (p. 405). Only then does the baker break open a dark loaf of bread and have them smell and taste it, in a scene that resembles the breaking of bread in communion. Ann and Howard seem blessed by this act. For a while, at least, the weight of loneliness that presses in on them is overcome: 'They ate what they could. They swallowed the dark bread. It was like daylight under the fluorescent trays of light. They talked on into the early morning, the high, pale cast of light in the windows, and they did not think of leaving' (p. 405).

Now we can summarise the requirements that Carver finds necessary for negotiating the move from event to significance, from individual initiative to general usefulness. First, it requires recognition or confession that one's own language or narration is insufficient to the task. Second, the effort to find a larger language and a larger meaning for experience requires a complementary, not a single, effort. Third, it often requires a new view of social enclosures. Speaking of the narrator in 'Cathedral', Kirk Nesset writes, 'the narrator begins to realize just how exhilarating confinement can be, once one sees beyond the narrow enclosure of self that larger, more expansive enclosure of society'.[13]

We see in 'Cathedral' just how much works against this hopeful social interaction and productive narrative work. The work environment of the main characters in 'Cathedral', as in so many of Carver's other stories, is both understated and important. The narrator's wife had worked for Robert, her blind friend, before her previous marriage: 'She read stuff to him, case studies, reports, that sort of thing', our narrator tells us. 'She helped him organize his little office in the county social-service department' (pp. 356–7). The language of the narrator ('stuff', 'that sort of thing') suggests that such administrative work was as strange to him as his wife's attempts to write a poem once or twice a year. In the first of two other occasions on which we hear about work, the narrator summarises his and Robert's early, polite conversation: 'From time to time, he'd turn his blind face toward me, put his hand under his beard, ask me something. How long had I been in my present position? (Three years.) Did I like my work? (I didn't.) Was I going to stay with it? (What were the options?) Finally, when I thought he was beginning to run down, I got up and turned on the TV' (p. 365). The second occasion comes after the narrator can't find anything else on and switches back to the public television programme on cathedrals. After he watches for a few minutes, he wonders if Robert knows anything about cathedrals and what they looked like – how they were different, say, from a Baptist church. Robert replies, 'I know they took hundreds of workers fifty or a hundred years to build ... I just heard the man say that, of course. I know generations of the same families worked on a cathedral. I heard him say that, too. The men who began their life's work on them, they never lived to see the completion of their work. In that wise, bub, they're no different from the rest of us, right?' (p. 370).

There is nothing about the narrator's or Robert's comments on work that should surprise a reader of Carver's short stories. Carver seemed to realise 'work's centrality and its place in the disarray of modern civilisation'. The phrase belongs to Simone Weil, who worried in the 1930s and early 40s that the 'rootless citizen opted for escapism rather than responsible engagement' and that wrong ideas about and situations for work led to this rootlessness.[14] For Weil, 'the modern worker is a homeless person, even though there is a place of residence. The lack of belonging promises to produce apathy and withdrawal from social responsibility. Where workers are "homeless in their own places of work," she warns, "they will never truly feel at home in their country, never be responsible members of society" '.[15] The urgency of Carver's narrators should be read as a desperate attempt to understand this apathy and to break through their habitual withdrawal from social responsibility toward social interaction. A bad work situation and a bad view of work encumber most of these attempts – which makes them more rather than less important to us. For work produced without meaningful exchange or association seems to be a primary obstacle to the social interaction and meaningful discourse these characters seek. 'No society', Weil warns, 'can be stable in which a whole stratum of the population labors daily with a heart-felt loathing'.[16] The characters in 'Cathedral' and 'A Small, Good Thing' position themselves as part of that stratum but then find new possibilities for exchange in their narrative labour.

Work, companionship and the public sphere

In locating the rise of the public sphere in the coffee shops and salons of the early eighteenth century, Habermas pointed to a historical era that was richer than our own in the groups and associations that make up civic society, but he did not consider the workplace as one of those associations. Nor did he consider the church as an important association within civic society, despite its considerable literacy campaigns. Both work and belief fell to the side of the private sphere, despite the fact that both are deeply tied to economic and political life and despite the challenge both make to the rule of the nuclear family. Carver's fiction makes clear how much work has to do with his narrators' ability to move outside a personal sphere of freedom or victimisation. Surprisingly, given Habermas' neo-Marxist background, the connection between work and the public sphere can more easily be seen in John Calvin's writings on economic exchange than in Habermas' account. Calvin's analysis of the importance of work and belief to the public sphere provides an important qualification to the historical emphasis in Habermas. Further, what Calvin says about economic exchange gives us a helpful perspective on the goals of linguistic exchange as well, even as we see that exchange at work in Carver's short stories.

Labour without companionship figures importantly in Carver's stories of failed understanding, whether as symptom or as cause. And that seems to be as true for narrative labour as for labour in the marketplace. The narrative efforts of Carver's storytellers mirror, even as they try to overcome, their lack of meaningful exchange in the rest of their workaday world. Their labour, whether physical or narrative, leads to one of the goals of work, production, but not to the other, companionship. Max Weber argued that the historical roots for our modern emphasis on production could be found in the rise of bourgeois capitalism under the influence of Calvinism. Weber's hypothesis might be true if applied to the seventeenth century, but Calvin himself never saw production as an independent value. 'God has created man so that man may be a creature of fellowship,' Calvin wrote. This was no more a religious than an economic claim. Andre Bieler summarises Calvin's emphasis on a faithful economics this way: 'Human fellowship is realized in relationships which flow from the division of labor wherein each person has been called by God to a particular and partial work which complements the work of others'. Bieler continues, 'Companionship is completed in work and in the interplay of economic exchanges'.[17] What Calvin wrote about labour also applies to the construction of speech. Social intercourse is the larger goal of both labour and language. And it is only through social intercourse that we can achieve both individual initiative and general usefulness. For Calvin, these were the dual requirements one found in looking back to a creation order and in looking forward to a new order, the Kingdom of God. Indeed, Calvin's insistence on the importance of companionship and exchange is an example of the Reformation's influence on the development of the modern public sphere.

In his writing on Calvin and the Protestant ethic, Weber distinguished between two dimensions of legitimate order. That distinction may also help us articulate why Carver's narrators so seldom arrive at an understanding of the events that trigger their narratives. Weber claimed that order included both the *structure* of social relations and the *authority* or *command* that society follows. A social structure, on this view, does not provide order by itself but only in tandem with a legitimate authority or command. When a social structure becomes its own authority or follows a misguided authority, it does not provide order.[18] This is what bears in upon Carver's characters: they suddenly understand that they no longer know by what authority – if any – their social relationships are structured. In light of Weber's analysis, we can say that Carver's characters feel the force of the social structure without being able to articulate, and hence resist, its authority. The lack of companionship, the difficulty of complementarity, the failure to pursue rational discourse to its end warn us that the lifeworld of these characters has been twisted by structures that have become their own authority or that have followed a misguided command. In this reading, the greatest social problem the tellers express is not planned obsolescence or idle desiring or family breakdown or the problem of addiction, but the difficulty of creating and sustaining a discerning discourse with one's fellow citizen. We must learn to be auditors. As Nesset writes, 'The coming out of hardened insularity involves intensive listening. ... For this narrator, significantly, the process of coming out involves *going into* the narrative of another, involves entering imaginatively into a discourse which, arising [out] of the communal act of storytelling, is at once familiar and unfamiliar'. Second, one does not leave confinement for an unconfined liberty but for a larger, social enclosure. As Nesset said about the narrator of 'Cathedral', confinement can be exhilarating 'once one sees beyond the narrow enclosure of self that larger, more expansive enclosure of society'.[19] This is the promise of the public sphere, a space for rational discourse about the enclosure of society that requires appropriate structures and answerable authority.

Its lack can be seen in Carver's images of emptiness. One of his most haunting comes from 'Blackbird Pie', one of the last stories Carver wrote. It's about the companionship of marriage, though its commentary on a failed marriage might extend to work and other associations as well. The amateur historian who narrates this bizarre tale realises that he is not going to get beyond the narrow enclosure of self by himself:

> It could be said, for instance, that to take a wife is to take a history. And if that's so, then I understand that I'm outside history now – like horses and fog. Or you could say that my history has left me. Or that I'm having to go on *without history*. Or that history will now have to do without me – unless my wife writes more letters, or tells a friend who keeps a diary, say. Then, years later, someone can look back on this time, interpret it according to the record, its scraps and tirades, its silences and innuendos. That's when it dawns on me that autobiography is the poor man's history. And that I am saying good-bye to history. Good-bye, my darling. (pp. 510–11)

This is the move all Carver's narrators seek to make, the move from auto-biography to some shared history, even though most of them fail. Earlier images of emptiness seemed to imply other possibilities, for a gift ('Sacks'), a home ('Why Don't We Dance?'), a lunch room ('Feathers'). And some images didn't show emptiness but the extraordinary quality of ordinary life: the peacock in 'Feathers', the cathedral in 'Cathedral', the bread in 'A Small, Good Thing'. We find a similar contrast between emptiness and the extraordinary quality of ordinary but shared life in two new stories Carver and his wife, writer Tess Gallagher, placed last in his final collection. 'Errand', the concluding story of *Where I'm Calling From*, reads like a historical account, perhaps answering the anti-history of 'Blackbird Pie', placed immediately before it.

'Errand' tells the story of the night of Chekhov's death. The carefully shaped narrative slowly reveals how the extravagant but humble act of Chekhov's doctor and the attentive courtesy of the room-service boy help Chekhov, his wife, his doctor, the mortician and the room-service boy face the facts of death together. Between 2 and 3 a.m., after Chekhov had stopped him from ordering oxygen, 'sa[ying] quietly, "What's the use? Before it arrives I'll be a corpse" ', the doctor orders the best bottle of champagne from the hotel at Badenweiler where Chekhov was staying. Once the room-service boy, wakened by his superior, arrives with the champagne,

> the doctor went about the business of working the cork out of the bottle. He did it in such a way as to minimize, as much as possible,

the festive explosion. … He then took the glasses of champagne over to the bed. Olga momentarily released her grip on Chekhov's hand – a hand, she said later, that burned her fingers. She arranged another pillow behind his head. Then she put the cool glass of champagne against Chekhov's palm and made sure his fingers closed around the stem. They exchanged looks – Chekhov, Olga, Dr. Schwohrer. They didn't touch glasses. There was no toast. What on earth was there to drink to? To death? Chekhov summoned his remaining strength and said, 'It's been so long since I've had champagne.' He brought the glass to his lips and drank. In a minute or two Olga took the empty glass from his hand and set it on the nightstand. Then Chekhov turned onto his side. He closed his eyes and sighed. A minute later, his breathing stopped. (pp. 519–20)

After the doctor leaves, agreeing to give Olga some time alone with her husband before announcing his death to the authorities, Olga goes back to Chekhov's bedside. In Carver's shaped history, which sometimes, as here, quotes from Henri Troyat's biography or from Maria Chekhov's *Memoirs*, '[s]he sat on a footstool, holding his hand, from time to time stroking his face. "There were no human voices, no everyday sounds," she wrote. "There was only beauty, peace, and the grandeur of death"' (p. 521).

Though Chekhov was more Carver's model than any other author, the story is not first of all a tribute to the writer but to the uncommon attentiveness of all those in the room to the life and now the death they conducted together, not least of all a tribute to the attentions of the flustered room-service boy, with his three yellow, long-stemmed roses, his tactful retrieval of the cork that had popped out of the champagne bottle and his conveyance of Olga's wishes to the mortician (the 'errand' of the story's title). This is not a picture of loneliness or of heroism but of the stubborn and sometimes awkward efforts of companionship and exchange. In this room, imagined at the same time as Carver was imagining his own death, we see Carver's characters create in their speech and actions a sign for each other of a different authority, and a different structure, that they will establish between them for this life and this death. This sign of hope, toned down, deliberately understated, was Carver's final gift to his wife and readers. It encourages us to exercise the same humble, sometimes awkward, attention needed to carry on, in whatever public forums we can join or recreate, a rational discourse about the order of our lives.

Notes

1 S. Terkel, *Working* (New York: Random House, 1974) pp. xxiv, xxii.
2 Ibid., p. 222.
3 K. Herzinger, 'Introduction: On the New Fiction', *Mississippi Review*, 40–41 (Winter 1985), 7.
4 Rpr. in R. Carver, *Where I'm Calling From: New and Selected Stories* (New York: Random House, 1989) p. 139. Stories that Carver included in this final collection of his work will be cited from this edition and parenthetically noted.
5 M. Chenetier, 'Living On/Off the "Reserve": Performance, Interrogation, and Negativity in the Works of Raymond Carver', in M. Chenetier (ed.), *Critical Angles: European Views of Contemporary American Literature* (Carbondale: Southern Illinois Univ. Press, 1986) p. 166.
6 L. McCaffery and S. Gregory, 'An Interview with Raymond Carver', in S. Gregory and L. McCaffery (eds.), *Alive and Writing* (Urbana: Univ. of Illinois Press, 1987); rpt. in E. Campbell, *Raymond Carver; A Study of the Short Fiction* (New York: Twayne Publishers, 1992) p. 111.
7 Quoted by Tess Gallagher in her introduction to Carver's last book of poems, *A New Path to the Waterfall* (New York: Atlantic Monthly Press, 1988; rpt. Random House, 1989), p. xxix. Gallagher reported that the *Guardian* also referred to Carver as 'America's Chekhov' in its obituary.
8 *What We Talk about When We Talk about Love* (New York: Alfred A. Knopf, 1981; rpt. Random House, 1982) p. 37.
9 Ibid., p. 39.
10 Ibid., pp. 42–3.
11 Ibid., p. 45.
12 'The Art of Fiction LXXVI: Raymond Carver', *Paris Review*, 25 (Summer 1983) 210.
13 K. Nesset, 'Insularity and Self-Enlargement in Raymond Carver's *Cathedral*', *Essays in Literature*, 21 (1994), 127.
14 C. Fischer, 'Simone Weil and the Civilisation of Work', in R. H. Bell (ed.), *Simone Weil's Philosophy of Culture* (Cambridge: Cambridge Univ. Press, 1993) p. 189.
15 Ibid., p. 193.
16 Ibid., p. 197.
17 A. Bieler, *The Social Humanism of Calvin*, P. T. Fuhrmann (trans.) (Richmond, VA: John Knox Press, 1964), pp.17–18; quoted in D. Little, *Religion, Order, and Law; A Study in Pre-Revolutionary England*, The Library of Religion and Culture (New York: Harper & Row, 1969) p. 60.
18 See Little's discussion in chapter 2, 'Religion, Order, and Law and the Thought of Max Weber', ibid., pp. 6–32.
19 Nesset, 'Insularity and Self-Enlargement', p. 119.

8
Sherman Alexie: Walking with Skeletons

Janet Blumberg

There are things you should learn. Your past is a skeleton walking one step behind you, and your future is a skeleton walking one step in front of you. Maybe you don't wear a watch, but your skeletons do, and they always know what time it is. ...

Sometimes your skeletons will dress up as beautiful Indian women and ask you to slow dance. Sometimes your skeletons will dress up as your best friend and offer you a drink, one more for the road. Sometimes your skeletons will look exactly like your parents and offer you gifts.

But, no matter what they do, keep walking, keep moving. And don't wear a watch. Hell, Indians never need to wear a watch because your skeletons will always remind you about the time. See, it is always now. That's what Indian time is. The past, the future, all of it is wrapped up in the now. That's how it is. *We are trapped in the now.*[1]

Rush-hour commuters who tuned into National Public Radio stations across North America on 27 September 1993 heard these words recited during an unusual interview conducted by Linda Worthheimer with Sherman Alexie, then 26, a writer-poet who grew up on the Spokane/Coeur d'Alene Tribal Reservation in Washington state. In twelve minutes of air time, Alexie painted an unforgettable portrait of Indian life on the North American reservation in taut and driving cadences both bardic and contemporary. Listeners were probably as arrested by the voice as by the words, while hearing Alexie answer questions and perform selections from his volume of prose-poems called *The Lone Ranger and Tonto Fistfight in Heaven* (1994). Alexie's voice was that of everybody's kid brother, young, fresh and familiar, and he conversed with Wertheimer in an unaffected high school idiom sprinkled with 'yeahs' and 'heys'. Yet whenever he began to perform his work, Alexie's voice grew edgy and compelling, revealing a ferocious intelligence at times crackling with rage, at times staggering under an enormous weight of despair. At the same time listeners were made to know they were in the presence of an artistic medium much older than the printed page, a way of speaking for which the written word would always remain nothing more than a scant and inadequate means of representation. For all its otherness, the work's poetic power and its connection with its non-tribal hearers were there in spades. Emily Dickinson once wrote that you *knew* something was poetry 'if it knocked the top of your head off'. Alexie's words did.

Through the agency of this remarkable voice, moreover, listeners found themselves engulfed, with torrential force and immediacy, in the lifeworld of 'the rez', suddenly becoming near-inhabitants of what previously must have been, for many, only a shaded area designated on the local roadmap. Wertheimer asked, for instance, about an incident in the 'Indian Education' chapter of *The Lone Ranger and Tonto*, when the narrator tells how, as a second-grader in the tribal school, he was kept in from recess for fourteen days straight by a red-haired missionary teacher named Betty Towle. The teacher had given him a spelling test designed for junior high, and, when he spelled every word correctly, crumbled up the sheet of paper and made him eat it. 'Yeah, that story is true', Alexie told Wertheimer. 'It happened to me.' In the vignette, the day after the teacher tells him to cut his braids and 'learn respect' or her God will punish him for being 'indian, indian, indian', the child's parents come to school with him and drag their braids across Betty Towle's desk. '*Yes, I am*', the child thinks to himself. '*I am Indian. Indian, I am*'.[2] Alexie's revelation of the world-within-a-world that is the reservation – on the one hand so materially deprived that little girls buy a box of food colours at the BIA commodity store to colour their meagre fare of potatoes red and yellow and blue, and on the other hand so richly poignant, funny and human, at once so agonisingly like and so unlike the society surrounding it – must have comprised another powerful shock for many listeners.

Of those commuters who heard Sherman Alexie on NPR, some who lived in the Puget Sound area no doubt found occasion to attend the poetry readings Alexie often gave at the Elliott Bay Book Company in Seattle's downtown Pioneer Square district. There, they would have observed even more markedly than in the interview the high degree of hostility and distrust Alexie exhibited toward the general American society surrounding the reservation subculture. His performance pieces, reminiscent of the work of the best stand-up comedians on the night-club circuit, only better, were calculated to convey with haunting effect the bleakness of the reservation situation and the on-going culpability and cruelty of white society toward Native Americans. Alexie frequently made his white audiences squirm.

In contrast, he exuded a sense of warm rapport with the members of his own ethnic community who were in his audience, along with those he viewed as fellow victims of genocide, notably persons of African or Jewish descent. While championing these groups, his bitter-sweet comic monologues and his poignant anecdotes of Indian experience were aimed squarely at the culture represented in the persons of the rest of the audience – persons whom Alexie pointedly warned before-hand against asking questions after the reading. He clearly expected to find the questions unbearably patronising and derogatory. On some occasions, Alexie simply looked at an audience and announced that he would take no questions at all. His resentment was in some ways understandable: he recalls, for example, one white interviewer who asked this highly trained storyteller and myth-maker if his parents were 'literate'. In any case, detaching the rawness of Alexie's anger and scorn from the explosive brilliance of his performances would have been impossible. Still, Alexie's palpable dislike, distrust, even hatred toward his non-Native audience created a curious and fascinating contradiction.

To attempt to speak to the perpetrator culture as a member of a despised and humiliated subculture – Alexie does not hesitate to use the term 'holocaust' for what Native Americans have experienced and continue to experience at the hands of the European settlers of the Americas – entails an inevitable contradiction in terms. At the same time, it constitutes a tremendous act of faith. Entering the public sphere to speak to the larger society assumes belief that a genuine hearing is possible, even from the very persons one endemically distrusts. In the journey of Sherman Alexie, therefore, we can examine the difficulties of entering the public sphere experienced by members of groups with high degrees of alienation, hostility and distrust toward the dominant culture. Yet, despite some agonising interior contradic-tions, Alexie has gone on to devote his full energies in recent years to the possibility of revitalising the public sphere, the arena in which Habermas believes the world's best (and last) hopes for social justice and human survival depend. The case of an artist such as Alexie tests alike our hopes for a reconstituted public sphere and our notions of the role of literature in that reconstruction.

A rising star

Since the Wertheimer interview in 1993 and his early readings at Elliott Bay Book Company, Alexie's productivity has been astounding and his rise to artistic prominence meteoric. After those early volumes of poems and short prose pieces, Alexie turned to the novel: the highly acclaimed *Reservation Blues* was published in 1995 by Atlantic Monthly Press, followed by his bestselling murder mystery, *Indian Killer*, in 1996. That June, Alexie was named one of America's 20 best young novelists by *Granta*.[3] From fiction, Alexie turned to screenwriting. His first film, adapted from a story in *The Lone Ranger and Tonto* and tagged by Alexie as the 'first ever all-Indian road movie, with all the white guys played by Indian actors', has been produced by Seattle-based Shadow Catcher Productions with a Native American director, screened at Sundance (where it won the Filmmakers Trophy and the Audience Award), and picked up for distribution by Miramax in 1998. Alexie's second screenplay, a film adaptation of *Indian Killer*, is currently under production at Shadow Catcher.

As Alexie's artistic range and popular reputation have steadily increased, he has taken to speaking and appearing in a rich variety of civic venues, ranging from his columns in the *Seattle Weekly* to editorial commentaries on the Jim Lehrer News Hour, from local and national benefits and artistic convocations to writers' workshops on reservations all over the country. He has opened himself deliberately to public contact by publishing his phone number in *Indian Killer* (and returning phone calls), and he has sponsored and worked with a student literary journal in a white high school, as well as standing for hours ladling out sauce at spaghetti-dinner fund-raisers for reservation youth groups. Alexie has thus emerged not only as a literary voice whose work has entered the public sphere through the medium of books and film, but also as a civic voice in those sorts of venue belonging more particularly to the public sphere itself and to its most important function, contributing to the formation of genuine public opinion.

These experiences in reaching out to the society around him have occasionally borne out Alexie's distrust of 'making treaties with white guys', a leading theme of *Reservation Blues*. In this novel Alexie invents the 'first all-Indian Catholic rock band', hailing from the Spokane Reservation, and traces its exploitation at the hands of unscrupulous New York record producers. After undergoing robbery and rape, the band members give up hope for a voice in mainstream American culture. In real life, when Alexie attempted to pitch his first screenplay *This is what it means to say Phoenix, Arizona* to the major studios, he found executives who 'liked the story' but wanted him to make the main characters white. Alexie almost abandoned the project, until he heard of a small film-making enterprise newly established in Seattle by self-declared renegades from the Hollywood scene. None the less, even after Shadow Catcher's sensitive and responsive handling of the Indian-produced, Indian-directed and Indian-acted movie ('no Italians with long hair'), the film's integrity suffered one last indignity at the hands of its distributor Miramax, which unilaterally decided it would release the film (in the summer of 1998) under a new title evoking all the traditional stereotypes: *Smoke Signals*.

In spite of such setbacks, Alexie's early alienation from the larger culture has evolved into a complicated and fascinating pattern of conversations and (even) conversions. For example, as the second part of an unusual double billing in February of 1995, Alexie appeared at the University of Washington to read from a just-published book of love poems for his wife Diane; the first half of the programme, extraordinarily enough, dealt with European Romantic opera. Alexie, after sitting through the first hour's lecture (which was accompanied by two tenors performing arias), rose and commended the lecture as 'the best one-hour introduction to Romanticism' the audience might ever hope to hear. He then launched, after some hilarious Valentine's Day patter about ineptitude in love, into a reading of his love poems, after which he acceded to a request from the audience that he perform the title poem from *First Indian on the Moon* ('The first Indian on the moon / Is a woman').

Because Alexie is an oral poet who carries his work in his head, frequently reworking and improving it regardless of its published form, he willingly concluded the programme with the requested lyric, and with, of course, its final line, a line in which the speaker declares his love in his native Salish dialect. Throughout the evening, Alexie kept going out of his way to draw the diverse halves of the programme together, first reprising the lecture's main points about European Romanticism and then pointing out, as he read his own poems, the presence of similar moods and tendencies. You see, he commented, the emotions of lovers are in many ways the same, whether they are

Indian lovers or European. Needless to say, on this occasion no members of the audience felt constraint about asking questions or talking with the poet afterwards.

But Alexie's edge has not disappeared. He continues to disturb and confront white culture, and in an interview at the end of the cassette version of *Indian Killer* (read by Alexie), he notes that his own people resist the way that he brings their anger into the open. Particularly vociferous have been Alexie's attacks on 'eyedropper Indians': those whose Indian blood would fill, he says, at most an eyedropper, who do not look like Indians and who have no Indian experience, yet still try to claim a spurious kinship. A prominent example of Alexie's outrage over this tendency is his bitterly satiric depiction of Jack Wilson, a white writer in *Indian Killer* who cashes in on his spurious Native ancestry by penning a popular series of mysteries featuring an Indian detective. On the cassette version of *Indian Killer*, Alexie explains that he thinks every non-Native writer about Native experience cuts into the market for this kind of writing, and that the least such writers can do is to donate a percentage of their royalties to Indian colleges, to help produce genuine Native writers in the future. 'That would be a very Indian thing to do,' Alexie comments wryly, 'and we would admire them for it'.[4]

Another instance of Alexie's stubborn resistance to cultural 'making nice' is his declining to smooth things over with the non-Native novelist Barbara Kingsolver, whom he has criticised for her portrayal of Indian characters and reservation life in such popular novels as *Pigs in Heaven* and *Animal Dreams*. 'After she finishes writing for the day, she goes out and buys groceries as a white person. I have to go out and buy groceries as an Indian', he notes. Alexie's identity politics insist that Indian physiognomy and Indian experience distinguish the authentic voices of Native American experience. Their opportunity to address the larger society must not be encroached upon by non-Native writers, however able and sympathetic such writers might be. Alexie also disagrees strongly, as is best seen in *Indian Killer*, with the practice of non-Native adoption of Native American babies, which is presented positively in several Kingsolver novels.

Race, identity, and song

Throughout his work, Alexie has wrestled with the issue of the racial construction of identity. In an early vignette called 'Freaks', he imagines a visit to Seattle by a young Yakima, 'the Indian tourist with half-braids and a wallet full of money'. On the Seattle waterfront, the visitor encounters 'three Indians sharing a bottle of wine and a can of Spam', with whom he identifies as an Indian, although not as a tourist. After spending time with his fellow outcasts, 'I say goodbye with handshakes and walk down the waterfront, passing by white tourists who don't care if they ever know my name. I walk all day, looking for just one more kind face'.[5] Yet when the usual physical identification of himself as an Indian fails, Alexie finds himself at a strange loss. During a trip to New York he discovers:

> Everyone walking past me, through me, in the streets, on the subway, had darker skin. I have been Native American all my life and now I was Chicano, Puerto Rican, Chinese, Japanese, Iraqui, a non-practicing Jew. ... Walking down aisles of the pharmacy across the street from Lincoln Center – the white clerk didn't watch me closely, expecting me to shoplift. For that, I almost missed Spokane, the city where I was born and which reminds me continually of my dark eyes and hair and skin. Could it be true? Am I Native American only when I am hated for it? Does racism determine my entire identity?[6]

In spite of this deep identification with his ethnic origins and people, Alexie refuses to sentimentalise his Native American identity. He never glosses over the chronic ills of tribal life or the indigenous atrocities of Native history. The skeletons that walk by his side are many. In the Wertheimer interview, for example, he frankly detailed his own years of alcoholism and spoke tellingly of the early deaths – stemming from drinking, drugs and violence – of many childhood friends. Elsewhere, he has pithily refuted what he views as the liberal and New Age romanticising of Native life and traditions, earning himself enemies on his own reservation.

Alexie's sense of his own ethnicity is constituted by a complex blend of identifying moments, both positive and negative, poignantly captured, for example, in the opening piece of *First Indian on the Moon*. Here the speaker remembers himself as a small boy in a car parked outside a bar, entertaining his little sisters by inventing stories of a warrior woman who will save them all, including their drunken parents. His imaginary red-haired Saviour is a response to the children's palpable sense that an incalculable catastrophe has befallen 'all Indian kids' and has 'disappeared' their parents and the other members of their decimated communities:

> We waited in the car
>   outside the bar
>   my sisters and I
> 'for just a couple drinks'
>   as we had heard it
> so many times before
>   as Ramona had said
> like all Indian kids
>   have heard
>   before

from their parents, disappeared into the smoke and laughter of a reservation tavern, emerging every half-hour with Pepsi, potato chips, and more promises. And, like all Indians have learned, we never did trust those promises. We knew to believe something when it happened, learned to trust the source of a river and never its mouth. But this is not about sadness. This is about the stories …

> ... those rough drafts
> that thundered the walls
>   of the HUD house
> as my sisters and I lay awake
> after we finally arrived home
>   and listened
> to my mother and father dream
>   breathe deep
> in their sleep, snore
> like what you might want me to call drums
>   but in the reservation dark
>   it meant we were all alive
>   and that was enough.[7]

From earliest memory, Alexie has identified himself as Native American, but also as one who is compelled to tell stories and to make poems, to utter the words that might sustain life on behalf of his people. While several of the reservation characters who crop up from book to book seem to be Alexie *alter egos*, it is the tormented story-teller Thomas Builds-the-Fire who expresses the most painful aspects of the storytelling identity Alexie embraces:

> Thomas Builds-the-Fire walked through the corridors of the tribal school by himself. Nobody wanted to be anywhere near him because of all those stories. Story after story.
>
> Thomas closed his eyes and this story came to him: 'We are all given one thing by which our lives are measured, one determination. Mine are the stories which can change or not change the world. It doesn't matter which as long as I continue to tell the stories. My father, he died on Okinawa in World War II, fighting for this country, which had tried to kill him for years. My mother, she died giving birth to me, died while I was still inside her. She pushed me out into the world with her last breath. ... I learned a thousand stories before I took my first thousand steps. They are all I have. It's all I can do'.[8]

Thomas knows that his stories have been given to him for healing. Yet he wonders how stories as bitter as his own can ever heal anything. His own tribe hates to hear his stories. Still, he continues to tell them.

Alexie's early identity construction, as one designated an Indian by his physical appearance and a child of the reservation by his history and experience, included an urgent personal calling to be a storyteller. This aspect of his formation connected him with what Paul Tillich would call the 'depth dimension' of his culture. But paradoxically such a depth dimension, in which his connections to his own culture are the strongest and deepest, may also have helped to open up Alexie in his process of personal formation to the depth dimensions of other cultures, however alien those cultures might appear on the surface. Alexie's metaphor for the human connection to a cultural depth dimension is the image of song, and song includes (as for European bards from Homer to Milton) every mode of the singing and playing we call art. Alexie's song is, like Milton's, 'sacred song', divine and originary.

Alexie's musical theology of cosmic sustenance and renewal is embodied throughout *Reservation Blues* in the semi-mythical figure of Big Mom (reservations often have a Big Mom). In the beautiful opening passages of the novel, Alexie's Big Mom, who lives on a mountain above the little reservation town of Wellpinit, hears the horses she had long ago taught to sing now begin to scream. The allusion is to the slaughter in 1858 of the Appaloosa horses of the Nez Percé and other Salish-speaking tribes (including Alexie's own), 800 of which were confiscated and rounded up by the US Cavalry and shot to death, first serially and then, when that proved too slow, *en masse* by continuous rifle fire. From her mountainside above the Spokane Reservation, Big Mom listens as her vanished horses begin to sing a new song:

> She had taught all her horses to sing many generations before, but she soon realized this was not a song of her teaching. The song sounded so pained and tortured that Big Mom could never have imagined it before the white men came. ... In 1992, Big Mom still watched for the return of those slaughtered horses and listened to their songs. With each successive generation, the horses arrived in different forms and with different songs, called themselves Janis Joplin, Jimi Hendrix, Marvin Gaye.[9]

This is the new song that Big Mom will teach to the Indian Catholic rock band at the end of the novel, after they have relinquished their hopes for artistic careers in the corrupted mainstream commercial media. 'Big Mom taught them a new song, the shadow horses' song, the slaughtered horses' song, a song of mourning that had become a song of celebration: we have survived, we have survived'. Through the sustaining depth of this new music by which they will now live, the surviving members of the band are able to leave the reservation and travel toward their menial jobs in Spokane feeling that, although they can foresee no public or artistic future, 'songs were waiting for them in the city. Thomas drove the car in the dark. He drove. Checkers and Chess reached out of their windows and held tightly to the manes of those shadow horses running alongside the blue van'.[10]

Alexie's segue from tribal creation songs to the legendary singers of the blues and rock-and-roll demonstrates how cross-cultural communal identifications can function to open up a predominantly ethnic identity formation. Alexie's stories are replete with characters who identify passionately with counter-cultural figures who have entered the mainstream of American popular culture, from Billy Jack or Mohammed Ali to the legendary blues guitarist Robert Johnson whose story is told in the 1989 film *Crossroads* and who figures prominently in the plot of *Reservation Blues*. In *The Lone Ranger and Tonto*, embittered young Victor and his ravaged, alcoholic father are bound together by the memory they carry in common, which is also the title of a chapter: 'Because My Father Always Said He Was the Only Indian Who Saw Jimi Hendrix Play "The Star-Spangled Banner" at Woodstock'.

Alexie's devotion to the blues and its role in his early formation is evident in his depiction of Victor's childhood:

> On those nights I missed him most I listened to music. Not always Jimi Hendrix. Usually I listened to the blues. Robert Johnson mostly. The first time I heard Robert Johnson sing I knew he understood what it meant to be an Indian on the edge of the twenty-first century, even if he was black at the beginning of the twentieth. That must have been how my father felt when he heard Jimi Hendrix. When he stood in the rain at Woodstock.[11]

Here we see the efficacy of music to open up identity formation and ultimately facilitate public discourse. In fact a scene from *Crossroads* dramatises the possibility that music can play a vital role in the American public sphere. Johnson and his young white guitar-playing admirer are on the road together, and when they split up to work the bars in a segregated Southern town, a striking contrast occurs. The redneck bars where the white adolescent seeks an audience have no public venue operating at all, just hard-drinking private parties united only in their suspicion of outsiders; the Negro bars, on the other hand, are surging with rhythm and blues in which everyone vocally participates in delighted counterpoint. The performance space is clearly held by everyone present as an opening for dialogical public discourse, and as the scene progresses it demonstrates the way performance can function as a means for arriving at collective opinion formation. Both jazz and rock-and-roll, Alexie suggests, reach participants on a deep communal level and might frequently play an important role in developing and sustaining genuine public discourse.

Alexie's own communicative roles and interactions have continued to broaden and produce genuine fruit. Although his tribal, Native identity is crucial, Alexie also marks out and calls attention to his connections with many aspects of the larger culture. Alexie consciously shares much with all the members of Generation X, regardless of ethnicity. The same comic books have been ubiquitous, and the same television programmes, even when the TVs were ancient and unreliable black-and-white models, sitting on rickety tables in unfinished HUD houses or in the corners of trailers on the reservation. In *Smoke Signals*, for example, Alexie's reservation scenes and road scenes alike resonate with popular culture icons such as Nike or Mary Lou Retton. Reflexively, Alexie's membership in Generation X has heightened the power and appeal of his work and allowed him to continue to evolve and change cross-culturally, and that has enabled him to carry his ethnic identity into the civic arena even while that identity continues to become more syncretic. His story demonstrates the ways in which individuals, like cultures, are complicated intersections of many identifications both particular and diffuse, identifications that work against simple identity politics and thankfully do not always dwell easily with one another.

Conversions, prayers, and bitterness

Perhaps the most intriguing of Alexie's cross-cultural conjunctions is his recent embrace of Roman Catholicism, the religion of his Native American wife Diane, who was a devout Catholic when they married in 1992. Alexie, not surprisingly, has made much of the ironies implicit in his acceptance of the faith of some of those very European settlers who inflicted so much damage upon his people, even in the course of their attempted ministries. Alexie had a field day, for example, reporting in the *Seattle Weekly* on the trip he made with Diane to Italy, the ancient seat of his new-found religion. There, he describes their adventures in conversation with jaded Italians who tell them that the church is *passé* and has nothing to offer the world any longer. Alexie gets in some wonderfully funny barbs at the expense of the 'Catholic Disneyland' of Vatican City, where 'Jesus Christ has become a commodity, a tourist attraction, an economic opportunity'. He also records this internal soliloquy: 'What have white people done to their religion? To the religion they forced upon my tribe? To the religion I have somehow come to love?'[12]

Alexie's sense of Jesus as a counter-cultural exemplar and as a divinely-grieving witness to the healing needed by our deeply fractured contemporary society remains. In *Indian Killer*, for example, Father Duncan, a Native American Jesuit priest, serves as mentor and father-figure to the child protagonist, John, who was snatched as a newborn baby from his reservation birth-mother and delivered by helicopter to a wealthy white couple in Seattle. Duncan takes John to view the Chapel of the North American martyrs in downtown Seattle, where scenes of Jesuits murdered by Indians are depicted:

> John was confused. He stared at the martyred Jesuits. Then he noticed the large crucifix hanging over the altar. A mortally wounded Jesus, blood pouring from his hands and feet, from the

> wound in his side. John saw the altar candles burning and followed the white smoke as it rose toward the ceiling of the chapel.
>
> 'Was Jesus an Indian?' asked John.
>
> 'He wasn't an Indian,' said the Jesuit, 'but he should have been'.[13]

In the conversation which ensues, we see that Big Mom has been joined by her human-divine brother in testifying to the facts of oppression and perhaps in teaching us the songs of survival. ('The Jesuit held the baby John in his arms, sang traditional Spokane songs and Catholic hymns, and rocked him to sleep'.[14]) Still, when John is seven years old, Father Duncan disappears from sight into the desert, seemingly turning his back on a society and on a religious role whose contradictions are no longer bearable.

Alexie's syncretic identifications, none the less, have laid the foundations for his corresponding act of faith in seeking a place in the public sphere for the voices of his people. The Czech underground novelist Ivan Klima, invoking Kafka's dictum that 'writing is prayer' as he wrote secretly within his communist-ruled homeland, noted that, whenever we commit the inner landscape of the life we know to the written word, 'we turn to someone whose existence and hence also whose language we can scarcely surmise'.[15] Alexie's writings and performances, directed as they are at a mainstream audience, are in this sense striking acts of faith, and especially so, given the experiences of callousness and indifference he has recorded so compellingly.

Perhaps the most difficult question raised by Alexie in terms of the renewal of the public sphere is the threat to public discourse occasioned by the bitterness and alienation that he expresses. When 'the songs of the slaughtered horses' enter the mainstream, as all blues-lovers know, they might well 'sing the skins off our backs'. How does the dispassionate rhetoric of the public sphere accommodate and respond to such pain, and to such embittered speakers? Biting, distempered and disturbing elements plague the act of communication any time that the subaltern gets a chance to make the hegemony hear 'good and loud', as the Simpson jury verdict so tellingly demonstrated. None the less, bitter stories are precisely the stories necessary for the healing of democratic societies, if the democratic base is to be expanded to include those formed by these bitter stories. Such stories and people subsequently need to be assimilated into the mainstream of public opinion through conversations, commentaries, interpretations and analyses offered in a plethora of public and semi-public venues.

As a Christian, Alexie must deal with the issues of hatred and forgiveness on a religious level. He frequently addressed such issues even
before he converted to Catholicism, and it will be interesting to
observe how the development of his faith will play out in his future
writing. Alexie has always displayed a tendency to correct his own
excesses, even when they were a direct moral response to the excessive
cruelty and persecution he encountered and saw others suffer. For
example, in a brilliant poetic sequence called 'Firestorms' in *First
Indian*, he employs his master-metaphor for racial hatred – the image
of fire – in a stunning *tour de force* about the annihilation of Indian
personhood in white society. But he ends the sequence with a piece
called 'Fire Sale: a sale of merchandise damaged in a fire', in which he
offers himself in the image of a living holocaust and burnt offering, a
self none the less complicit in its own conflagration: 'Here I offer what
I own / Grief, like a burning bush / That cries, forgiveness, / And never
forgives'.[16]

As a child on the reservation, Alexie recalls, he was 'beat up' regularly
by the bigger kids, until he learned how to beat up people with his mind.
'In a way', he admits in the *Indian Killer* interview, 'I'm still doing that,
with my words'. Alexie is well aware of his vengeful desire to even the
score, and he worries along with Thomas Builds-the-Fire that his sad and
bitter stories will never heal anything. In this context, it is particularly
interesting that in his first feature film, *Smoke Signals*, the intertwined
themes of fire and hatred are not dealt with directly in terms of white
society at all, but in relation to the anger of reservation sons against their
fathers, and the question it leaves us with crosses all cultural boundaries:
'and if we forgive *them*, what is left?'

Growth and the public sphere

Sherman Alexie's journey suggests a certain parallel between the psychological development of a public artist and the inter-subjective development of a healthy public sphere. By stepping into a plethora of mixed
venues, Alexie has experienced the kinds of participation in a wider lifeworld that are requisite to effective participation in the public sphere.
Habermas has theorised that individual participation in democratic
processes can emerge only out of personal and social growth that results
from experiencing solidarity with a variety of groups and 'publics'. Only
those individuals who have engaged in the process of speaking and being
heard, and also of listening and being persuaded, in a number of communities, learn to exercise those discursive assumptions and practices,

and internalise that confidence in personal agency necessary for vital participation in the public sphere. It would seem, then, that individuals who have identified with only one collectivity or who are formed only in non-democratic collectivities inevitably lack the psychological formation and intellectual assumptions through which they might become participants in public deliberation on the common good. Perhaps, if the survival of the public sphere is predicated upon the fact that social collectivities always are, in fact, overlapping, and if no one's subjectivity comes to be formed strictly through only one identification, it may be the role of music, art, religion and literature to ensure that the contemporary lifeworld's complexity is registered and its existential depth dimensions powerfully tapped.

Habermas' theory of growth is surprisingly similar to that invoked by the Trappist priest Thomas Merton, who has argued that only truly autonomous individuals can make up a functioning society. Only such a person possesses 'a sense of one's own reality' and a sense of one's ability to give him or herself to society, 'or to refuse that gift'.[17] The profound sense of personal agency Merton describes registers its own deeply rooted identifications, but simultaneously, and equally, opens to the experience of contradictory solidarities that separate one in complicated ways from one's primary roots. It may be that only in this painful way do persons and societies grow, and restrictively dominant structures become less rigid and monolithic, more porous and adaptive, even as suppressed identifications and silent grievances are given voice and integrated into a larger dialogue. Handicapped by the absence of an internalised sense of self that comes only from experiencing the roles of both speaker and hearer within collectively functioning publics, a person's efforts to find a public voice for his or her experiences may result only in a kind of exclusionary identity politics that cannot, by definition, vitalise the public sphere, but only batter and assault it.

When it comes to producing public voices out of deeply alienated communities, it may not matter whether we are thinking of Native Americans on their reservations, or of any of the other isolated and distrustful enclaves within hegemonic cultures. The problems of emergent self-expression may be the same whether the collectivities we refer to are relatively readily identifiable subcultures such as the African-American community, or nearly invisible fellowships such as the victims of childhood sexual violence. In this context, acts of faith and growth such as Alexie's might be seen as perhaps the *sine qua non* of public life, however fraught with bitterness, distrust and anger they may be, however offensive and dislocating their content to the established fabric of public life. But it is only *in the hearing* of those voices, paradoxically, that those voices can develop adequately to function as sensors for the larger society. Only with a myriad of small decisions on the parts of many persons will an embittered minority grow into a complex and fruitful factor in the larger weave of democratic communal life, or will that life remain genuinely democratic.

Daily and weekly, the newspapers of the Pacific Northwest carry stories that reflect the changing culture Sherman Alexie is helping to create. A judge bows to the request of tribal elders and assigns two adolescent offenders to tribal supervision in a traditional exile to a remote island. Four members of a high school football team participate publicly in a 'shaming' ceremony to show their penitence for vandalising a totem pole standing in front of a rival high school. The pole was a gift from a tribal artist; now the young men are working with that artist to harvest a tree and shape it into a new piece of art to replace the original gift. Alexie attends the memorial service and public reading to honour internationally famous poet and Seattle resident Denise Levertov. Inter-tribal debates over casinos, Indian rights to salmon and other legal battles are respectfully reported. An appreciable impact on regional life might well be attributed, not in small part, to the unflinching honesty and galvanising power of the literary work and the civic activity of Sherman Alexie.

While Alexie says that a traditional Spokane does not tell outsiders about the sacred things of the tribe, he has found a way to write about the mysteries of communal identity experienced by many faith communities. He has done so in a 'public' language which is not dis-passionate, but none the less has a lucid case to make (in the ways that literary art makes its cases), and which is, most of all, a language guardedly open to response. Most important, perhaps, he appears to have done so without the loss of artistry, message, ethnic identity or sense of personal integrity. Despite his ambivalences – about his identity, his bitterness, his audiences and his notoriety – Alexie has become a public figure and spokesperson capable of communicating across immense barriers of difference.

Through his art, the excruciating and irreplaceable gift of his story-telling and picture-painting, and equally through his public discourse and interactions, Alexie has opened up a space in which persons who are in many ways radically 'other' from one another can stand together and engage in truly dialogical exchange. When we walk with skeletons beside us, we must give them voices and those who hear us must learn to see them, too. But when we gaze closely at the flames that have consumed and yet made us, we must give those flames back their human features. Literature, film, music and religion provide existential languages that give us access to the depth dimensions of human life-worlds through which all of us might connect with cultures and persons other than ourselves. These conjunctions might even, as in Alexie's case, operate powerfully enough upon identity formation in contemporary societies to disrupt the self-enclosure of hermetically sealed collectivities or individuals. Only lively processes of personal formation that tap deeply into cherished forms of rootedness, while also opening outward into a complexity of 'peripheral' associations,[18] can produce artists and citizens capable of sustaining the richly dissonant and painfully varied exchanges of a genuine public sphere. Reciprocally, only the disparate voices and stories which thus emerge in a public sphere can deliver the hegemonic and subaltern together from their lonely structures of self-defence and retreat.

Notes

1 S. Alexie, *The Lone Ranger and Tonto Fistfight in Heaven* (New York: HarperCollins, 1994) pp. 21–2.
2 Ibid., pp. 172–3.
3 *Granta: The Best of Young American Novelists*, 54 (1996).
4 *Indian Killer as read by the author* (San Bruno, CA: Audio Literature, 1996).
5 S. Alexie, *First Indian on the Moon* (Brooklyn, NY: Hanging Loose Press, 1993) p. 49.
6 Ibid., p. 81.
7 Ibid., pp. 9–10.
8 Alexie, *The Lone Ranger and Tonto*, pp. 72–3.
9 S. Alexie, *Reservation Blues* (New York: Atlantic Monthly Press, 1995) pp. 9–10.
10 Ibid., p. 306.
11 Alexie, *The Lone Ranger and Tonto*, p. 24.
12 'Going Native: A visitor's guide to exploring the Northwest's Native culture and history', *Seattle Weekly*, 3 July 1996, pp. 18–21.
13 S. Alexie, *Indian Killer* (New York: Atlantic Monthly Press, 1996) pp. 14–15.
14 Ibid., p. 13.
15 I. Klima, *Love and Garbage* (New York: Alfred A. Knopf, 1989) p. 86.
16 Alexie, *First Indian*, p. 28.
17 T. Merton, *Thoughts in Solitude* (New York: Farrar, Straus and Giroux, 1956) p. 13.
18 M. C. Bateson, *Peripheral Visions: Learning Along the Way* (New York: Harper Collins, 1994).

9
Denis Johnson's Strange Light

James Champion

> At the bottom of the heart of every human being, from earliest infancy until the tomb, there is something that goes on indomitably expecting, in the teeth of all experience of crimes committed, suffered, and witnessed, that good and not evil will be done to him. It is this above all that is sacred in every human being.
>
> Simone Weil, 'Human Personality'[1]

There is a new product you can purchase called 'Bibleopoly', a board game in which players can compete to build churches, not hotels. It is marketed by retailers who claim religious goods are badly needed in a world hell-bent on secular values. Many, pleased by such products, see in them something like faith at work. Others, rendered empty, might see demonic mediocrity triumphant. In other words, some recognise a hell of a different making, one marked above all by the disappearance of the dimension of depth in contemporary society.

To grasp the nature of this loss is to recognise related developments, including the erosion of the public sphere and the effacement of the human self. These changes can in turn be connected to a variety of factors, such as the dissolution of language into information systems, the monopolising of the means of manipulation of public opinion and the rise of a monolithic entertainment industry in the Americanised global marketplace. Perhaps the impact of these changes becomes most glaring in the religious sphere, where literalists take advantage of the spiritual vacuum left by conspicuous consumption and the trivialisation of ultimate questions. As Cornel West has said, we live in 'an increasingly market-driven world in which the hunger for meaning and community tends to yield to more authoritarian strategies to satisfy it'.[2]

To counter new authoritarian strategies, while still facing up to the condition of loss, we need a far-reaching perspective on human culture, a view that takes note of the public and religious levels of this domain. It's worth noting, however, that the domain of culture is often dismissed – and not only by those who, like the infamous Nazi minister, feel a need to reach for their pistols upon hearing the very word. Religiously committed people may wish to avoid dealing with culture because examination of its dynamics can reveal the conditioned side of truth. Those in anti-religious camps, on the other hand, often adhere to another sort of defence. In the academic world, for example, it is significant that 'cultural studies' has come to dominate conferences and publishing. Yet this movement, its name and vital research notwithstanding, studiously avoids incalculable areas of experience. It is surely easier to maintain an aura of analytic power when you treat religious phenomena – soul or ritual, say – as constructs or sign-systems primarily. As constructed signs these things are already prepared for dissection at the 'cutting edge' in a marketing game intellectuals prefer to play.

If we can speak of a dimension of depth in our world still – that is, of a range of human experience that is not movie-ready or efficiently translated into commodified terms – we can expect to glimpse it on the border regions of life. And when artists try to re-enact such experience in their cultural creations, we can expect them to use unstable and fragmented forms. For as Paul Tillich, a theologian of culture, once pointed out, there are times when covert 'spiritual substance' breaks through cultural forms.[3] And if this happens – if some element of ultimacy irrupts into experience – it is not conveniently contained. In short, when the depth of life appears, standard forms fail to domesticate the disclosure.

This is not to say that such moments must be grandiose or humourless. Unheroic disclosures of depth occur from time to time in the very sad and very funny writings of Denis Johnson. In the stories, novels and poems of this contemporary American author, the vicissitudes of particular lives find startling expression. Through this expression, Johnson's works retain literature's historic capacity to call a public sphere into being, albeit one riddled with profound loss. For the characters Johnson writes about are often, as he has acknowledged, 'twisted losers who don't contribute much to society'.[4] They barely function on the social margins, but they come alive at the heart of imaginative works that proffer alternatives to the corporate fictions and pseudo-realities that increasingly structure our world.

The trash of government buildings

I want to turn first to Denis Johnson's poetry. In particular, I wish to focus on the title poem of a volume in which he has collected earlier books of verse: *The Throne of the Third Heaven of the Nations Millennium General Assembly*. This name is taken from the work of James Hampton, a visionary African-American artist and self-proclaimed saint.[5] Between the end of World War II and his death in 1964, Hampton constructed a gold-and-silver-foil-covered setting for the Last Judgment. His 'Throne' – virtually an indoor environment – is symmetrically composed of almost two hundred objects, each of which is constructed of select items of junk. Privately scavenged and assembled, the work has been installed for public viewing in the National Museum of American Art in Washington, DC. The artist, meanwhile, has been elevated for the public to the status of folk-art hero. It should be remembered, however, that Hampton created this work in obscurity and isolation. He made the entire 'Throne' in a garage in an impoverished part of DC, and he survived by labouring as a janitor in government office buildings.

Johnson's poem, composed in three sections, interprets and pays tribute to Hampton's creation. Yet it also foregrounds the artist's loneliness and refuses to cover up signs of Hampton's derangement. The first section of the poem recounts a pilgrimage, a journey that unfolds through the speaker's images, dreams and confessions. The journey begins in Key West, Florida, and ends at the speaker's home in Massachusetts. But the heart of the poem lies between in a record of encounters, first with Hampton's birthplace in South Carolina, and finally with 'The Throne of the Third Heaven of the Nations Millennium General Assembly' in the capital of America.

The observer in Johnson's poem feels disoriented when first facing Hampton's work: 'It was in a big room. I couldn't take it all in, / And I was a little frightened'.[6] Yet the unusual light of the 'Throne' and its overarching inscription – 'Fear Not' – seem to open up the beholder and draw him into reflection. His thoughts and responses gradually disarm before the scope of another man's vision and the details of this same man's anguished life. The observer, feeling his own life interpreted by Hampton's work, finds

> ... I was his friend
> As I looked at and was looked at by the rushing-together parts
> Of this vision of someone who was probably insane
> Growing brighter and brighter like a forest after a rain –

> And if you look at the leaves of a forest,
> At its dirt and its heights, the stuttering mystic
> Replication, the blithering symmetry,
> You'll go crazy, too. If you look at the city
> And its spilled wine
> And broken glass, its spilled and broken people and hearts,
> You'll go crazy. If you stand
> In the world you'll go out of your mind. (p. 201)

As it evokes 'mystic' comparisons to a forest and a city, and as judgements emerge, 'The Throne' is something other than an official museum piece. Here, on public display, is the Revelation unmediated by state or ecclesiastical authority. Made from detritus, here is a vision pointing beyond itself, yet to no easy transcendent referent. What looms largest is close at hand in the everyday terror of Hampton's world, a world ironically portrayed by an inscription which he tacked to a board on his 'Throne': 'Where There Is No Vision the People Perish'. This *is* the world of the perishing, as the observer notes, a realm of 'shaken earthlings' clutching bottles, dice, ivory crucifixes, cards, newspapers – dispersed 'clues' which cannot tell them where they are inside their programmed destitution. These are the inhabitants of the underside of the nation's seat of power, a nation whose 'pure products', as William Carlos Williams once said, 'go crazy'.[7]

Yet Johnson's poem does more than toss off requisite political indictments. As one man encounters another's apocalyptic vision, questions of the heart become urgent. The enigma of the meaning of lost lives enters the poem at its deepest level of response:

> But it's all right,
> What happened to him. I can, now
> That he doesn't have to,
> Accept it.
> I don't believe that Christ, when he claimed
> The last will be first, the lost life saved –
> When he implied that the deeply abysmal is deeply blessed –
> I just can't believe that Christ, when faced
> With poor, poor people aspiring to become at best
> The wives and husbands of a lonely fear,
> Would have spoken redundantly.
> Surely he couldn't have referred to some other time

> Or place, when in fact such a place and time
> Are unnecessary. We have a time and place here,
> Now, abundantly. (p. 201)

At this juncture, the extremity of condition in Hampton's life comes into alignment with unembellished biblical truth. The paradoxes of Christ's Sermon on the Mount are suddenly present, unpostponed and embodied. The principle that a society will be judged by the way it treats the poorest in its midst bears hard on the current moment.

Such biblical overturnings and paradoxes do not become doctrinal in Johnson's poem. At the aesthetic level, they join with a host of unexpected associations and images of reversal appearing throughout. In section three, for example, we find the 'ALPHA AND OMEGA' in 'an empty garage', and we learn of a design by Hampton depicting 'the Virgin Mary descending / Into Heaven' (p. 202). Witnessing to such surprising formulations is itself a 'making', a poetic making companionable with Hampton's own. It is utterance that prepares the way for the poem's overarching reversal. For a kind of healing and acceptance does come to the speaker on this pilgrimage. But it arrives in the end by way of an empty, glittering chair, a revelation that is, in large measure, a painstakingly constructed scream of absence.

In grief and amazement

Johnson is an author who repeatedly turns to face, and who teaches us to see, the 'abundance' of broken lives here and now. As in Hampton's 'Throne', there is a kind of light in his work that – strange to say – illuminates absence. No doubt cultural institutions would rather see artists engage in more uplifting ventures. But in a world rushing to the millennium, truth-telling about what is displaced, torn and irretrievably gone can become a threshold to the discovery of what is actually present, and what is yet to come. In other words, Johnson shows us a world of diminished and even shattered meaning. But it is the honest portrayal of this condition that occasions moments when we enter the possibility of moving beyond it. Such moments are fragmentary and unrelentingly lowly; they are also sacred in their outside chance of overturning meaninglessness.

Johnson's way of combining emptiness with liminal reversals of loss makes for some remarkable reading. It has led more than one commentator to note something 'deeply new' going on in this body of work. As

Padgett Powell puts it, these writings 'take loss through some kind of sound barrier'.[8] It's a breakthrough that matters, not least of all because it offers an alternate voice to the conglomerate of books, movies and television shows that traffic in human loss. Such exploitation is endemic to an entertainment industry that regularly supplies cynical or infantilised audiences with recreational gazes at the down and out. In fact, cashing in on the seamy side, as Michiko Kakutani points out, amounts to 'a thriving new brand of tourism. Documentaries like *Kids*, musicals like *Rent* and movies like *Trainspotting* give audiences a voyeuristic peep at an alien subculture and let them go home feeling smug and *with it*'.[9]

The spiritual reach of Johnson's work is likely to prevent it from becoming a 'tourist' stop. In focusing on that religious element here, however, I do not want to discount the sheer aesthetic pleasure of reading this author's texts, nor to sequester them in an overly pure realm of high art. My point is that, in Johnson's stories about the hardcore drug underworld (*Jesus' Son*), or in his poem about James Hampton, or in his novel about dispossessed souls in Central America (*The Stars at Noon*), or in his essays on subaltern American communities,[10] something is at stake which voyeuristic entertainment precludes. Differently put, any art work that highlights the question of whether the 'deeply abysmal' is eternally 'blessed' is not likely to reach massive distribution behind a surge of cultural capital investment.

Fictional narrative can still provide an imaginative space in which writers such as Johnson can recast the religious news. But this news speaks to the tenor of experience in the post-modern world, a world in which everything can seem vaguely unhinged. Like other innovative contemporary writers, Johnson experiments with narrative techniques that re-enact life realistically, but he often opts for an expressionist realism that has aims far beyond verisimilitude. For instance, *Fiskadoro* (1985), one of Johnson's early novels, is set in the future in southern Florida after cataclysmic nuclear destruction. Readers slowly find their bearings in this half-familiar, amnesiac place by following the lives of a few displaced characters, including a curious, black 13-year-old boy called Fiskadoro. We also meet a remnant of survivors who are attempting to forge rituals and new understandings of what's true by piecing together broken symbols, historical traces and scavenged information. As the novel unfolds around this activity, it becomes a study of the role that mythic construction plays when humans act within a shattered culture to renegotiate the terms of life and death. A further purpose lies in the novel's fleeting views of 'the End of the World', and, beyond that, of the abyss at 'the bottom of everything'.[11] Yet these glimpses turn out to be doorways instead of points of closure, for the author emphasises the utterly ambiguous nature of final things. To use Victor Turner's term, these final things are marked by 'liminality', a transitional quality which is constantly at hand in Johnson's fictional worlds. It figures into the apocalyptic side of this author's work in consecrated, indeterminate moments between old configurations and a new reality. It is virtually embodied in the character of Fiskadoro, for example – especially in the moment when he realises that he has lost any hold on his life. At this point, late in the novel, we are told: 'His memory left him and he looked up at the giant desolation in grief and amazement once again, but also for the first time'.[12]

Border lines and transitional states also figure prominently in Johnson's recent work, *Already Dead* (1997). The novel opens with one dispossessed character, Van Ness, driving 'past the small isolated towns along US 101 in Northern California'. These towns exert a vague pull on the driver 'because he sensed they were places a person could disappear into. They felt like little naps you might never wake up from – you might throw a tire and hike to a gas station and stumble unexpectedly onto the rest of your life, the people who would finally mean something to you, a woman, an immortal friend, a saving fellowship in the religion of some obscure church'.[13]

Johnson's concern with the liminal is steadily evident in his explorations of human selfhood. His characters, who recall the grotesqueries of Flannery O'Connor's fictions, tend to reel between one set of pathological traits and another. These people can seldom voice their own tragedies. Moreover, they rely on delusions, instead of any solid sense of identity, to make it through the random catastrophes of life. But Johnson – and here he parts company with a number of postmodern writers – nevertheless depicts these characters as careening towards a transformed sense of self. In other words, while Johnson does not represent the self as some sort of Cartesian cogito perduring over time, neither does he treat identity as just another delusion. He does not dismantle the human self only to reveal arbitrary constructs. The worst misfits in his fiction insinuate that there is something in the seeking soul that is more than the sum of prevailing linguistic and social codes.

While discarding the idea of the self as a fixed entity, Johnson retains a sense of personhood as open to the possibility of apprehending itself differently over time. It is a take on the human core perhaps best designated by Paul Ricoeur's term 'narrative identity'.[14] The narrative self may become radically decentred and broken down, yet through novel emplotments of its journey it can still retain a strange cohesion. Such a view stresses the entwinement of life with narrative, and it has implications for both literature and life. For one thing, it clashes with the idea that life is primarily about information, an assumption currently serving electronic discourse in its colonisation of the private sphere. An endorsement of the function of story, by contrast, would maintain a place for the special powers of fictional narrative and, equally important, for the role that the reader plays in the imaginative recreation of a fictional world. Because readers must draw on their prefigured understandings of their own lives as they approach works of fiction, such narrative has the capacity to remain rooted in the common world of action.

Granted, many readers coming to a novel like Johnson's *Angels* (1983) will not find a world they immediately have in common. For here again is the nowhere side of American life, an ex-con's world of endless Greyhound bus rides and indistinguishable trailer parks, a thoroughly depressed landscape whose locals are generally failing at marriage, detox and armed robbery. Yet with Johnson's portrayal of the main characters in this novel, Jaimie Mays and Bill Houston, readers can connect with two inner lives. For we see psychological forces and sense a dimension of unconsciousness that makes the decisions and feelings of these figures all too recognisable.

In the character of Bill Houston, moreover, Johnson portrays someone who is on his way towards deliverance. Figuratively and quite literally, it is a redemption of the flesh of a man who comes to have a long, atoning dream of God as 'the Unmade ... the incredible darkness, the huge blue mouth of love'.[15] The dream comes in the last scenes of *Angels*, but with no moral competency rushing in at the end to explain it. Instead, we see the execution of Houston through 'the machinery of law and circumstance' at the Arizona State Prison Complex about eighty miles west of Tucson. Assorted families and onlookers gather outside the prison as witnesses to the occasion. They come in part because they want to know what death row is like and 'to draw close to the ceremonies of a semi-public death'. They also come because they sense 'that why they themselves had not been executed' was inexplicable, a miracle'.[16] They wait through the night, into the dawn, and then under the morning's burning sun. It is this sun that becomes for a moment the common symbol in vastly different lives. You could try to explain it as the spiritual resource transcending all the individual egos. In the imagery of this fiercely redemptive novel it becomes the 'negligent powerful breath of the day's coming heat, the heat that burns away each shadow and incinerates every last particle of shit inside the heart'.[17]

An apophatic way

In his fiction, Johnson re-enacts the complexities of the narrative self by including radical dissonance in the daily plot of lives. This emphasis on dissonance is in tandem with the post-modern critique of the tendency in our world to affirm presence unduly. We privilege presence and cover up absence when we believe we are fixed personalities inside an order of language that is transparent to our controlling meanings. We privilege presence and cover up absence when we give tacit assent to the power of consciousness to override the *aporias* of history and to master our secret fears.

With its truth-telling about what is absent, Johnson's authorship corroborates this critique. Yet his inspirations clearly diverge. He does not write criticism born of the resentment of presence, and he does not compose poems that revel only in the play of signifiers. His imagery and thought consistently take a theological turn, although, here again, it is towards post-modern theology of a distinctive sort.

One can elaborate this distinction ontologically. When presence and meaning are affirmed in Johnson's writings, they appear, so to speak, as the *negation* of absence. Put in these terms, being appears as a 'double negation', which is, of course, merely an abstract formulation. But the experience of this negation could not be more concrete, for the felt reality is as immediate as life. More exactly, this is life experienced as uncalculated grace, or, as Johnson once described it in an interview, it is life unexpectedly 'rescued' from 'hell' and various forms of living death.[18] It's life that gives rise to vision, but vision that forgoes metaphysical representations of God – that edifice of pure presence unquestionably in back of it all, forever identical with itself.

The intense focus on absence in Johnson's work is also apparent in a number of contemporary thinkers who are discovering new paths in storytelling and in religious reflection. You can see it in recent theological works. For example, in *Tragic Vision and Divine Compassion*, Wendy Farley discusses redemption in a manner that stresses its 'fragmentary' nature and its vulnerability 'to defeat'. Noting that redemption cannot nullify the destructiveness of sin and radical suffering, she states: 'precisely in the depth of this destruction a power remains to resist it, to thwart it, to preserve the possibility of healing'.[19] In a related vein, consider Peter Hodgson's *Winds of the Spirit*. In a chapter entitled 'The Challenge of Postmodernity', Hodgson describes the Christian cross as 'a question mark or a cancellation sign, a large "X"'. This sign, he goes on to say, 'must be written across the shape of the basileia, reminding us that its vision of inclusive wholeness, of a liberated communion of free persons, will forever remain marginal in this world, unable ultimately to dislodge the economy of domination and violence'.[20] Hodgson soon adds more positive assertions, but the acknowledgement of such limits is telling in a work whose subtitle is *A Constructive Christian Theology*. The attention both Hodgson and Farley pay to marginality and to actual anguish in the world clashes with metaphysical theologies intent on pronouncing victory over evil.

Honest looks at profound absence can also be found in New Testament scholarship. For example, in *Jesus: A Revolutionary Biography*, John Dominic Crossan makes it clear that the death of Jesus was, among other things, a harrowing political execution in an ancient police state. Crossan examines ways that the early church communities and their designated authors may have recast some of the details of this event.[21] Mark least of all, however. There is a broad consensus in New Testament studies that Mark's Gospel probably ended originally with chapter 16, verse 8. This means that the Good News according to Mark closes with the word 'afraid', and without incorporating post-resurrection appearances.

A reading of Mark that pays attention to these absences might be called apophatic. I mention this term from medieval theology not to conjure up some arcane practices, but as a way of naming in broad terms religious thinking that attempts to give the negative its due. For instance, such an approach would not see a threat to Christian faith in studies of the differences between John, Mark, Luke and Matthew. For the Gospels are not straightforward renderings of events, but disclosures of the *significance* of those events – significance that reaches its more profound strata precisely through radical gaps and lacunas.

The unusual vision in Denis Johnson's poetry and fiction could also be called apophatic. He does not convey such a stance in a propounded theory, but rather through portents and voices that come and go in his works. You hear it, for example, in 'The Rockefeller Collection of Primitive Art', a poem which questions the order privileged by the powers of sight:

> ... we freely admit how powerful sight is,
> we say the eyes stab and glances rake,
> but it is not the sight
> that lets us taste the salt on someone's shoulder in the night,
> the musk of fear in the morning,
> the savor of falling in the falling
> elevators in the buildings of rock,
> it is the dark that lets us it is the dark. (p. 141)

Epiphanies of the dark are nearby. As deployed by Johnson, they bear an immediacy that reflects his relations to certain medieval mystics. In his recurring motif of redemptive fire (reminiscent of Richard Rolle), and in his use of paradox, silence and unexpected details to convey precious truths, he shows affinities with figures such as Hildegard of Bingen and Meister Eckhart. In Johnson's portrayal of his characters' conflicted spiritual yearnings, he seems to share, in particular, Eckhart's understanding of the soul. 'The spark of the soul', according to Eckhart, is dimly aware of its exhaustibility, yet it 'is not satisfied with the simple immobile divine being that neither gives nor takes. ... It wants to penetrate to the simple ground, the silent desert where distinction never gazed, where there is neither Father, nor Son, nor Holy Spirit'.[22]

Eckhart's description of this primordial longing – like his famous prayer to God 'to free us of God'[23] – apparently posed a threat to religious authorities in his day. But in our secular culture and with our public sphere (however waning), there is no need for inquisitions to suppress such apophatic ideas. Theological talk about a longing to penetrate to the ground of God will not be viewed as a problem if it remains a personal religious matter.

Yet religion is unlikely to remain bound to the personal in the contemporary world. In the resurgence of public religion today there is evidence of a hunger for existential knowledge and for a language of the soul, and these have more than merely private ramifications. Any attempts to come to terms with the disappearance of the public sphere in our commodity culture must take this resurgence into account. Perhaps an acknowledgement of mystery and of something incalculable in the depth of our common life would do more to reconstitute the public sphere than any highly rational communicative project.

To conclude: whenever the incalculable is acknowledged, and when the negative is given its due, there will be a place for apophatic utterance and for works like Johnson's which insist on showing profound fragmentation and loss. There will be a place for those who tell of the tragic dimensions which underlie human exchange. It is these same truth-tellers, though, who may bring religious vision back to the ideal of a societal conversation. In a society devoted to 'self-sufficient finitude',[24] renewal of the public sphere, lest it perish, may come from unexpected sources.

There are others, in the meantime, who will find in alternate discourses and in apophatic words doorways to unconditional healing truths. This will occur under our culture's veneer of incessant innovation and despite the fact that our reigning idol of the market allows little room for the silence needed to address spiritual signals.

But literary works will continue to offer such room. They still hold spiritual promise today because they allow us to respond experientially to the imaginative worlds they propose, the worlds to which, in our creative reception of texts, we momentarily grant ontological status. Through this process of imaginative recreation, literature can always become an invitation to something deeper. Readers who proceed to those depths may lose themselves, and then rediscover themselves in a strange light. They might even find themselves uttering words like those of the narrator of Denis Johnson's novel *Jesus' Son*: 'I had never known, never even imagined for a heartbeat, that there might be a place for people like us'.[25]

Notes

1 S. Weil, 'Human Personality', *The Simone Weil Reader*, G. A. Panichas (ed.) (Wakefield, Rhode Island: Moyer Bell, 1977) p. 315.
2 C. West, *Prophetic Thought in Postmodern Times* (Monroe, Maine: Common Courage Press, 1993) p. 18.
3 P. Tillich, 'On the Idea of a Theology of Culture', *What Is Religion*, J. L. Adams (trans.) (New York: Harper & Row, 1973) p. 164.
4 *Columbia University Record*, 31 March 1995.
5 In a review of this work, Karen Volkman points out that 'in titling 20 years of his passionate, incisive poetry after Hampton's creation, Denis Johnson declares his loyalty to the mad American visionary and outsider who scavenges a life of meaning from peculiar leavings'. *Boston Review*, 21, 1 (February/March 1996) 4–5.
6 D. Johnson, *The Throne of the Third Heaven of the Nations Millennium General Assembly* (New York: HarperCollins, 1995) p. 200. Subsequent references to this poem are noted parenthetically in the text.
7 W. C. Williams, 'For Elsie', *The William Carlos Williams Reader*, M. L. Rosenthal (ed.) (New York: New Directions, 1966) p. 17.

8   Quoted on the cover of D. Johnson, *Jesus' Son* (New York: Harper Collins, 1992).

9   M. Kakutani, 'Slumming', *New York Times Magazine,* 26 May 1996, p. 16.

10   See, for example, Johnson's profile of 'Bikers for Christ' as a gathering of religious outsiders: 'Change Your Life Forever: God's Warriors in the 3rd Millennium', *Salon,* 10 *<www.salonmagazine.com/10/features/bikers1>* (5 May 1998).

11   D. Johnson, *Fiskadoro* (New York: HarperCollins, 1985) p. 216.

12   Ibid., p. 188.

13   D. Johnson, *Already Dead* (New York: HarperCollins, 1997) p. 3.

14   P. Ricoeur, *Oneself As Another*, K. Blamey (trans.) (Chicago: Univ. of Chicago Press, 1992) p. 113.

15   D. Johnson, *Angels* (New York: Vintage, 1983) p. 204.

16   Ibid., p. 203.

17   Ibid., p. 202.

18   D. Wojan and L. Hull, 'The Kind of Light I'm Seeing: An Interview with Denis Johnson', *Ironwood,* 25 (1988) 34.

19   W. Farley, *Tragic Vision and Divine Compassion: A Contemporary Theodicy* (Louisville: Westminster, 1990) p. 132.

20   P. C. Hodgson, *Winds of the Spirit: A Constructive Christian Theology* (Louisville: Westminster John Knox, 1994) p. 264.

21   J. D. Crossan, *Jesus: A Revolutionary Biography* (San Francisco: Harper, 1994).

22   See the translation by B. McGinn, 'Love, knowledge, and Mystical Union in Western Christianity: Twelfth to Sixteenth Centuries', *Church History,* 56 (1991) 73–81.

23   See the translation by M. Sells, *Mystical Languages of Unsaying* (Chicago: Univ. of Chicago Press, 1994) p. 188.

24   P. Tillich, *The Religious Situation*, H. R. Niebuhr (trans.) (New York: Meridian, 1956) p. 59.

25   D. Johnson, *Jesus' Son*, p. 160.

10
The Fate of French Poetry

Glenn W. Fetzer

The popular magazine *Granta* recently devoted an entire issue to the state of French culture. In an editorial, Ian Jack sketches a dismal picture of the country known throughout the world as the birthplace of modern ideas and enduring human values. Then in short order he asks, 'Where is the place of French writing in all this?'[1] For Jack, the response is inevitable: French literature, once pre-eminent in the west, has failed miserably. Regrettably introspective, narrow, and unpopular, French novels, in his view, reflect a society whose lustre has long since tarnished. Jack is not alone in his assessment, however, nor is fiction the sole literary expression suffering such an ignoble fate. Poetry is acknowledged to be in even more dire straits. Readership is off, the willingness of publishers to market books of poems is dwindling at an alarming rate, and, for the general reading public, few figures stand out as the unquestionably leading poets of our time. Almost everyone involved with French poetry – editors, poets, booksellers and critics – laments its condition.

One of the more vigorous critiques of the current state of French poetry comes from the pen of Jacques Darras, a poet, essayist and editor who, in confronting directly the thinning of poetry's ranks, absolves neither publishers, government and cultural institutions, the literary public nor even poets themselves of responsibility for poetry's sluggish existence.[2] His prescriptions to remedy the situation, moreover, are bold and far-reaching: in his view the place of poetry will not improve either until such time as critical language sheds its romantic trappings or until such time as poets themselves become – in his words – less 'byzantine' in their expectations of art and more predisposed to being inventive. The questions loom large. Simply put: can poetry – a very private expression that has been increasingly marginalised – speak to us today? And if so, do the insights it offers have the potential to engage the public sphere? If these questions can be answered affirmatively, I believe that the perceived *crise de vers* might just turn out to have a silver lining.

Poetry under siege

At the beginning of the twentieth century French poetry flourished along with the expansion of France's industrial base and cultural dominance in Western Europe. But beginning with the post-war period and perhaps even earlier, poetry has undergone a process of marginalisation both in terms of artistic expression and in readership, eventually becoming inaccessible to the general reading public. At the risk of over-simplifying, let me attempt an overview. By the advent of the Second World War the great periods of poetic creativity of the nineteenth century, namely romanticism and symbolism, were long past and their principal heirs in the early twentieth century – Paul Claudel, Blaise Cendrars, Charles Péguy, Paul Valéry and Guillaume Apollinaire – had passed from the scene. The dominant avant-garde poetic energies that emerged from the First World War were concentrated in the projects of dadaism, briefly, and then of surrealism. With emphasis on automatic writing, verbal strings and non-logical compulsiveness, surrealism initially attracted some interest on the part of the public in the 1920s, but it was an interest that waned shortly thereafter. Despite the numerous and significant voices of surrealist poetry – including those of André Breton, Paul Éluard, Max Jacob, Henri Michaux, Benjamin Péret and Philippe Soupault – by mid-century, surrealism had become too arcane for most readers.

By the outbreak of war in 1939 surrealist poets were still writing, but their work had lost much of its public appeal. True, not all the major voices of poetry in mid-century had strong surrealist connections; the works of Pierre Reverdy, Pierre-Jean Jouve, René Char and Saint-John Perse, among others, carried the torch for poetry during its leaner years. And although during the war poetry *did* experience an upswing, ultimately that renaissance proved to be short-lived and even prejudicial to its future. In the wartime efforts to circumvent the occupying censors, for instance, many writers and even a good many novelists turned to poetry in the search for a voice of political engagement, be it anti-Nazi, pro-Communist, avowed Stalinist or most immediately pro-Resistance. Even some of the dyed-in-the-wool surrealists – poets such as Louis Aragon and Robert Desnos – returned to rhythms and forms that they had long before abandoned. As currents of patriotism swept throughout France, poets and prose writers banded together clandestinely to publish poems written expressly for the purpose of rallying the flagging morale of the citizens. Journals carrying titles such as *Confluences, Les lettres françaises* and *Fontaine* sprang up at short notice and folded almost as quickly after the war. Thus, although the Resistance succeeded in heralding a new day for verse, it was arguably a verse artistically compromised and laden with a political agenda. Somewhat ironically, the many efforts that the rallying cry of *patrie* had elicited in verse seemed to foist upon poetry in France not only a role traditionally not its own, but, more insidiously, a legacy all-too-soon irrelevant and thus short-lived.

As the later forties and fifties came to be dominated by playwrights and novelists of various existentialist stripes, poetry had difficulty recouping the edge it had lost. In an age in which Malraux, Camus, Beckett, Sartre, Anouilh and Ionesco were welcomed with open arms by publishers, André Breton and the latter-day surrealists were unable to muster any semblance of unity let alone to avoid an impasse in creativity. The fifties, however, did see the emergence of some isolated poets whose work signalled a return to the enduring project of poetry: recovering the voice of the world and of life. This is the decade in which the French began to become acquainted with the early work of André du Bouchet, Yves Bonnefoy, Eugène Guillevic, Jacques Dupin and Bernard Noël.

By 1960, at the height of the drama of Algerian Independence and in the wake of the collapse of the French colonial empire, the commitment to literature as art was taken up once again, this time by Philippe Sollers with the founding of his journal *Tel Quel*. The ensuing movement (known as 'Tel Quel') came to dominate the literary life of France until the mid-seventies. It arose, thus, as an apolitical reaction to *littérature engagée* and early on established its focus as that of a literature intent on excluding any philosophical or political content. The partisans of *Tel Quel* rejected writing oriented around accepted notions of nature, tragedy and humanism and instead embraced the ludic, playful side of language. Although the movement's most well-known poetic voice was that of Denis Roche, contributors to the journal included Francis Ponge and Marcelin Pleynet, poets with preoccupations focused on the phonemic dimensions of language.

History does have the tendency to repeat itself, however, and *Tel Quel*, in its overwhelming embrace of *écriture* as an experimental practice linked to social and economic revolution, soon found itself trapped in many of the same patterns that had sounded the deathknell for surrealism years earlier. As a result, poets of the sixties and seventies became reticent to form any groups. A diverse group of poets and poetic projects emerged, a group whose numbers have swelled during the past two decades to the point where any attempt to classify French poets on their poetic affinities seems foolhardy. Contemporary poetic projects range from lyrical and a-lyrical, minimalist and objectivist, to ontological, hermetic and metapoetic. Any sense of shared affiliations stems more from convenience, pragmatic working relationships and formal similarities among individual poets than from any strong commitment to shared ideology.

The variety of opinions and practices regarding contemporary French poetry is vividly revealed in *Poésies Aujourd'hui: Aspects d'un paysage éditorial* (1990), a book edited by Bruno Grégoire and produced as a joint effort of the *Direction du livre et de la lecture* and the *Maison des écrivains*. Providing a general guide to poetry in France, *Poésies Aujourd'hui* includes a list of publishers of poetry, brief backgrounds to the founding of the publishing houses, the names of some of the poets published by each and descriptions of the types of submission welcomed. The collection also presents descriptions of literary reviews focusing on poetry, the annual and biannual prizes which recognise poets and their works, and a sampling of poems from thirty-six younger poets. Most revealing, though, is the volume's inclusion of the varied responses to a survey inquiring about the nature of poetry, its status throughout history and its function in society. We can identify at least four perspectives on the current alleged crisis in poetry in these responses.

The first, articulated by Michel Deguy, attributes poetry's so-called 'desertion' of literary culture not to external phenomena but to internal factors. Deguy's line of thinking is this: by abandoning its traditional domain of prescribed poetic conventions and language, poetry has left itself vulnerable and empty of referents.[3] In short, this view links the current malaise to an underlying stagnation caused by poetry's own indirection and lack of self-identity. A second point of view seeking to explain the marginalisation of poetry insists that poetry is and always has been inherently private. If poetry is excluded from cultural life, proponents of this view note, it is not a recent phenomenon. Poetry has always been on the fringes of cultural life due to both its anti-institutional character and its inherently private nature as *écriture*. Among those who espouse this perspective is Jacques Dupin who, in his essay *Éclisse* (1992), attempts to locate poetry solely in language and defends its 'absence' from the literary marketplace. In reacting strongly to the inference that the status of poetry in contemporary society may have slipped and that, as a consequence, poetry has absented itself from the lifeworld, Dupin claims that poetry has occupied a tenuous place in culture ever since Plato excluded it from his *Republic*. Unlike Deguy, who attributes the crisis in poetry to its own regression, Dupin views poetry as anti-institutional, highly personal and private, and yet intensely alive.[4] There is no crisis in the status of poetry, according to Dupin, for poetry's proper place has always been inevitably isolated.

Pierre Dubrunquez, director of *Poésie 90*, recasts the question of a crisis in poetry in terms of the centuries-old debate over the significance of poetry's public image. As long as poets are writing, what difference does it make whether the public holds poetry in high esteem or not? In differentiating between the appeal that poetry holds for practitioners, on the one hand, and the readiness of the public to read poetry, on the other, Dubrunquez cites an important phenomenon: despite the diminishing presence of published poetry in the market-place, the increasing indifference on the part of major publishers in publishing volumes of poems and poetry's declining readership, never before have there been as many people writing poetry as there are today.[5]

A fourth point of view – one articulated by Christian Prigent, editor of *TXT* – is not totally different from the one expressed by Dubrunquez. Where Prigent distinguishes himself, however, is in the extent to which he locates the question within the broader issue of culture and the public sphere. Prigent sees the crisis of marginalisation as intrinsic not only to poetry but, on a broader scale, to literature itself. For Prigent, whether one seeks to confront the impossible intersection of the real in language by means of poetry or, more generally, by some other literary expression is immaterial: for him, the crisis touches all of literature and involves, first of all, the invention of a language of poetry within language more broadly perceived, and then the place of that invention in language as it is written, spoken, published and read. The crisis concerns, as well, the relationship of these languages (these *écritures*) to structures of social interaction.[6] The resulting uneasy alliances, or 'crises', Prigent asserts, are not confined to only a few poets but rather constitute normal working contexts for all writers who aspire to confront the 'impossible' of the real in language. Deliberately working on the periphery of society, such poets inevitably understand writing as a crisis. Prigent thus distinguishes between a popular poetry impervious to any hint of a cultural or ideological crisis and a more existential poetry characterised by a self-conscious uneasiness with the notion of poetry itself. For those 'bystanders' interested primarily in the public face of poetry, the crisis is at best superficial; the true crisis lies within poetic language itself.

The challenge of dissonance

What is demonstrated by the various responses to the questions, first, of whether or not French poetry is undergoing a period of crisis, and second, of whether this crisis is profound or superficial, is a confusion over poetry as an aesthetic object and poetry as an economic product. That is to say that the perceived theoretical crisis in poetry relates both to questions concerning the nature of poetic writing, on the one hand, and to issues related to marketing, on the other: readership, publication, subventions and distribution. These are the very questions engaged by public sphere theorists who suggest the existence of a growing impasse between the steering systems of contemporary civilisation and the lifeworld. In brief, if we choose to focus on the lack of volumes of poems coming from publishers who previously published a great amount of poetry, we are privileging the steering systems of culture. If, however, we view poetry as an integral part of cultural tradition and, more importantly, of personal expression and identity, then we must – as Dupin, Dubrunquez, Deguy and Prigent apparently do – acknowledge poetry's true place as anchored firmly in the lifeworld. No declines in readership – however precipitous they may be – would be able to threaten the place of poetry in the lifeworld.

For many, the chief indicator of poetry's faltering status is its growing absence from economic or steering system structures such as the media industry and government support. Ironically, however, the withdrawal of poetry from marketable prominence may very well signal a literary environment more conducive to the Habermasian model of the public sphere. In his early work, we recall, Habermas attributed the breakdown of that sphere to undue external influence, political and social as well as economic. In the French context, since the publicly subsidised publication of works by poets has become increasingly financially problematic, the cultural sector and commercial interests are forcing poetry back to its aesthetic domain. That is to say that once the external props are removed – the subsidies, the officially sanctioned recognition and the purely economic concerns of publication and dissemination – the potential for poetry to redefine itself in a vibrant civil society is actually enhanced rather than curtailed.

If we shift our focus from publicly funded and distributed poetry, the supposed crisis may not be as severe as we thought. Although mainstream publishing houses such as Albin Michel, Grasset, and Laffont as well as the avant-garde press Les Éditions de Minuit do not customarily involve themselves with volumes of poems, and although Flammarion, Gallimard and Mercure de France publish far fewer poets than they did thirty years ago (with the flagship publisher Gallimard increasingly relegating its publication of poems to the *Collection poésie* series), dozens of poets each year are none the less seeing their work in print, albeit in limited press runs. In 1996, for example, poets found their works issued by small presses such as Autres Temps, La Bartavelle, Cahiers de l'Égaré, Cheyne, Deyrolle, La Délirante, La Différence, Éditions du Tiroir, Empreintes, Folle Avoine, Obsidiane, POL, Rougerie, Spectres familiers and Le Temps qu'il Fait. Such presses admittedly wield far less economic clout than publishers of fiction, but this list is by no means insignificant, either. Besides small presses that are coming to fill the gap left by the major publishers, another avenue for the distribution of poetry is one whose presence is just now beginning to be known: the World Wide Web. Poets, members of poetry clubs and others interested in poetry are establishing websites that contain discussions, bibliographies and anthologies of poetry, as well as new poems.

Poetry thus continues to play an important social role in French culture, despite its economic marginalisation. Public access to poetry persists, and the very existence of public concern over the perceived 'crisis' demonstrates an enduring social role. French poetry still holds a significant place on the cultural landscape. The evident concerns over the historical development of the poem as genre, of the public response to and opinion of poetry, and of the public's access to poetry all stem from the question of the capacity of a society to reproduce itself culturally. These issues all reflect in some way the means and effectiveness by which a society retrieves artefacts from its cultural past and transmits to successive generations both those artefacts and also the creative practices embodied by that heritage. In supporting the concept of a society that integrates the lifeworld and steering systems, Habermas distinguishes between the material reproduction and the social reproduction of societies. On the one hand, societies need to oversee the successful metabolic interchange between biological members and their physical environment. But on the other, Habermas advocates the successful reproduction of a society's symbolic identity, transmitting to its new members its frameworks of perception and interpretation. To this second aspect of society's reproduction – the social – belongs the perpetuation of a society's cultural life. Any perceived marginalisation of poetry thus evokes by extension the question of the success of French society in reproducing its cultural identity, as well as the question of the current status of that identity. Seen in this light, the state of contemporary French poetry, the debate over the existence of a crisis, in itself expresses and so reproduces a key aspect of French culture.

But what are the hallmarks of French culture? The common view among non-Europeans is that, unlike American culture, which is defined by pluralism, French culture is monolithic, uniform in nature and in its cultural expressions. But stereotypes aside, one of the most prominent characteristics of French culture is dissonance. Mario Vargas Llosa, for example, defining French identity for *La Nouvelle Revue Française*, focuses on individualism. Llosa notes the plurality of voices, interests, styles and preoccupations of the French throughout history and sees in that pluralism a cultural unity founded on differences and contradictions.[7] At any given historical point, French culture has accommodated numerous distinct expressions, styles and aesthetic projects under the single rubric of 'French culture'. The conceptual aggregate of French culture is a loose framework with many constituent parts, whose configurations are unpredictable and whose relationships are increasingly problematic. Linguistic debates abound concerning the extent to which English has eroded or enriched the French language and culture, and further dissonance is caused by the unsettling question of the place of 'foreignness' in French cultural identity. For some observers the extent to which France assimilates artists from outside the Hexagon compromises the accepted boundaries of French culture. Any attempt to articulate common cultural ground in post-war France proves daunting; for example, how could we imagine a coherent linking of the cuisine of Joel Robuchon with *le fast food*, I. M. Pei's pyramid at the Louvre with Disneyland Paris, l'Académie Française with *verlan*, or *les prix littéraires* with protectionist laws prescribing acceptable ratios of English to French broadcasts?

Given this refractive image of contemporary culture, it is not surprising that poetry deviates from the expected monolithic course. As we have seen, the French public both expects that the government will financially support creative efforts and recognises the unwieldy burden such subsidies have imposed. Tensions continue to grow between partisans of a highly intellectual strain of art (perceived by many as elitist and doomed) and the champions of a more accessible, spontaneous art of greater popular appeal and consumption. The problem might not be so much one of the marginalisation of poetry, as one of a great disparity between romantic nostalgia and current realities: that is, between the public's longing for an art that fulfils certain well-defined expectations and the reality of an art that follows its own course and is by nature subtle, inventive, unorthodox and even renegade. Ironically, what is currently perceived by some to be a crisis in poetry actually demonstrates the achievement of a society in reproducing its cultural heritage. Where independence and difference have been among the hallmarks of the cultural tradition, independence and difference have been cultivated. These are values that poets have long incorporated, and French poetry today reflects French society's success in transmitting those values.

If poetry in France can be thought of as a metaphor for cultural dissonance, we can also contend that by both its essential characteristics and its place in the literary fabric of society it holds the potential to play a role in the re-establishment of civil society. A society whose poetry may be read as a metaphor for cultural dissonance is a society confronting significant social upheaval and malaise. But it is also a society that can find in that discord the possibility for engaging the public sphere. To appreciate that potential, however, we must consider briefly some characteristics of dissonance as well as some key features of poetry. Dissonance, of course, implies a plurality of non-assimilated elements, elements that by the very fact of their diversity highlight separateness and individual autonomy. But dissonance is more than simply multiplicity. It also connotes conflict, competing interests and a resistance to cohesion. At the heart of the concept of dissonance, however, is the awareness of something distinct from oneself, an 'other' with which the self constructs an identity barrier and with which it enters into a relationship of alienation. At the most elemental level, therefore, those cultural phenomena that evidence dissonance assume the presence of a cultural other, and even define themselves in terms of this alterity.

Poetry, however, expresses something other than simply the reflection of alienation. As we shall see, much of the endeavour of poetry today is to point to that which lies beyond the self, whether that 'other' be art, metaphysics, history, language or reality. Furthermore, one of the hallmarks of poetry in France has also been the concern for bridging the gap between what is known and what is unknown or unexperienced. Thus we say that, in pointing to the other, poetry often takes on characteristics of the sacred: religious concerns pertaining to reality and to the ethics of relationships. Both in terms of recognising and depicting instances of *alterity* and in its attempts at *reconciliation*, contemporary French poetry reveals glimpses of rapprochement and reconciliation.

Poems of reconciliation

In French poetry today, the perceived *crise de vers* may very well harbour signs of revitalisation. French poets occasionally make use of a poem to comment upon the nature of text as poem. Much more infrequent, however, is the poem which purports to speak for all of poetry, as does the following piece from Robert Marteau's collection *Louange*. These lines suggest the capacity of poetry to imply fullness in the face of apparent hollowness:

> Toute la poésie est faite de faux bruits.
> Elle est illusion. Elle ne sert de rien
> Et ne doit pas servir. Elle n'existe pas,
> Mais son service exige un souci sans partage.
> Elle a perdu la rime avec la raison. Elle
> N'a plus de gens de métier, ni d'amateurs, ni
> D'admirateurs, hors les poètes, qui s'admirent
> D'avoir le génie, et qui causent du moderne
> Qu'ils sont censés mettre au monde. La poésie
> Est une conque sonore où on croit entendre
> Le ressac de la mer, les tourments de l'amour,
> Le cri de la parturiante, un rossignol,
> Une Iliade racontée au prétérit,
> Le dernier soupir extirpé par Othello.

> All of poetry is made of false noises.
> It is illusion. It serves as nothing
> And must not serve. It doesn't exist,
> But its service demands an undivided concern.
> It has lost rhyme along with reason. It
> No longer has experts, nor hobbyists, nor
> Admirers, except for poets, who admire themselves

> For having genius, and who talk about the modern
> Which they are supposed to bring to life. Poetry
> Is a sonorous conch where we believe we hear
> The ocean surf, the torments of love,
> The parturiant's cry, a nightingale,
> An Iliad recounted in the preterit,
> The last sigh rooted out by Othello.[8]

Written in July of 1990, the piece occurs in a compendium of 553 other poems, all penned between New Year's Day 1990 and 31 December 1992. A cursory reading is enough to note that this poem stands apart from the others, all of which celebrate the cyclical rhythm of nature and the solemnity of religious rite. By contrast, this poem seems oddly incongruent, dismissing poetry as mere illusion, devoid of all usefulness and bereft of its traditionally defined features. Situated among lexically rich alexandrine sonnets that take their reference in classical mythology and whose every line reflects a consideration for the alliterative value of language, the poem opens on an ironic note. Poetry, it claims, has lost its form, its usefulness and its public – 'except for poets', whose self-admiring talk accomplishes little.

But in the poem two voices are heard. In the first nine lines, the voice is that of the collective public seduced by the denizens of practicality and all too eager to accept unquestioningly the truism of poetry's alleged irrelevance to contemporary culture. Marteau's lines evoke Christian Prigent's query 'A quoi bon encore des poètes?' As Prigent notes, this very question is couched in the language of a consumerist public. What that question actually means, Prigent claims, is not merely one of utility – 'What are they [used] for?' – but rather, 'Why is this even here, *this*, rather than nothing at all?'[9] Yet in the last six lines we hear the poet giving voice to a very private, existential experience in a language suggestive of the *rhétoriqueurs*. In contrast to the voice of the popularised notion that poetry is vacuous, the voice of these lines seems to imply the opposite: namely, that in poetry can be found the capacity for fullness without the risk of ever being replete. As we might infer from Marteau's image of the conch – the shell which is the sign of a departed organism – poetry affords the space, the moment or the occasion which had once been occupied, filled or had taken place. Expansive, inexhaustible and inclusive, poetry is able to bring together the most disparate of times and spaces. It is the plane of convergence, the dimension where (in the words of the poet) tropes common in literary history, such as the ocean surf and the nightingale, and hallmark themes in literature – the torments of love, for instance – intersect with figures from all eras of the poetic tradition, from Homer's *Iliad* to Shakespeare's *Othello*. Such reconciliation embraces otherness, and the conventions that Marteau respects throughout the entire volume – the twelve-syllable alexandrine lines of French poetry gathered in sonnet form – signal not only the poet's allegiance to tradition but also his inventiveness in linking to his art the prose of *lisibilité*.

A second example, from the work of Eugène Guillevic, further illustrates the unexpected movement towards convergence by acknowledging the intersection between poetry and religion. In many respects the work of one of France's major poets might be thought an odd choice to comment on the relationship of poetry to the sacred. After all, Guillevic is avowedly atheist and has always been fascinated by the word as object. His distinctive view of language can be understood to some extent by his orientation to Marxist materialism. In recent decades Guillevic has become one of France's most highly respected poets, in part perhaps because of his iconoclasm; perhaps, as well, by the veneration which comes with age. Born in 1907, he has been publishing for over fifty years; the last thirty, in particular, have been especially productive. Just since 1990, for instance, he has published several volumes, including *Maintenant* (1993), *L'Été* (1994), *Du Silence* (1995) and *Possibles futurs* (1996).

One of Guillevic's key interests in writing is epistemology. In his view the one who writes does so in order to know the world external to himself.[10] This ongoing project sheds light on the common characteristics of his work: convergence or rapprochement – the ceaseless movement on the part of the knower to embrace (or understand, or experience) the unknown. Self-knowledge is a prerequisite to knowing the world, and Guillevic's poetic voice is one of attentive watchfulness, as is illustrated in this poem from *Du Silence*:

> C'est le silence
> Qui m'apporte, qui me donne
> Le souffle du monde.
> Il me permet
> De me connaître en lui
>
> Il m'ouvre une porte
> Sur un espace de calme
> Où s'éclaire la présence
> Indispensable.

> It is silence
> Which brings to me, which gives to me
> The breath of the world.
> It permits me
> To know myself in him
>
> It opens to me a door
> Onto a calm space
> Where presence shines forth
> Indispensable.[11]

Three words or word phrases stand out: *silence, souffle du monde, présence* (silence, breath of the world, presence). These three reveal several characteristics of Guillevic's poetry. First of all, it is primarily a poetry of discovery. Depicting a perceiving presence facing the world, the poem assumes the existence of relationships consisting primarily in exploring those avenues of interaction. Throughout *Du Silence* and the remainder of the work, in fact, the perceiving presence plays a rather passive role. Here it is silence that unobtrusively and non-threateningly sets in motion the process of awareness, while the speaking voice submits to the gradual (and inevitable, it would seem) world consciousness. Second, although Guillevic is far removed from the poets of cosmic grandeur, 'the breath of the world' of which he speaks signals a belief in the existence of some life-giving force, a fullness that when experienced makes everything right. Third, the 'presence [that] shines forth' suggests the nearness of intimacy, or else at the very least is indicative of ontological being. As a matter of fact, on more than one occasion Guillevic has expressed his interest in the notion of communion – both in the personal, existential sense as well as in the religious context. Although Guillevic observes that the kind of knowledge that informs his work as a whole is both cognitive and experiential, he takes pains to emphasise the spiritual nature of the goal of convergence. 'Ultimately', he claims, 'poetry and the sacred merge'. He goes on to say that, if poetry is sacred, then the individual poem is a sacerdotal monument.[12] Guillevic's choice of the word 'monument' is, I believe, important, for it suggests the publicising of a moment, an event or a phenomenon that is not experienced by all. A monument stands for all to witness what is known privately, or by only a few. It marks the entrance of the personal into the public.

For Guillevic the poet enjoys a priestly role; in his office as a person of language, the poet is there to make the sacred live. The poet is there to

ensure that the poem is not only a monument, but a sacerdotal one –
a public expression set apart to the service of something other. Language
itself is not sufficient to invoke the sacred, Guillevic asserts. Only
inasmuch as language is at the disposition of poets, however, is it
possible to draw near to the sacred.[13] It would seem, then, that poetry
does indeed serve a function other than, let's say, the communication of
an ideology or the private expression of a personal experience. As the
case of Guillevic suggests, even when the poet is admittedly secular,
definitely a-theological or, as the case may be, even atheist, poetry
retains the potential for fostering communion and for translating some
private knowledge into the public domain. Moreover, in a world whose
structures and practices are inimical to meaning, poetry – even in those
instances in which we least expect it – conveys by its religious character
the hope of bridging previously disconnected parts and the inclination
towards reconciliation.

That hope can enter the public sphere by means of poetry, as our
third example demonstrates. Ironically, for all his defence of poetry as
a private endeavour, Jacques Dupin often illustrates by his creative
work the belief that literature is indeed able to contribute to the
network of communicable information and ideas that in some way
affects public opinion. Throughout his career, Dupin has sought in the
visual art of sculptors and painters those principles of artistic engagement that he might in turn present to the reading public and that his
own poems incorporate. From Alberto Giacometti, Joan Miró, Kasimir
Malevich, Henri Laurens to Jean Capdeville, Jean-Paul Riopelle, Joseph
Sima and many others, Dupin's poetry probes the connections
between art and poetry, the verbal and the visual and, more
importantly, reality and its perception. In this preoccupation with
works of art, Dupin is not alone. Indeed, one of the continuous hallmarks of belles-lettres in France has been the interest of writers in the
visual arts and in exploring the connections between image and word.
In the eighteenth century, for instance, Denis Diderot's critical reviews
of exhibitions at the Salon Carré, reviews which were to become
known as his *Salons* at their publication some years after his death in
1784, set the groundwork for other writers to practise art criticism.
Working in the nineteenth century, Stendhal, Baudelaire and Zola
further developed the genre which, in the twentieth century, by and
large came to be the domain of poets, including René Char, Henri
Michaux, Yves Bonnefoy and Claude Esteban.

Dupin's *Matière du souffle* (1994) is a poetic discourse on visual art,
especially the paintings of the Catalan artist Antoni Tàpies. The

collection's poems are preceded by a frontispiece sketch by Tàpies of an animal – a rodent, possibly – above which lies a small cross (or an *x*). The text that follows refers to the sketch in particular, and the entire artistic project of Tàpies in general. Between the aesthetics of Tàpies and Dupin there are a number of similarities. Both share some basic presuppositions about reality and its artistic depiction. Both rely upon materiality to present the essence of art. Both suggest that the work of art is, by nature, spiritual.

As most of Dupin's work, *Matière du souffle* is anchored in preoccupations with ontology. Unlike that of many of his collections, however, the subject here is not so much the elusive *réel* as something beyond the poem itself, as it is the very language of poetry. For the poet, as for the painter, the engendering force of the work derives from breath *(souffle)*:

> Le souffle arme le bras, la main, et ajuste le geste, la visée aveugle, le suspens du souffle, et l'arrêt de mort, au ras du sol, à portée de main. ... Sous la montagne et dans le réseau des nerfs est accroupi un millénaire de méditation, de désirs, de connaissance, et de pourriture sacrée.

> Breath equips the arm, the hand, and adjusts the act, the blind sighting, breath withheld, and death sentence, skimming the ground, within arm's reach. ... Under the mountain and in the network of nerves is crouched a millennium of meditation, of desires, of knowledge, and of sacred rottenness.[14]

The breath that engenders the creative endeavour is not, however, the breath of silence that for Guillevic takes the form of unobtrusive presence. For Dupin, that which equips the arm and forces one to focus attention is the breath of determination and sheer will, the force of gathered energies and single-minded resoluteness of the artist. The impulses behind this breath are tightly wound and give rise to a flood of utterances.

From the beginning of the volume, the image of a wall is used to invoke the art of Tàpies, and in so doing serves to link the work of the poet to that of the artist. 'Un mur marqué de croix, de lettres, de signes, de balafres, qui l'agrandissent et le transfigurent, qui le déplacent à travers le temps. [A wall marked by crosses, letters, signs, scars, which enlarge it and transfigure it, which displace it throughout time]'.[15] Scored, marked and disfigured, these walls announce the characteristics of the poet's work in the rest of this collection: a pre-occupation with materiality, with the thickness of language in all its lexical diversity – its assertions, its retractions and its revisions. The image of the wall carries for Tàpies further significance and, by extension, for Dupin as well. Emblematic of contemporary life, the wall signals for the painter not an obstacle but rather an assemblage of surfaces through which the more hermetic meanings of life might be approached.[16] Tàpies believes that reality as signified is never presented directly in the painting but is, rather, created in the mind of the viewer through a process of association.[17] For him, what we call reality in the picture is in fact merely a cryptic symbol of the real. With the multi-layered application of pigments to the canvases, the impasto paintings for which Tàpies is known reflect his aim of penetrating beyond the superficial appearance of things to the darkness that, for mystics, brings to light new perceptions and knowledge. Tàpies' connection of materiality to meaning provides the occasion for Dupin to draw similar inferences about language and life.

> Tàpies, un nom de mur devenu un mot dans l'espace, d'un coup de brosse ou de tête, qui plonge dans l'inconnu comme une écriture inventée, avant de s'écrire, de condescendre à ce morne et merveilleux rectangle de toile qui dénie le drame pour incorporer le signe.

> Tàpies, name of a wall become a work in space, by a brush stroke or a head, which plunges into the unknown as an invented creature, before being written, condescending to that gloomy and marvelous canvas rectangle which denies drama in order to incorporate the sign.[18]

In his inclination to read the work of the painter in terms of writing, Dupin demonstrates the possibility for poetry to bridge the gap between visual art and language. Furthermore this poet evidences what might be for some the surprising capacity to acknowledge the potential of art (whether it be painting or poetry) to point to new awareness and knowledge: 'Négligent et relâché, le noeud de Tàpies n'est encore qu'un avatar de la matière, un débordement de la surface, une prise de conscience du vide vivant qui le traverse et qui nous porte. [Negligent and relaxed, Tàpies' knot is yet but an avatar of matter, an overflowing of surface, an awareness of the living void which crosses it and which carries us]'.[19] Although unassuming and private, Dupin shows in his work not only a sensitivity to other media of aesthetic expression but, more importantly, the understanding that art and life are inextricably linked.

All three poets share an assumption about the nature of poetry. For these poets the term *poetry* refers not to the physical texts but to that lying outside the texts. Yves Bonnefoy elaborates this point first by differentiating textuality and poeticity, and then by distinguishing reader as consumer from reader as contributor.[20] According to Bonnefoy *poetry* in this larger sense is something other than a text whose various levels of signification may be unearthed by skilful exegesis. It is, rather, that which is suggested by the text but not exhausted by it, that toward which the text points but can never (nor ever dares attempt to) name. The text is not poetry's true place, he asserts, but is only the path poetry followed a moment earlier. Thus the poem can be thought of as signalling the alterity of poetry, that *other-consciousness* that is set in motion but never fully achieved by the poet, that which is maintained by the physical text but exists even when the reading of the text is suspended.

It is perhaps relevant at this point to recall that Guillevic insists on the centrality of the sacred in poetry. A poet who relies heavily on the materialism of language none the less recognises an otherness to which language can only point. For him that otherness is religious. It is a dimension on the other side of language for which the individual poem is mediator. Naturally, a perspective that acknowledges a religious dimension in poetry makes certain demands on the poet and on the reader. It demands an awareness of the limitations of the printed page. As has long been the case in France, this perspective on poetry demands of the reader in particular and of society, by extension, certain values – patience, tolerance and a willingness to accept that which is significantly other. And I would contend that just as Habermas includes not only art and literature but also religion in his assessment of what is capable of translating private experience into public discourse, so also do the values which art and literature elicit on the part of the public include those values intrinsic to religion.

What, finally, does poetry have to do with the renewal of the public sphere? Little, if we measure the success of published poems by marketing indicators. On the other hand, if, freed from the external constraints imposed by economics and government influence, we give attention to the social element intrinsic to poetry, then those dimensions of public dialogue concerning the amorphous entity commonly known as French culture will be enhanced. Expressions of dissonance, awareness of alterity and otherness, and moments of reconciliation emerge in the writing and reading of contemporary French poetry.

Notes

1 I. Jack, *Granta: France the Outsider*, 59 (1997) 11.
2 J. Darras, 'Situation de la poésie en France', *Esprits*, juin 1995, pp. 37–49.
3 M. Deguy, in B. Grégoire (ed.), *Poésies aujourd'hui* (Paris: Seghors, 1990) p. 110.
4 J. Dupin, *Éclisse* (Marseille: Spectres familiers, 1992) pp. 17, 22.
5 Grégoire, *Poésies aujourd'hui*, pp. 111–12.
6 Ibid., p. 113.
7 M. V. Llosa, 'L'Identité Française', A. Bensoussan (trans.), *La Nouvelle Revue Française*, 517 (1996) 26–33.
8 R. Marteau, 'Laboissière-en-Thelle, jeudi 26 juillet 1990', in *Louange* (Seyssel: Champ Vallon, 1996) p. 91. Unless otherwise indicated, all translations are my own.
9 'Pourquoi y a-t-il quand même *ça*, ça plutôt que rien (plutôt que seulement le toutvenant qui occupe les boutiques et les tréteaux médiatiques)?' C. Prigent, *A Quoi bon encore des poètes* (Paris: P.O.L.) p. 16.
10 E. Guillevic, *Choses parlées: entretiens* (Seyssel: Champ Vallon, 1980) p. 73.
11 E. Guillevic, *Du Silence* (Seyssel: Champ Vallon, 1995).
12 E. Guillevic, 'A la limite, poésie et sacré se confondent', *Vivre en poésie* (Paris: Stock, 1980) pp. 158, 160.
13 Ibid., p. 158.
14 J. Dupin, *Matière du souffle* (Paris: Fourbis, 1994) p. 14.
15 Ibid., p. 9.
16 B. Catoir, *Conversations with Antoni Tàpies* (Munich: Prestel-Verlag, 1991) p. 32.
17 Ibid., p. 76.
18 Dupin, *Matiére du souffle*, p. 28.
19 Ibid., p. 34.
20 Y. Bonnefoy, 'Lifting Our Eyes from the Page', J. Naughton (trans.), *Critical Inquiry*, 16.4 (Summer 1990) 797–9.

11
Woza South Africa! A Postcolonial Public Sphere

Susan VanZanten Gallagher

One night during the apartheid era in South Africa, two actors on a township tour sat on a crowded cast bus and talked about creating a play that would go beyond the broad entertainment of township musicals to address some of the more serious concerns of their lives. After hours of discussion, Percy Mtwa and Mbongeni Ngema found their subject in the pages of the Bible. What would happen to Jesus Christ, they speculated, if he returned to South Africa? How would the South African government, whose apartheid policies were supposedly justified by something called 'Christian Nationalism', react to the Second Coming? Such was the genesis of one of South Africa's most successful dramatic works, *Woza Albert!* Developed in collaborative workshops with Barney Simon, then artistic director of the Johannesburg Market Theatre, *Woza Albert!* performed to sold-out venues in both white urban centres and black townships in South Africa, was an acclaimed entry in the 1982 Edinburgh Festival, had a successful London run that fall, and eventually toured Germany and the United States, playing to standing ovations every evening. The play's dramatic and musical energy, innovative style and forceful anti-apartheid stance proved remarkably successful both at home and abroad.

The success of *Woza Albert!* demonstrates one role of religion and literature in the public sphere. The play provides a powerful venue in which personal experiences achieve public expression by drawing on both literary and religious resources. Such conjunctions between religion and literature occur frequently in postcolonial settings. In his account of the way in which religion 'went public' in the 1980s, Casanova says that 'the widespread and simultaneous character of the refusal to be restricted to the private sphere' occurred in all 'three worlds of development', but his five case studies include only one that we might call postcolonial: Brazil.[1] However, the significant influence of Protestantism and Catholicism in colonisation, the major role that culture, particularly literature, played in fabricating a colonial mindset and society, and a rapidly evolving postcolonial distrust and questioning of modernity has resulted in both religion and literature decisively claiming a place in the postcolonial public sphere.

Calling South Africa a postcolonial country is admittedly problematic, but I would argue that we can certainly describe the society and nation currently occupying the southern tip of the African continent as postcolonial, perhaps with a vengeance. The term *postcolonial* is notoriously imprecise, and there is the danger of obscuring important political and theoretical distinctions among local situations by using it. None the less, I will follow the increasingly common usage of referring to the postcolonial as that historical period in which a people who were once colonised (politically, economically and culturally) now have some form of political independence and are attempting to establish a new national identity.[2] From one point of view, post-1948 South Africa can be termed postcolonial, since at that time a once-colonised people (the Afrikaners) achieved political independence and consolidated their national and cultural identity. After a prolonged struggle against British political rule and cultural influence, and the imposition of the English language, highlighted by the second Anglo-Boer War (1889–1902), Afrikaners eventually gained complete control of the South African government in 1948, with an overtly nationalistic campaign slogan of '*Eie volk, eie tall, eie land*' – our own people, our own language, our own land.

However, from the point of view of the majority of its inhabitants, South Africa remained colonial during the very time when the rest of Africa was experiencing decolonisation. Inspired in part by the democratic principles of the Atlantic Charter of 1941, a steady stream of independent nations emerged throughout the African continent during the fifties and sixties. Yet, as grand apartheid spread its tentacles everywhere in South African life in the years following the victory of the Afrikaners' National Party, the majority of South Africans were denied the rights of citizenship, were forbidden basic human freedoms and were exploited economically as sources of cheap labour. For these people, each of whom was assigned a particular non-European racial label, South Africa did not move towards post-colonialism, politically speaking, until the historic elections of 1994, which recognised for the first time the citizenship of all South

Africans. None the less, the postcolonial process in South Africa has obviously only begun, as thousands of economic, educational, cultural and social inequities remain to be addressed.

Since the 1994 elections South Africa has begun to create a new civil society in which a true public sphere is emerging, with the assistance of both religion and literature. During the apartheid years, such a full public sphere did not exist, although various counter-public spheres were generated by anti-apartheid impulses. Several of these counter-public literary arenas were formed with the assistance of religion, as we shall see. The political transformation of the nineties has witnessed the birth pangs of a true public sphere in South Africa. As Fraser notes, 'something like Habermas' idea of the public sphere is indispensable to critical social theory and to democratic political practice'.[3] This chapter will examine briefly the history of the development of the public sphere in South African society, with special attention to the interplay of religion and literature in two particular literary forms: the oral praise poem and the township drama. It will then briefly discuss the reality of the new South African public sphere and the continuing role that we can expect literature and religion to play.

The ghostly South African public sphere

During institutionalised apartheid, in the period from 1948 to 1990, the public sphere that existed in South Africa was – from one point of view – very small; from another point of view, non-existent. At times it materialised briefly, a pale reflection of a flesh-and-blood public sphere, only to fade quickly from sight. South Africa never officially denied the existence of public discourse; it just constructed its society and crafted its legislation in such a way as to make such discourse virtually impossible. Within the ideal public sphere, Habermas says, 'access is guaranteed to all citizens', who are allowed to speak in an unrestricted fashion, unhindered by social status or rank.[4] As Joan Landes, Mary Ryan and Geoff Eley, among others, have demonstrated, however, the eighteenth-century public sphere, despite a rhetoric of publicity and accessibility, was exclusionary, denying admittance both to women of all classes and to the working class male. Such people were not considered either citizens or of sufficient 'rationality' to participate in the conversation, although alternative ways of gaining access to public life and discourse did exist, subaltern counter-public spheres.[5]

Similarly, South Africa for many years had a limited definition of 'citizen', which included only a small fraction of its almost forty million people, determined by supposed racial lines. Following the Nationalist Party's 1948 victory, the vast engine of apartheid began to accelerate, slowly but steadily limiting access to the public sphere by re-defining 'citizenship'. Previously South Africa had had a limited franchise for the Indian and Coloured populations, which the new government soon abolished. In 1950 the Population and Registration Act was passed, by which all South African people were officially classified according to race – often by such means as a curl of hair, the size of a lip, a tone of complexion, or the slope of a shoulder. Those who were labelled African, Indian, or Coloured were not only denied the vote but were also subject to a vast system of control – determining where they could live and work, and even whom they could marry. The National States Citizenship Act required that in due time all blacks would be designated as 'citizens' of one of the black 'homelands' and subject to deportation. The goal, said one Cabinet minister in 1978, is that 'there will not be one black man with South African citizenship'.[6]

The majority of South Africans were further hampered from entering the public sphere by means of the educational system. In the early part of the century, educational opportunities for black Africans had been provided by the mission schools. Before 1948, the syllabi of African and white secondary schools were essentially the same; all students received a Western, English-language schooling. However, only a select number of black Africans were enrolled, since education was not compulsory for blacks and the government spent about six times as much per white student as per African student. However, with the 1953 Bantu Education Act, control of African education was given to the Native Affairs Department, and all schools operated by churches or missions were given the choice to adopt a government-mandated curriculum or to lose their government subsidy. Bantu Education deliberately prepared Africans solely for manual labour. Dr Hendrik Verwoerd, the architect and first minister of Bantu Education, told the South African Senate, 'A Bantu [black African] pupil must obtain knowledge, skills and attitudes which will be useful and advantageous to him and at the same time beneficial to his community. ... There is no place for him in the European community above the level of certain forms of labour. ... For that reason it is of no avail for him to receive a training which has as its aim absorption in the European community'. A mission school education, Verwoerd continued, 'drew him away from his own community and misled him by showing him the green pastures of European society in which he is not allowed to graze'. And, in one of his more famous pronouncements, Verwoerd asked, 'What is the use of teaching the Bantu child mathematics when it [*sic*] cannot use it in practice?'[7] Similar limitations were imposed in other subjects that might facilitate access to the public sphere: English-language instruction; courses in composition, rhetoric, speech and debate; and the study of political or economic theory. Denied suffrage, their citizenship under siege and blocked from access to the kind of education that would train them for standard forms of rational discourse, the majority of South Africans found themselves unable to enter the public sphere.

Whether that space for conversation existed at all in South Africa at this time is questionable, however. Apartheid South Africa certainly never promoted 'a discourse of publicity touting accessibility, rationality, and the suspension of status hierarchies', as Fraser describes the public sphere.[8] Rather, South African social life and public discourse were explicitly governed by status hierarchies. Furthermore, even those who were acknowledged as rational citizens (because of their skin colour and ancestry) often could not enter freely into public discourse. The South African government, ostensibly a parliamentary, democratic institution, exercised the kind of state control over private life more typical of a feudal or authoritarian state. The sphere of private autonomy, particularly with respect to public discourse, was deliberately limited. One of the early legislative coups of the National Party was the passage of the Suppression of Communism Act in 1950, which not only outlawed the Communist Party of South Africa but also prohibited all but the most innocuous protests against the state. This act gave the Minister of Justice the right to limit, by means of banning, the freedom of movement and speech of any person deemed to be opposing the state. Banning orders shut down all pretence of an open public sphere: a banned person could not write or publish anything, could not be quoted or cited in any publication, could not be with more than one person at a time other than family, and could not communicate in any way with another banned person. The Suppression of Communism Act applied to both blacks and whites alike, both 'citizens' and 'natives', and was broadly interpreted as pertaining to anyone who was too zealous in opposing the government. A public sphere where political and artistic matters could be openly discussed did not exist, except sporadically for brief moments between an individual's banning orders, or when a particular person fell through a governmental crack.

Besides banning targeted individuals, the massive state censorship practised in South Africa under the aegis of the Publication Control Board further limited public discourse. Habermas notes that, in the twentieth century, 'newspapers and magazines, radio and television are the media of the public sphere', replacing the eighteenth-century coffee houses, intellectual broadsheets, and novels.[9] But South African radio and television were state-owned and controlled media, tools of propaganda, not open chat rooms, while all printed material was subject to an elaborate system of censorship. Some 15,000 books, magazines, pamphlets, calendars, and posters were banned before 1982. South African newspapers regularly appeared with large sections of white space, indicating that material had been censored. In the perpetual States of Emergency that existed in South Africa throughout the 1980s, the liberal model of the public sphere as a medium of public discourse, open and accessible by all, did not exist, even for the privileged few. However, as in similar circumstances around the world, a few counterpublics continued to exercise strategies of resistance – through underground publications; allegorical, symbolic or coded writing; and overseas publication of manuscripts smuggled out of the country.

Such strategies of resistance often originated and were practised within religious, particularly Christian, contexts. Almost 80 per cent of the South African population identify themselves as professing Christians, and most take that belief very seriously. South African journalist Allister Sparks says, '[the country] is as universally religious as it is socially divided'.[10] In another unusual historical permutation, religion in South Africa during the modern era did not undergo privatisation; in fact, the development of South Africa's first postcolonial stage (post-British control) was premised on a powerful civil religion. For years, South Africa was a self-proclaimed 'Christian' country, and the Dutch Reformed Church played a crucial role in originating and justifying the practice of apartheid, with public theological pronouncements serving the cause as effectively as social or political commentary. Given this legacy, and given the marked intrusion of the Afrikaner state into the traditional lifeworld, it is not surprising to find alternative forms of Christianity entering the public sphere to work against apartheid. Black Africans are a majority in the Anglican, Baptist, Lutheran, Methodist, Presbyterian and Roman Catholic Churches, and approximately 3.5 million belong to one of the 3000 independent churches.[11] These Christians proclaim a theology affirming the common humanity of all people, God's compassion for the poor and suffering, and a biblical call for justice. Archbishop Desmond Tutu, the Rev. Frank Chikane, and the Rev. C. F. Beyers Naudé all served as influential leaders in the anti-apartheid movement. Sparks recalls that, in the anti-apartheid movements of the eighties, South African clergy 'were everywhere in the forefront, organizing, supporting, interceding, and providing advice and relief services. Churches became meeting places and centres of information. Clergymen provided leadership at both national and local levels ... Nowhere else in the world except perhaps in Poland is the Christian church so closely identified with a people's struggle for freedom'.[12] Religion has been a crucial aspect of the South African public sphere for many years.

Literature and the counter-public sphere

The struggle for freedom thoroughly permeated the literary realm as well as the religious; for many years South African literature was predominately a literature of protest, dwelling under the powerful shadow of apartheid. It is an irony of history that the same conditions permitting only a phantom public sphere – state censorship and lack of education – none the less contributed to the development of significant new literary forms, primarily oral in nature. Kelwyn Sole explains, 'In a situation where publishing and the media were in the hands of the white establishment or liberal white patrons at best, performance came to be seen as a way to have immediate political effect on a black audience in a manner which, due to its ephemerality, could at the same time evade the stringent limitations placed on political utterance'.[13] Sermons, eulogies, hymns, choral chants and ritual dances are only a few of these performance genres that grew in importance during the apartheid period. But perhaps the two most popular performance genres were contemporary praise poetry and the township drama, both of which employed religious and literary elements as a means of making their case.

Emerging in the seventies, with growing popularity in the eighties, praise poetry was part of a cultural movement trying to bring uneducated, often illiterate, workers to political consciousness. Contemporary praise poetry has its historical origins in a prized traditional oral form, *imbongi* poetry, in which a praise singer recounts the achievements of a great ruler. Employing but transforming this traditional oral form, today's praise singers comment on, celebrate or lament current events, usually focusing on the lives of ordinary people rather than great rulers. These energetic, improvisational performances are typically chanted or sung in vernacular Zulu or Xhosa, with equally energetic responses from the audience. The spontaneous songs, ululations and audience participation create a potent communal experience strikingly similar to indigenous black church services. Within the time and space of performance (which can last anywhere from five minutes to several hours), a unique public sphere is created, a South African version of the eighteenth-century coffee house, the nineteenth-century novel, or the twentieth-century MTV event.

One popular oral performer is Mi S'dumo Hlatshwayo, who became a poet as a result of his participation in one of the largest indigenous African churches, St John's Apostolic Church, or the *eCibini*. Known for its emphasis on healing rituals and dramatic services, St John's gave Hlatshwayo both a literary form and a theological impetus: 'In that independent African church of the poor, he experienced for the first time in his life a community of concern and care. ... He also experienced in the church's emotional gatherings his baptism in "words of fire": the lay-preachers, men and women who were imbued with a prophetic and messianic vision, and had integrated the *imbongi* tradition of Nguni poetry in their religious sermons. He was dis-covering there the power of language and poetry'.[14] In 'The Tears of a Creator', co-written with Alfred Temba Qabula (commonly hailed as the father of the contemporary revival of *imbongi* poetry), Hlatshwayo speaks of God's identification with the poor:

> O maker of all things
> Grief
> Assails you from all sides
> Each step forward you take
> Brings enmity nearer
> What is the nature of your sin?
>
> In the factories
> Your enemy suffocates you
> On this side: the bosses
> On that side: the boss-boys
>
> Attackers and assailants
> Stalk you
> From all chambers
> And channels ...
> Permits and money

> Become the slogans
> Through which
> They pounce on you
> What is the nature of your sin?[15]

Qabula's own performances also demonstrate Christian influences. In 'Migrants' Lament – A Song' he keens in the manner of the Psalmist:

> If I have wronged you Lord forgive me
> All my cattle were dead
> My goats and sheep were dead
> And
> I did not know what to do
> Oh Creator forgive me
> If I had done wrong to you
> My children: out of school
> Out of uniforms and books
> My wife and I were naked – naked …

In the opposite emotional vein, Qabula sings praise – not to a traditional leader, or to the common people, but to Africa itself:

> Oh, I thank the Creator
> For molding and placing me
> In Africa
>
> When my eye rests on you Africa
> You are indeed
> A bride on her wedding day
> Plumed in all the treasures
> Found in you:
> The gold, the silver, the copper and aluminum
> The diamond, the lead and iron …
> Recounting them would take us
> To infinity

In contemporary praise poetry, traditional forms and current concerns, indigenous practices and Christian beliefs, merge to form a new public mode of literary and religious expression.

Township theatre has many similarities to oral performance poetry in terms of its traditional roots, its cultural resistance to apartheid, its communal nature and its Christian influences. Even as contemporary praise poetry would not exist without the influence of trade unions and Christianity, so township theatre would not exist without the emergence of the polyglot culture of the township, the new urban village created in the 1950s by apartheid. Drawing large crowds to the churches, schools or community centres in which it is performed, township theatre has been a commercial success. Its aesthetic forms have been adapted to its location: play titles have to be short, so that they can be painted on banners that are hung between two poles to advertise the performance. Venues are limited, with little professional lighting, few fixed seats, no room for elaborate stage settings or spectacular special effects. Township theatre is noisy: babies cry, friends call to each other, drunks heckle the actors, acoustics are terrible. Consequently the performances are broad, loud and rely heavily on music and dance, with an unusual blend of realism and stylisation. Township plays tend to have a multiplicity of short, action-filled episodes creating a montage effect. Sole describes the typical township troop: 'Traveling around the townships in combis [vans] with impromptu sets, they performed a melodramatic and spectacular form of drama which highlighted the use of more accessible oral forms such as music, song and dance. Episodes in everyday township life were presented, and a number of stereotyped characters (the gangster, the venal priest, the policeman) were introduced for audience recognition and amusement. Some characters spoke in the tsotsitaal patois endemic to the townships'. Initially, Sole notes, 'while reflecting accurately many of the hopes and frustrations of township life, this theater tended to remain politically quiescent', but with the Black Consciousness movement of the seventies, such drama was increasingly used as a means of raising workers' consciousness.[16] More sophisticated forms of local theatre emerged in the eighties, according to Loren Kruger, that attempted 'to adumbrate an alternative public sphere, in which participants may realize their potential agency'.[17]

Similar to oral performance poetry, many township plays were based upon Christian concepts and employed Christian symbols, although no other play achieved the success of *Woza Albert!* Using the dramatic conventions of township theatre, *Woza Albert!* created a communal public experience of rejuvenation and hope. Presentational rather than representational in style, the play features two actors who depict all the characters, defined only by gestures, voices and largely symbolic costumes, such as huge white clown noses. With unparalleled miming ability, the actors magically conjure up a jazz combo, a train trip into Soweto, a ride on the back of a lurching coal truck and the manoeuvres of a military helicopter. The episodic structure of the script, according to Anne Fuchs, resembles the folk tales of Nguni culture, with a series of vignettes repeating a basic motif, 're-creating in a different way all the plays that have gone before, repeating again and again the same function formulas in different sequence combinations'. Further re-creation takes place through improvisations: 'rarely having as reference a text, each evening the actors modify and refine the performance'.[18] Another type of re-creation lies in the play's re-enactment of the biblical narrative, with repetition of scenes such as the Last Supper, Judas' betrayal, Jesus walking on water and the triumphal entry into Jerusalem. Like most township drama, *Woza Albert!* is a linguistic polyglot, referring to Jesus Christ with the Zulu word *Morena*, and featuring a fantastic blend of Zulu, Xhosa, Afrikaans, English and street slang. Most resistance theatre tended to be heavy-handed and historically ephemeral, producing in its worker-audiences the shock of recognition and a resolution to fight oppression. *Woza Albert!*, however, is unusual in its high degree of humour and in the lasting power that it has demonstrated in the post-apartheid age.

Opening with an itinerant musician sent to prison for a passbook violation, the play introduces the idea of Jesus as a comforter of the oppressed in its first song. After a day of hard labour, the musician sings: 'Morena walks with me all the way / Watching over me all the day / When the night time comes he's there with me / Watching over, loving me'.[19] Assailed by the other prisoners for singing 'bloody hymns', the musician confidently claims that Morena is in prison with them.

Subsequent scenes show other scoffers who do not believe in Morena, but the Saviour soon arrives in glory, on a South African Airways jumbo jet. The ruling party, secure in their Christian nationalism, jump to claim the saviour as their own, with the President appearing on national television and proclaiming,

> Thank you very much, thank you very much. My people, Morena is back and South Africa has got him! I hope that the free world will sit up and notice whose bread is buttered and where! Let them keep their boycotts, their boxers, rugby players, and tennis racketeers. Stay home Larry Holmes! Stay home John McEnroe! We have got Morena! But there is already rumours going around that this is not the real Morena, but some cheap impostor. And to those that spread such vicious rumours I can only say, 'tough luck friends! He chose us!'[20]

Morena, however, quickly finds his way to the township, identifying with the hungry, the suffering, the outcast. Visiting the homelands, Morena hears the laments of the women and children abandoned by husbands and fathers who are working in the cities. Soon perceived by the formerly friendly authorities as a threat to stability, Morena is arrested and brought to the notorious John Vorster Square for interrogation. He escapes through a miracle, floating through the air with the angel Gabriel in a heavenly parody of the many detainees who 'jumped to their death' from the tenth floor of John Vorster. Desperate to destroy the troublemaker, the government eventually shoots Morena with a nuclear missile, detonating a massive explosion that completely destroys Capetown and Table Mountain. Three days later Morena shows up in a cemetery, walking around the graves and commanding martyred African leaders to 'Woza!' – 'Rise up!' He begins by raising Chief Albert Luthuli, a devout Christian who was President of the African National Congress and awarded the Nobel Peace Prize in 1961. This prosaic account does scant justice to the energy and hope that a production of *Woza Albert!* raises, even seen on videotape.[21] Despite an undercurrent of lamentation, *Woza Albert!* sounds a strong chord of hope arising from the liberating quality of the Christian ideas, images and rhetoric.

Contemporary performance poetry and township resistance drama represent two examples of ways in which counter-public spheres emerged in apartheid South Africa, despite the absence of a civil society and an open public sphere. Throughout the seventies and eighties, the apartheid system clamped down on public expression in one arena only to find it bubbling out in another. Both genres exemplify new and creative alliances between literature and religion, tradition and modernity, and both genres have continued to make an impact on the emergence of the public sphere that has occurred in the nineties.

Religion, literature and an emerging civil society

The South African political chrysalis that appeared to have been petrified for so many years showed its first signs of cracking on 2 February 1990. Despite the almost unanimous expectation that change in South Africa would occur only in a hail of guns, blood and bodies, a relatively peaceful transformation process was initiated with a historic speech by F. W. de Klerk that opened a protracted period of diplomacy resulting in the democratic elections of 1994. During these years of negotiations, a true public sphere began to emerge for the first time, in part because both the NP and the ANC were consciously employing the media – by making public statements, leaking information and holding press conferences – in an attempt to win public support. For the first time, a free press served as 'a mediator and intensifier of public discussion' in the crucial process of creating a common good.[22]

As the South African public sphere began to materialise, an extraordinary exchange known as the Albie Sachs debate occurred. Habermas cites the emergence of relatively autonomous cultural institutions as one of the crucial components for the creation of a public sphere in the eighteenth century, and it is precisely this topic – autonomous cultural institutions – that is at the heart of the Sachs debate. The subsequent impassioned fervour and wide-ranging participation in this discourse demonstrate the fertile ground waiting for the public sphere in the new South Africa, as well as the crucial role of literature in that sphere. On the very same day that F. W. de Klerk made his unprecedented announcement, the Johannesburg *Weekly Mail* published 'Preparing Ourselves for Freedom', a thought-provoking essay on the future of art in a new South Africa by Albie Sachs, a white ANC lawyer living in exile. Sachs's essay thus moved into the public domain as the opening volley of a prolonged rhetorical battle.

Sachs's primary concern was the role that art should play in the new South Africa: how literature, in particular, might contribute to the development of a civil society. As a new South African nation struggles 'to give birth to itself', what role should culture (and literature) play? Sachs then argues that ANC members should give up the slogan that culture is a weapon of the struggle and instead employ culture as a means of reflecting and creating 'who we are, how we see ourselves and the vision we have of the world'.[23] As 'a rainbow nation', South Africa will have an art that both draws on past traditions and incorporates new revolutionary elements, an art that embraces 'African tradition, church tradition, Ghandian tradition, revolutionary socialist tradition, liberal tradition, all the languages and ways and styles of all the many communities in our country' (p. 22). Sachs continues, 'South Africa is now said to be a bilingual country: we envisage it as a multi-lingual country. It will be multi-faith and multi-cultural as well. The objective is not to create a model culture into which everyone has to assimilate, but to acknowledge and take pride in the cultural variety of our people' (p. 24). Sachs thus envisions the creation of a liberal public sphere in which numerous counter-public spheres participate, including those influenced by faiths and religions.

Sachs returned to South Africa in 1990 and participated in a series of public forums, and numerous cultural organisations conducted vociferous debates about his proposal. One observer comments, 'Albie Sachs's paper ... evoked a response unrivalled in our recent cultural history'.[24] Liberals and radicals, creative writers and literary critics, trade workers and university academics all participated. Within a year, two books were published that chronicled and continued the public discussion. The Albie Sachs debate provides a glimpse of the process of the emergence of a public sphere in a postcolonial situation. It is an excellent example of the use of public discourse – a paper, the media, response papers, meetings, resolutions, books – to debate a matter related to the public good. Within that debate, auditors were concerned to develop an inclusive definition of South African identity and art. Drawing on their individual positioning as members of disparate publics, they none the less deliberated as peers across lines of differences about a question of what is equally good for the whole. The participants in the conversation assumed what Fraser calls 'an orientation that is *publicist*', understanding themselves 'as part of a potentially wider public'.[25] In their attempt to re-define South African identity, they turned to literary culture, recognising that it had been a potent part of the movement against apartheid and would continue to play a key role in the evolution of a new country.

The question of the forms and concerns of post-apartheid art was a common one in South Africa during the nineties. Short story writer Njabulo Ndebele poses a question similar to that of Sachs: 'with the demise of grand apartheid now certain, what are South African writers now going to write about?'[26] The evidence so far suggests a new interest in historical accounts, confessional autobiographies, nature poetry and fiction about the South African Defence Force. Frank Schulze-Engler sees the recent literature of South Africa as attempting to address the problem of the lack of a civil society, with authors such as Coetzee and Gordimer moving from depictions of speechlessness and the breakdown of communication (pre-apartheid) to considerations of the obstacles and potentials of civil communication (post-apartheid). He contends, 'it would be misleading to conceive of the relationship between literature and civil society in terms of cultural identity. ... Strengthening civil society ... amounts to establishing procedural rules and creating conditions of possibility rather than to furthering particular political or cultural agendas'.[27] However, within the Albie Sachs debate, as well as in numerous other instances, we can identify a strong drive to redefine South Africa, to craft a new national identity in cultural terms. A central part of that process continues to be the role of a Christian religious vision.

Perhaps the most visible instance is occurring with the work of the Truth and Reconciliation Commission (TRC), established to explore the violation of human rights that took place during the apartheid era by providing an official public forum for the stories of victims and the confessions of perpetrators. Grounded in a Christian vision of the need for confession, reconciliation and forgiveness, the work of the TRC is intended to help South Africa forge a new identity by remembering the past and acknowledging its wrongs. South African church leaders played a major role in designing the Truth Commission. The TRC's principal architect, Dr. Alex Boraine, and its chair and chief confessor, Archbishop Desmond Tutu, are both prominent religious figures. Charles Villa-Vicencio, a theologian from the University of Cape Town, serves as the TRC's Director of Research. The TRC was endorsed by a number of such different religious organisations as the Research Institute on Christianity at the University of Cape Town, the faculty of Religion and Theology at the University of the Western Cape and the South African Council of Churches.

The public process of the hearings into the violation of human rights contains much religious symbolism and rhetoric. Each session is opened with a prayer and the ritual lighting of a towering white candle representing truth. I attended two days of these hearings in Pietermaritzburg in 1996 and, with only one exception, every victim I heard testify talked about his or her life as part of the Christian story and described suffering and endurance in Christian rhetoric. Biblical citations, references to impassioned prayer, narrow escapes attributed to God's miraculous intervention were commonly heard. 'When I think of the things that have happened', one matronly woman said with great dignity, 'I just open the Bible and pray Psalm 71'. When each victim finished, one of the commissioners responded with a formal statement, summing up the story that had been told, affirming and thanking the witness, pronouncing on the evil that had been done. 'We have a system that needs overhauling, a system that needs to re-earn your trust', one said in thanks to the witness, 'testimony such as yours will assist in the process of creating a just system'. 'May the Lord help you through these hardships', concluded another.

The primary goal of the work of the TRC's Human Rights Abuses Committee is therapeutic: individuals, families and the country as a whole all need healing. By providing a public opportunity for victims of apartheid to tell their stories, the TRC is attempting to restore their human and civil dignity, bringing new forms of representation and agency into the public sphere. The formal, almost liturgical, tone of the proceedings provided a mechanism by which grief could be publicly expressed and experienced, and the Christian resonances added an even deeper significance for these victims. This public accounting of facts is also intended to help South Africa form a new identity as a civil society. Mass general amnesties, as were granted in some South American countries and which the National Party preferred, would not contribute to nation-building, the TRC designers argued. If the new South Africa is convincingly to affirm human rights and respect for the law, it cannot overlook the crimes of the past. It needs public condemnation of abuses. Rather than concentrating their efforts on punishing those who committed atrocities in the past, though, the new South Africa is attempting to rhetorically bring a new country into being through narrative, to deliberately provide a physical space in which a new civic and cultural entity can emerge.

Given the significant role that the Christian church played in both the creation of and the struggle against apartheid, it is perhaps fitting that this attempt to exorcise the past draws on the Christian tradition. South African theologian John de Gruchy notes, 'The Christian understanding of repentance, forgiveness and reparation is of fundamental importance in shaping a national consciousness that can heal the land, achieve genuine reconciliation and build a moral and democratic culture'.[28] In this public, communal act of confession, South Africa is beginning to write a new national identity. As the public hearings in which the victims tell their stories are broadcast weekly on South African television, a vast cacophony of previously silenced voices have entered the public sphere. The TRC proceedings are thus the writing of a new, collective, national oral biography of South Africa.

While such new literary forms continue to emerge, some apartheid-era works have survived, although they have undergone intriguing changes in their social and cultural functions. *Woza Albert!*, for example, remains a frequently produced piece, with new actors taking on the dramatic and physical challenges of the roles first created by Mtwa and Ngema. This popular play, however, now participates in what playwright Zakes Mda calls the 'theatre for development' rather than the 'theatre for resistance'. The theatre of development is a postcolonial manifestation that participates in the building of a new nation-state by creating community dialogue in both its creation and its reception. Its objective is to use the people's own performance modes to create dialogue and prompt critical analysis. Rural performances are to be followed by community discussion of the problem addressed in the play, such as AIDS, ritual circumcision or literacy.[29]

At the 1996 South African National Arts Festival in Grahamstown, a lively production of *Woza Albert!* was staged in a school gymnasium in the outlying township of Nombulelo. Although part of the official economy and aesthetic by means of its Festival affiliation, the play's unusual venue called attention to its township origins and continuing impact. A reviewer from the *Mail & Guardian* asked rhetorically, 'what does *Woza Albert* offer latter-day audiences, pinpointing, as it does, the political lie of the land in the 1970s and 1980s?' and concluded, 'Quite a lot, it seems, judging by the response of the largely young audience'. I attended a different performance of the same production and sat behind a row of twelve-year-old township boys, who anxiously glanced at their teacher during the most bawdy parts, but more often forgot themselves to laugh uproariously. None the less, I imagine that they had some provocative conversations with that teacher following the play. In the middle of the production, the two spotlights that provided all the stage lighting went out and, after a brief period of darkness and confusion, the play continued in the overhead lights of the gym, in true township theatre fashion.

The *Mail & Guardian* reviewer reflects, 'There was a distinct awareness that what we were watching was not as much theatre as it was a retrospective docu-drama; and this is where the production finds its home'. The lines and scenes that had previously spoken of protest and hope now referred to a courageous past, a celebration of strength in the face of adversity and a commonly shared heritage. The young audience was undoubtedly learning much about their nation's past and, as the reviewer puts it, 'the degree of loss and desperation of a generation that gets its identity from having fought for an identity'.[30] But the drama also embodied a vision of a loving and just community that incorporates all – women and children, urban and rural, Zulu and Xhosa. When Zulu Boy shares his simple meal of oil-and-vinegar chips and Coca Cola with Morena, the comic sacrament points to the future of South Africa even as it echoes its past. And when *Woza Albert!* concludes with the two actors holding their fists high as they sing 'Nkosi Sikelel' iAfrika' (God bless South Africa), they are no longer daring to sing a forbidden protest verse but rather concluding with part of the new national anthem of the democratic South Africa.

The postcolonial public sphere

The recent history of South Africa provides an extreme but intriguing example of the role of the public sphere in the postcolonial process. South African history is still far from resolved, but the evidence thus far does allow a few preliminary conclusions and observations about imperialism, postcolonialism and public spheres. Imperialism, by its very nature, constructed a limited public sphere: by definitions of citizenship, access to education, political control and economic dominance. Within differing local situations and with varying degrees of freedom, counterpublics were allowed to put forth contestational rhetoric, to oppose imperialism and the rule of the parent country. For the Afrikaners rebelling against British control, that freedom was fairly widespread, as they drew on the liberal tradition; for people of colour in South Africa, that freedom was much curtailed. During the process of decolonisation, liberal principles – often extant in rhetoric but not in structure – are frequently used to undermine imperialism. If a nation is to claim an identity as a democratic institution, despite distortions and failures, it must nevertheless promise equal access and open participation in order to exist. As Lambert Zuidervaart notes,

> Although few theorists today would deny that existing parliaments and political parties are exclusionary in their origins and in their current operations, pointing out these exclusionary tendencies amounts to a form of immanent critique: the critical theorist appeals to the normative principle promised by the organizational premises of such institutions. Supposedly democratic political institutions purport to be egalitarian and participatory. One task of 'subaltern counterpublics' is to hold such institutions to their own premises.[31]

Through the actions of such subaltern counterpublics, including those arising from the religious community, decolonisation is facilitated (although obviously other economic and material factors also enter into this complex process).

The success of political decolonisation and the achievement of a national identity, however, have often resulted in new forms of imperialism and silenced public spheres. Nationalism, as the record of the twentieth-century sadly demonstrates, often becomes frozen in a new oppressive state. One of the founding texts of postcolonial studies,

Franz Fanon's *The Wretched of the Earth* (1963), is almost prescient in its anticipation of 'the pitfalls of national consciousness' with respect to the unfolding story of Africa.[32] Fanon cautioned that 'from nationalism we have passed to ultra-nationalism, to chauvinism, and finally to racism' (p. 156). In the process of liberation, previously colonised countries, he warned, could all too easily resort to tribalism, religious rivalry and ethnic divisions. 'If nationalism is not made explicit, if it is not enriched and deepened by a very rapid transformation into a consciousness of social and political needs, in other words into humanism, it leads up a blind alley. The bourgeois leaders of underdeveloped countries imprison national consciousness in sterile formalism' (p. 204). Similarly, Edward Said warns, 'to tell a simple national story is to repeat, extend, and engender new forms of imperialism'. While insisting on the value of nationalism to fuel protest, resistance, and independence movements, Said, following Fanon, advocates a 'pull away from separatist nationalism toward a more integrative view of human community and human liberation'.[33]

A key contributor to the failure of democracy in many new nations has been the unwillingness of previously colonised people to permit the development of a true public sphere and autonomous cultural institutions. Fanon identifies three stages in culture that occur during the process of decolonisation, each of which we might relate to the concept of the public sphere. First, the colonial power denies the existence of a native culture, distorting and devaluing the realities of the past, disallowing the indigenous voice to enter the public sphere. Counterpublics may exist, to some degree. Second, the native intellectual, as part of the liberation process, embraces the suppressed past and embarks upon a 'passionate search for a precolonial national culture' (p. 209), demanding that the public sphere be accessible and amenable to traditional ideas, perhaps at the cost of Western ideas. A new limited public sphere is substituted for the old one, even as, in Fanon's famously inevitable stage of physical violence, one form of violence is needed to combat another: 'The violence of the colonial regime and the counter-violence of the native balance each other and respond to each other in an extraordinary reciprocal homogeneity' (p. 88). In the third step, a synthesis is achieved. The native intellectual realises that a return to an Edenic, idealised past is impossible (and often becomes a fetishised nativism), and that a nation and its culture must be built not only on the folklore of the past but on a continual and active movement toward the future. It is during this period that a true national culture evolves (as opposed to mere nativism), drawing on the past without denying the present. A fully developed national character is tolerant and flexible, 'will make such a culture open to other cultures and ... will enable it to influence and permeate other cultures' (p. 245).

Despite continuing and persistent calls for 'Africanisation', South Africa appears to be avoiding Fanon's second stage, primarily as a result of its apartheid history in which nativism was employed as a tool of apartheid. Instead, it is attempting to craft a civil society by allowing free and open public discussion, including input from religious sources. A national culture of identity and openness, a publicist orientation and counterpublic pride, can only be facilitated by the open, contentious and rational discourse of the public sphere. Within that discourse, literature and religion continue to play indispensable roles.

Notes

1 J. Casanova, *Public Religions in the Modern World* (Chicago: Univ. of Chicago Press, 1994) p. 6.
2 The difficulties with *postcolonial* as an identifying label have been frequently discussed; for example, see A. McClintock, 'The Angel of Progress: Pitfalls of the Term "Post-Colonialism"', *Social Text*, 31–2 (1992) 84–98; and V. Mishra and B. Hodge, 'What is post(-)colonialism?' *Textual Practice*, 5 (1991) 399–414.
3 N. Fraser, 'Rethinking the Public Sphere: A Contribution to the Critique of Actually Existing Democracy', in B. Robbins (ed.), *The Phantom Public Sphere* (Minneapolis: Univ. of Minnesota Press, 1993) p. 3.
4 J. Habermas, 'The Public Sphere: An Encyclopedia Article (1964)', S. Lennox and F. Lennox (trans.), *New German Critique*, 1 (1974) 49.
5 J. Landes, *Women and the Public Sphere in the Age of the French Revolution* (Ithaca: Cornell Univ. Press, 1988); G. Eley, 'Nations, Publics, and Political Cultures: Placing Habermas in the Nineteenth Century', in C. Calhoun (ed.), *Habermas and the Public Sphere* (Cambridge: MIT, 1992) pp. 289–339; and M. P. Ryan, 'Gender and Public Access: Women's Politics in Nineteenth Century America', in *Habermas and the Public Sphere*, pp. 259–88.
6 We can probably assume that black women wouldn't qualify either. J. Lelyveld, *Move Your Shadow: South Africa, Black and White* (New York: Penguin, 1985) p. 88.
7 G. Ziemer, *Education for Death* (London: Constable, 1952).
8 Fraser, 'Rethinking the Public Sphere', p. 6.
9 Habermas, 'The Public Sphere', p. 49.
10 A. Sparks, *The Mind of South Africa* (London: Heinemann, 1990) p. 278.
11 J. de Gruchy, *The Church Struggle in South Africa*, 2nd ed. (Grand Rapids, MI: Eerdmans, 1986) p. 246.
12 Sparks, *The Mind of South Africa*, p. 289.

13   K. Sole, 'Oral Performance and Social Struggle in Contemporary Black South African Literature', in D. Bunn and J. Taylor (eds), *From South Africa: New Writing, Photographs, and Art* (Chicago: Univ. of Chicago Press, 1987) p. 256.
14   Ibid., p. 278.
15   All quotes from transcriptions of oral performance poems are taken from Bunn and Taylor.
16   Sole, 'Oral Performance and Social Struggle', p. 255.
17   L. Kruger, ' "That Fluctuating Movement of National Consciousness": Protest, Publicity, and Postcolonial Theatre in South Africa', in J. E. Gainor (ed.), *Imperialism and Theatre: Essays on World Theatre, Drama and Performance* (London: Routledge, 1995) p. 159.
18   A. Fuchs, 'Re-creation: One Aspect of Oral Tradition and the Theatre in South Africa', *Commonwealth Essays and Studies*, 9.2 (1987) 38.
19   P. Mtwa, M. Ngema, and B. Simon, *Woza Albert!* (London: Methuen, 1983) p. 7.
20   Ibid., p. 13.
21   A videotape of *Woza Albert!* that contains an abridged performance and interviews with Mtwa and Ngema is available from California Newsreel.
22   Habermas, 'The Public Sphere', p. 53.
23   A. Sachs, 'Preparing Ourselves for Freedom', in I. de Kok and K. Press (eds), *Spring is Rebellious: Arguments about cultural freedom* (Cape Town: Buchu Books, 1990) p. 19. Subsequent references to this essay will be cited parenthetically.
24   *Exchanges: South African Writing in Transition*, D. Brown and B. van Dyke (eds) (Pietermaritzburg: Univ. of Natal Press, 1991) p. vii.
25   Fraser, 'Rethinking the Public Sphere', p. 15.
26   N. S. Ndebele, *South African Literature and Culture: Rediscovery of the Ordinary* (Manchester: Manchester Univ. Press, 1994) p. vii.
27   F. Schulze-Engler, 'Literature and Civil Society in South Africa', *Ariel*, 27.1 (1996) 35.
28   J. W. de Gruchy, 'Crimes and Reparations', *Christian Century*, 23 (Nov. 1994) First Search, online.
29   Z. Mda, 'Theatre for Development', unpublished talk given at the Grahamstown Festival, July 1996.
30   A. Wilson, 'Has Woza Albert stood the test of time?' *Mail & Guardian*, July 5–11, 1996, p. 31.
31   L. Zuidervaart, 'Civil Society, Practical Discourse, and Multiple Publics: Habermasian Revisions of the Public Sphere', unpublished manuscript, p. 10.
32   F. Fanon, *The Wretched of the Earth*, Constance Farrington (trans.) (New York: Grove, 1996) p. 148. Subsequent references are to this edition and will be cited parenthetically.
33   E. Said, *Culture and Imperialism* (New York: Knopf, 1993) pp. 273, 216.

12
Rushdie, Said and the Global Public Sphere

M. D. Walhout

In a recent issue of *The Nation*, columnist Christopher Hitchens recalls the following curious episode:

> One evening in 1988, while I was dining at the home of Professor Edward Said, a large box was delivered for him from a literary agency. Marked 'highly confidential', it turned out to contain the typescript of a novel called *The Satanic Verses*. An accompanying note from our mutual friend Salman Rushdie asked Edward if he could take a careful look. Salman was aware of the deep-running dispute within Islam between the literalists and the reformers, and he was taking counsel about it.[1]

Now this has to be one of the more intriguing ironies in the history of literature: Edward Said, the world's foremost critic of Western representations of Islam, vetting the novel destined to provoke more outrage in the Islamic world than perhaps any other book in history. We don't know what counsel Said may have given Rushdie, and we certainly shouldn't blame Said for the Rushdie Affair. Yet the irony gives one pause. Did Said, too, underestimate the fury of Islamic fundamentalists? Or did he share Rushdie's desire to 'shake up the Muslims'?[2]

The truth, if we can believe Said's own account, is that he simply didn't read Rushdie's novel as an insult to Islam. 'I am one of the people', he told W. J. Weatherby, 'who believe that *Satanic Verses* for all its irreverence and spoofing of the Islam [*sic*] world has been done with a certain amount of affection, not at all vituperative but done with tongue in cheek, knowingness and inwardness'. Moreover, he noted,

> A lot of what [Rushdie] has to say about Mahound and the story of
> the early years of Islam are to be found in early Islam [*sic*] texts,
> gossipy and malicious in character, most of it poking fun at divine
> providence. It's incredibly familiar to any Muslim. You can still buy
> on the streets of Rabat or Cairo scurrilous books, spoofs of Islam
> depending on early Islam [*sic*] accounts.[3]

But why, then, had Muslims reacted so violently to this latest spoof of
Islam, staging book burnings and issuing death threats? Ultimately,
Said's explanation was a geopolitical one: the Rushdie Affair, he
insisted, was an effect of Western domination of the global public
sphere.

Edward Said and the making of *The Satanic Verses*

We will return to Said's explanation of the Rushdie Affair at the end of
this chapter. First, however, it is important to note that his role in the
Rushdie Affair did not begin with the delivery of that mysterious box
in 1988. Said and Rushdie had first met in London after the publication of *Midnight's Children*, Rushdie's Booker Prize-winning second
novel, in 1980.[4] It's not hard to see why they quickly became friends:
both were immigrants from former British colonies with a smouldering
hatred of Western imperialism; both were masters of English prose
style with a flair for literate invective; both were confirmed secular
humanists with a deep suspicion of religious fundamentalists. Their
backgrounds, too, were similar. Both had been born into wealthy,
pious, well-educated families. Said's father, like his father before him,
was a member of the small Anglican community in Jerusalem, where
Edward was born and baptised; his mother was a Baptist from
Nazareth, where her father had founded the Baptist church.[5] Rushdie's
parents were observant, tolerant Muslims from Bombay.[6] Both Said and
Rushdie had been sent abroad at an early age to attend elite schools in
the West, where they later chose to live rather than return to Lebanon
(where the Said family had relocated after residing in Egypt for fifteen
years) or Pakistan (where the Rushdies had emigrated, contrary to
Salman's wishes).

It was not long before the two friends – one the leading theorist of
postcolonial writing, the other its most influential practitioner – were
regularly citing each other's work. In a 1984 essay on George Orwell,
for example, Rushdie announced that 'the zombie-like revival of the
defunct Empire' in such popular works as Paul Scott's *The Raj Quartet*

and David Lean's *A Passage to India* was merely the last gasp of the colonialist mentality that Said had analysed in *Orientalism*.[7] The following year, in an unpublished address on politics and religion, Rushdie again cited Said:

> The sloganizing of the term 'Islam' by the West in recent years has been extensively examined by Edward Said in his book *Covering Islam*. What 'Islam' now means in the West is an idea that is not merely medieval, barbarous, repressive, and hostile to Western civilization, but also united, unified, homogeneous, and therefore dangerous: an Islamic Peril to put beside the Red and Yellow ones. Not much has changed since the Crusades, except that now we are not even permitted a single, leavening image of a 'good Muslim' of the Saladin variety. We are back in the demonizing process which transformed the Prophet Muhammad, all those years ago, into the frightful and fiendish 'Mahound.'[8]

Rushdie's point was that this demonising process – which, ironically, he would later be accused of repeating in *The Satanic Verses* – belies the fact that modern 'Islam' is really a political phenomenon, one whose supposed unity breaks down along national lines.

As these references imply, Rushdie had digested Said's critique of orientalism by the time he started work on *The Satanic Verses*. Just as important to Rushdie, however, was Said's personal experience of exile – an experience Said recounted for the first time in his 1986 book *After the Last Sky*, a *cri de coeur* which Rushdie reviewed in *The Guardian* in September of that year. 'To those of us for whom the struggle between Eastern and Western descriptions of the world is an internal conflict as well as an external reality', he began, 'Edward Said's has been, for many years, a centrally important voice'. Yet *After the Last Sky*, he continued, marks a departure from Said's earlier books on the subject: 'The East–West dispute is still present, but it's no longer the centre. This is a very personal text, and a very moving one, about an internal struggle: the anguish of living with displacement, with exile'.[9] In fact, this internal struggle would be the main theme of *The Satanic Verses*.

Did reading *After the Last Sky* also confirm Rushdie's desire to thumb his nose at the fundamentalists? While his review was silent on the subject of religion, Rushdie must have been moved by Said's secularist lament for Palestine:

> We are drenched in religion. ... What a fate for Palestine: to have
> attracted the religious imagination and the dramas of the apoca-
> lypse not just once, but three times: Judaism, Christianity, Islam,
> the latter the most austere, least known, and most abominated. Lift
> off the veneer of religious cant – which speaks of the 'best and
> noblest in the Judaic, Christian, or Muslim tradition', in perfectly
> interchangeable phrases – and a seething cauldron of outrageous
> fables is revealed, seething with several bestiaries, streams of blood,
> and innumerable corpses.[10]

Surely the parallel between Palestine and India, with its 330 million
deities and its resurgent Hindu, Sikh, and Moslem communalism, did
not escape Rushdie's notice.

Yet Said struck an uncharacteristically reverent note when, having
decried the 'deranged imaginings' of the fundamentalists, he added
that 'there seems to be an absolute discontinuity between all that and
the dry Protestant atmosphere in which I was raised' – the memory of
which, he confessed, brings him acute nostalgia. He even recalled his
grandmother's Scripture reading:

> She was a literalist when it came to the Bible – it was God's word –
> but for her, as for us as children, it was the story that mattered, the
> exchanges between Moses and Pharaoh, Joseph and Potiphar's wife,
> Jesus and Pilate, exchanges that she led up to carefully and then
> rendered with a burning fidelity to the unadorned truth of how
> people – not plumed saints or imaginary heroes – could stand up for
> what they took to be right and just.

There was more to Said's loving portrait of his grandmother than
nostalgia; there was the hint of a gospel of human liberation, albeit
one that has 'disappeared in the swirl of noisy chiliastic visions that are
actually visionless with regard to the secular world of men and women
in society'.[11]

Coincidentally, Rushdie had just encountered the gospel of liberation during a visit to Nicaragua in July 1986 – a visit he recounted
in his first book of non-fiction, *The Jaguar Smile*, published in January
of 1987, some four months after *After the Last Sky*. While in
Managua, Rushdie visited the church of Santa Maria de los Angelos to
witness the Peasants' Mass and hear Father Uriel Molina, one of
Nicaragua's leading liberation priests. 'The texts for the day', Rushdie
remembered,

came from the book of Exodus, and, in his sermon, Father Molina wove them into an extended metaphor, in which the people of Nicaragua were equated with the Israelites in their Egyptian captivity. Somoza was cast as the Pharaoh, and the FSLN was likened to Moses, leading the people across the parted waters of the Red Sea into the Promised Land, while behind them, the God of the Poor closed the waters over the head of Rameses-Tacho and his National Guard.

Father Molina's sermon was followed by a rousing chorus of 'We Shall Overcome', which Rushdie joined enthusiastically before slipping out. 'Whether or not we would [overcome], I thought as I left the congregation, being unwilling to participate in the taking of body and blood, one certainly has to believe in the power of this new version of Christianity, and in its popularity'.[12]

Even so, Rushdie's encounter with this new version of Christianity did not cause him to rethink his own secularism. Nor did it impress Said enough to mention it in the long review essay on the Iran–Contra affair he wrote for the *London Review of Books* in May, which ended with praise for *The Jaguar Smile*. Instead, Said was preoccupied with the religious motives he detected behind the Iran–Contra Affair itself: 'The new forces [in the Middle East] are the motors driving Iran and Israel – states whose religious inspiration is barely assimilable to statehood. One of them, Israel, is the state, not of its citizens, but of "the Jewish people". The other, Iran, proclaims itself responsible for exporting a purified and resurgent Islam throughout the region'. As for 'the American obsession with Iran and Israel', Said charged that it 'is shaped by an increasing tendency to drive politics back to anti-secular, sectarian and atavistic roots. The revival of Christian fundamentalism in the US has been part of this tendency...'.[13] Thus the fuel of Christian fundamentalism, in Said's view, was powering Ronald Reagan's holy war against the demonic forces of anti-Americanism in Nicaragua and around the globe.

The real beneficiaries of the Iran–Contra Affair, Said insisted, were not the Contras but the Israelis, who had brokered the deal for their American patrons. When the Palestinian *intifada* broke out in the Occupied Territories on 9 December 1987, therefore, Said was ecstatic. Here, at last, was the popular uprising that would accomplish what the PLO had failed to accomplish: force Israel to end its illegal occupation and prepare the way for a secular, democratic state in Palestine. By March 1988, US Secretary of State George Shultz was asking to meet with Said in person to discuss the situation.[14] By November, Said was in Algiers for the historic *intifada* meeting of the Palestinian National Council (PNC), during which the delegates voted to declare Palestinian statehood, recognise Israel, and open negotiations on the future of the West Bank and Gaza.[15] It was in the midst of this flurry of political activity that Said received Rushdie's typescript of *The Satanic Verses*. 'My impression was that he was expecting the novel to have an impact', Said told Weatherby. 'He said it would shake up the Muslims. But he never expected it to bring about a threat to his life'.[16]

Said's defence of Rushdie in the West and the Middle East

Presumably with Said's blessing, *The Satanic Verses* was published in Britain on 26 September 1988. On 14 February 1989, the Ayatollah Khomeini issued his infamous *fatwa*. Said rose immediately to his friend's defence, assuming the thankless role of public mediator between Rushdie and his Islamic critics. On 22 February – the novel's official US publication date – the BBC aired a debate featuring Said and a variety of British and Muslim figures, including Shabbir Akhtar of the Bradford Council of Mosques, who defended the burning of the novel and called for a government ban on its distribution.[17] That same evening, Said addressed a pro-Rushdie rally in New York hosted by PEN, the international writers guild. In his prepared remarks, subsequently published in both British and American newspapers, Said tried to answer the question posed by many Muslims, namely, 'Why … must a member of our culture join the legions of Orientalists in Orientalizing Islam so radically and so unfairly?' Said's response was to insist that 'hybrids' like Rushdie cannot help but 'stir Islamic narratives into a stream of heterogeneous narratives'.[18]

Among those who took note of Said's remarks at the PEN rally was his old enemy Martin Peretz, the pro-Israeli editor of *The New Republic*. Noting 'the embarrassment of [Rushdie's] enthusiasms for Third World causes that turn out to be tyrannies', Peretz asked, 'What does he make of the fact that it is Margaret Thatcher, wittily satirized in his book *The Satanic Verses* as "Margaret Torture", who now offers him the protection of Western civilization against the anti-Western forces that would take his life?' As for Said, Peretz was highly amused at what he took to be his enemy's discomfiture:

Said's speech at the PEN meeting was a crimped and convoluted attempt to combine the obviously hateful behavior of the Muslim masses in many countries toward Rushdie and his book with Said's own decade-long apology for those masses. The Ayatollah really put the anti-Orientalist on the spot. Said, after all, wrote an entire book, *Covering Islam*, to demonstrate how America and the American media had contrived to misunderstand the Iranian revolution.[19]

For Peretz, then, *The Satanic Verses* was a convenient wedge to drive between First World intellectuals like Rushdie and Said and the Third World masses for whom they claimed to speak.

For Rushdie and Said, on the other hand, the battle over *The Satanic Verses* was symptomatic of an ongoing struggle within Islam itself – a struggle in which both Rushdie and Said continued to participate despite the *fatwa*. Thus when Rushdie published his next novel, *Haroun and the Sea of Stories*, in September 1990, Said insisted (in a review in *The Independent*) that

> this is *not* just an imaginative re-cycling of the Iranian *fatwa* against the author of *The Satanic Verses* and its lamentable effects. Instead, Rushdie's tale exuberantly fights over the Islamic terrain so rudely pre-empted by the *fatwa*, and shows that *another* narrative and spiritual source besides the *dicta* of dogmatic orthodoxy has fed the culture – namely the spirit of fun and storytelling so memorably embodied in the *Arabian Nights*. Islam is in those tales too, Rushdie seems to be saying, and that kind of experience can neither be severed from the whole tradition nor confined by clerical stricture.[20]

In short, Rushdie was letting the world know that he wasn't the enemy of Islam he'd been made out to be – that he was merely attempting to liberate true Islam from the stranglehold of the mullahs.

But then came Rushdie's meeting with a group of Muslim clerics on Christmas Eve 1990, followed by his surprising announcement that he had become a Muslim, promising not to permit new translations or a paperback edition of *The Satanic Verses*. Many of those who had defended Rushdie after the *fatwa* now took him to task for betraying his principles and his supporters. Said, however, was more forgiving of his misguided friend. The perilous circumstances of Rushdie's life since the *fatwa*, Said told *Newsweek*, are those in which 'people find religion'.

He guessed that Rushdie's announcement was merely his way of recon-
necting with his community of origin: 'It's a ritual, like the return of
the prodigal son'.[21] In any case, Rushdie's 'conversion' to Islam did not
alter Said's public defence of *The Satanic Verses* or his own strident
secularism.

As it happened, Rushdie's announcement of his conversion coincided with the Gulf War, during which Arafat aligned himself with
Saddam Hussein – a blunder that, in Said's view, merely added to the
PLO's already weak negotiating position with the US and Israel. By the
time the Madrid peace conference opened in October 1991, Said had
resigned from the PNC, increasingly critical of the direction of the
peace process he had helped launch at Algiers in 1988. But there was a
second, more personal factor behind Said's decision to withdraw from
politics: the discovery that he was suffering from a chronic illness that
threatened to cut short his life. It was the shock of this discovery that
prompted him to return to Palestine in the summer of 1992 – his first
visit since his exile in 1947.

It was a bittersweet homecoming. Everywhere he went, he witnessed
the ravages of fundamentalism. In Jerusalem, he discovered that the
Said residence,

> irony of ironies, bore the name plate 'International Christian Embassy'
> at the gate. To have found my family's house now occupied not by an
> Israeli Jewish family, but by a right-wing Christian fundamentalist and
> militantly pro-Zionist group (run by a South African Boer, no less, and
> with a record of unsavory involvements with the Contras to boot), this
> was an abrupt blow for a child of Palestinian Christian parents. Anger
> and melancholy took me over.[22]

Said encountered his share of Islamic fundamentalists as well – and
learned that *The Satanic Verses* was still very much on their minds.
After lecturing at Birzeit University on the West Bank, he got into a
lively discussion with his audience:

> In no time we were heavily into Salman Rushdie, whom I defended
> categorically, and political Islam, which I also criticized somewhat
> impetuously. I made, I think, one rather far-out analogy between the
> Israeli penchant for barbed-wire fences and the now current separa-
> tion of 'us' (Palestinians, Arabs, Muslims) from the West, saying that
> all cultures were in fact hybrid, and any attempt to push a homo-
> genizing line was not only false but demagogic.[23]

The following summer, Said returned to Birzeit, asking to meet with student leaders from Hamas and Islamic Jihad, the two main Islamic resistance organisations in the Occupied Territories. 'Jihad was clear', he noted, 'about wanting to kill anyone like Salman Rushdie who was an apostate (I had informed them that he was not only a good friend but someone whose writings I fully support); Hamas demurred but signalled he would suffer an unpleasant fate just this side of killing'.[24] No doubt these unsettling experiences brought home what Said had known all along: that Rushdie's cause was the cause of freedom throughout the Islamic world – including the newly independent but still homeless state of Palestine.

This was a point Said made explicitly in his contribution to a collection of essays by Arab and Muslim supporters of Rushdie. 'Rushdie', he declared,

> is everyone who dares to speak out against power, to say that we are entitled to think and express forbidden thoughts, to argue for democracy and freedom of opinion. The time has come for those of us who come from his part of the world to say that we are against this *fatwa* and all *fatwas* that silence, beat, imprison, or intimidate people and ban, burn, or anathematize books. ... His case is not really about offense to Islam, but a spur to go on struggling for democracy that has been denied us, and the courage not to stop. Rushdie is the *intifada* of the imagination.[25]

Ironically, this stirring statement was first published in the fall of 1993, when Arafat and Rabin were shaking hands over the Oslo Accords – the product of secret negotiations between the PLO and Israel. Said, who had grown increasingly critical of Arafat since Algiers, was outraged by this back-room 'Palestinian Versailles'. 'To be recognized at last by Israel and the United States may mean personal fulfillment for some', he fumed, 'but it doesn't necessarily answer Palestinian needs or solve the leadership crisis. Our struggle is about freedom and democracy; it is secular and, for a long time – indeed, up until the last few years – it was fairly democratic. Arafat has canceled the *intifada* unilaterally'.[26] In short, to be for the *intifada* was to be for Rushdie and against Arafat – to be for imagination and openness and democracy and against pragmatism and secrecy and autocracy.

In retrospect, one cannot help but wonder whether Said's *intifada* ever existed outside his imagination. That might explain why he now blames nearly everyone who supported the *intifada* for betraying the cause:

Arafat and his Palestinian Authority have become a sort of Vichy government for Palestinians. Those of us who fought for Palestine before Oslo fought for a cause that we believed would spur the emergence of a just order. Never has this ideal been further from realization than today. Arafat is corrupt. Hamas and Islamic Jihad are no alternative. And most Palestinian intellectuals have been too anxious to bolster their own case, following Arafat and his lieutenants in the abandonment of their principles and history just to be recognized by the West, to be invited to the Brookings Institution, and to appear on U.S. television.[27]

The truth, surely, is that the *intifada* was never about creating a 'just order' based on democracy and secularism; it was a spontaneous uprising against Israeli brutality that inspired, and was largely sustained by, the same Islamic activists who railed against Rushdie and his novel.

Said's explanation of the Rushdie Affair

In *Culture and Imperialism* (1993), Said stepped back from his direct involvement in the Rushdie Affair, explaining it as an effect of the Western-dominated 'world media system'. This system, he charged,

has an institutionalized tendency to produce out-of-scale transnational images that are now reorienting international social discourse and process. Take as a case in point the emergence of 'terrorism' and 'fundamentalism' as two key terms of the 1980s. For one, you could hardly begin (in the public space provided by international discourse) to analyze political conflicts involving Sunnis and Shi'is, or Kurds and Iraqis, or Tamils and Sinhalese, or Sikhs and Hindus – the list is long – without eventually having to resort to the categories and images of 'terrorism' and 'fundamentalism,' which derived entirely from the concerns and intellectual factories in metropolitan centers like Washington and London. ... Not Iran's official reaction to Rushdie's novel, or the unofficial enthusiasm for him among Islamic communities in the West, or the public and private expression of outrage in the West against the *fatwa* is intelligible, in my opinion, without reference to ... the overbearing system I have been trying to describe.[28]

Behind the 'concerns' of Reagan's Washington and Thatcher's London, in turn, lurked the spectre of 'Western Judeo-Christian triumphalism' – the age-old chauvinism of the Crusader reclaiming the Holy Land from the Infidel.[29]

No doubt there is a great deal of truth in Said's explanation of the Rushdie Affair. Still, one must be careful not to exaggerate the ideological uniformity of the global public sphere. Occasionally, at least, the public discourse on 'terrorism' and 'fundamentalism' that emerged in the 1980s was less ideological and more analytical than Said implied, even when it derived from the 'intellectual factories' of Washington and London. Take the ambitious Fundamentalism Project sponsored by the American Academy of Arts and Sciences and funded by the MacArthur Foundation. Under the direction of Martin Marty of the University of Chicago, the Project churned out a series of encyclopedic tomes on the world's fundamentalist movements. Marty has been called the 'Pope' of American Protestantism, but his international army of scholars bore more resemblance to a World Parliament of Religions than a new Crusade.

Moreover, to the extent that the Western-dominated media do reflect an ideological consensus, it is a consensus based on liberal secularism rather than 'Judeo-Christian triumphalism'. After all, it was not the Christian heritage of the West that Rushdie's Islamic critics condemned. On the contrary, it was the fact that the West had turned its back on that heritage, erecting in its place a godless culture that threatens to engulf the globe in a sea of seductive sounds and images. Only a permissive society that has lost its faith in God, they charged, could permit a novel like *The Satanic Verses* to be published. That is why Islamic leaders expressed such dismay when Christians joined the 'Liberal Inquisition' of Muslims (as Shabbir Akhtar described it) in the wake of the anti-Rushdie protests.[30]

In point of fact, a thoroughly secular public sphere is exactly what Said prescribes as the proper forum for social discourse. The true intellectual, he insists, is the enemy of religion, at least in its public forms; if one wishes to worship a god in private, that is one's own affair. As he proclaimed in his Reith Lectures, aired by the BBC in June 1993,

> In the secular world – our world, the historical and social world made by human effort – the intellectual has only secular means to work with; revelation and inspiration, while perfectly feasible as modes for understanding in private life, are disasters and even barbaric when put

to use by theoretically minded men and women. Indeed I would go so far as saying that the intellectual must be involved in a lifelong dispute with all the guardians of sacred vision or text, whose depradations are legion and whose heavy hand brooks no disagreement and certainly no diversity. Uncompromising freedom of opinion and expression is the secular intellectual's main bastion: to abandon its defense or to tolerate tamperings with any of its foundations is in effect to betray the intellectual's calling. That is why the defense of Salman Rushdie's *Satanic Verses* has been so absolutely central an issue.[31]

What's missing here is any sense that public religion in the modern world can be something other than the fundamentalism of a Khomeini. Surely it's possible to defend freedom of speech without insisting that religion be confined, in typical liberal fashion, to the private sphere. Granted, this modern form of public religion, with its respect for the hard-won Enlightenment freedoms of speech and religion, lacks the apocalyptic drama of a theocratic state arising out of the ashes of secular history. Even so, one ought not to discount the power of modern public religion to galvanise progressive social movements, as the careers of Gandhi, King, and Tutu remind us.

In his better moments, Said acknowledges the contributions made by particular religious traditions to the cause of human liberation, notably – and rather surprisingly, given his staunch anti-imperialism – some of the older Protestant missionary traditions of the Middle East. This is particularly true of the Quaker tradition of his wife Miriam and her father, Emile Cortas, the head of the Quaker community in Lebanon – a tradition that also produced Said's friend and role model Hanna Mikhail, a graduate of Haverford who, as Said noted in a moving tribute, retained his 'original Quaker modesty and plainness' throughout his years in the PLO.[32] In fact, Said has pointed to the Protestant churches of the Middle East as a prime example of the complex cultural legacy of imperialism – a legacy that, he insists, cannot be undone simply by disbanding these churches, which have developed their own hybrid identity over the years.[33] Of course Said is the product of a Protestant missionary tradition himself – a tradition he probably thought he'd left behind for good when he was expelled from Victoria College in Cairo and shipped off to America. But way leads on to way, and his autobiographical search for the mysterious thread of his own life has led him back, at long last, to his Protestant childhood in the Holy City, with St George's Cathedral at its centre.[34]

The problem, then, is not that Said is unappreciative of the social good done by particular religious figures and traditions. Rather, the problem is that his theory of the public sphere cannot accommodate his own best insights and experiences in this regard. Admittedly, it's not easy to think well of religion when your life and the lives of your people – not to mention friends like Salman Rushdie – are threatened on a daily basis by religious fundamentalists. The question, however, is whether secularism is an effective democratic response to the world's fundamentalist movements. If 'secularism' means staunchly opposing any state that violates basic human rights in the name of religion, then even religious democrats will agree that such opposition is necessary. If, however, 'secularism' means that the state must bar religion from the public sphere – as was the case until recently in Turkey, for example – then religious democrats will oppose such a policy. Not only is such an intrusion of state power into the realm of civil society undemocratic, but it serves to freeze and radicalise fundamentalist movements that might otherwise be transformed through participation in the public sphere. An example of such transformation is the new prominence of women in the Islamic movement in Turkey, where the public sphere has recently been opened to Islamists after decades of state-imposed secularisation.[35]

As it happens, Turkey was also the site of one of the most tragic events associated with the Rushdie Affair: a fundamentalist riot in Sivas in July 1993 that resulted in the deaths of some forty people. One of the mob's targets was Aziz Nesin, a secular journalist who had been publishing unauthorised excerpts from *The Satanic Verses* (and who, fortunately, escaped with his life). Afterwards, Rushdie made it clear that, while he deplored the behaviour of the fundamentalists, he also disapproved of Nesin's tactics:

> Ever since 1989, Iranian mullahs and Islamic zealots have been quoting and reproducing de-contextualized segments of *The Satanic Verses* to use as propaganda weapons in the larger war against progressive ideas, secularist thought and the modern world, in which the so-called 'Rushdie affair' is no more than a skirmish. I was appalled to find that these self-proclaimed Turkish secularists and anti-fundamentalists were using my work in exactly the same unscrupulous fashion, albeit to serve different political purposes. Once again, I was a pawn in somebody else's game.[36]

This may not be the best model of public intervention in local conflicts between secularists and fundamentalists. As Alexander Cockburn noted, both the style and the timing of Rushdie's statement implied a certain callousness with regard to the victims of the riot.[37] Nevertheless, Rushdie was right to insist that *The Satanic Verses* not be reduced to secularist propaganda by either party. One can only pray and work for a world in which novels like *The Satanic Verses* are seen for what they are: works that take the 'conflicting discourses' of the public sphere *'right inside our heads'*.[38]

Notes

 1 'Satanic Curses', *The Nation*, 22 December 1997, p. 8.
 2 W. J. Weatherby, *Salman Rushdie: Sentenced to Death* (New York: Carroll and Graf, 1990) p. 108.
 3 Ibid., pp. 183–4.
 4 Ibid., p. 182.
 5 E. W. Said, *The Politics of Dispossession* (New York: Vintage, 1995) pp. 175–85.
 6 Weatherby, *Salman Rushdie*, p. 10.
 7 S. Rushdie, *Imaginary Homelands* (New York: Penguin, 1991) p. 101.
 8 Ibid., p. 382.
 9. S. Rushdie, 'If I forget thee …', *The Guardian*, 19 September 1986, p. 11.
10 E. W. Said, *After the Last Sky* (London: Faber and Faber, 1986) p. 152.
11 Ibid., pp. 154–5.
12 S. Rushdie, *The Jaguar Smile* (New York: Viking Penguin, 1987) pp. 61–2.
13 E. W. Said, 'Irangate', *London Review of Books*, 7 May 1987, pp. 8–10.
14 Said, *Politics*, p. 138.
15 Ibid., pp. 145–51.
16 Weatherby, *Salman Rushdie*, p. 108.
17 S. Ahktar, *Be Careful With Muhammed!* (London: Bellew, 1989) pp. 48–9.
18 L. Appignanesi and S. Maitland (eds), *The Rushdie File* (Syracuse: Syracuse Univ. Press, 1990) p. 165.
19 M. Peretz, 'Embroiled Salman', *The New Republic*, 20 March 1989, p. 50.
20 E. W. Said, 'Shah of Blah rules OK', *The Independent on Sunday*, 25 November 1990, *Sunday Review*, p. 30.
21 E. Salholz, 'Rushdie Embraces the Faith', *Newsweek*, 7 January 1991, p. 52.
22 Said, *Politics*, p. 180.
23 Ibid., p. 198.
24 Ibid., p. 404.
25 E. W. Said, 'Against the Orthodoxies', in *For Rushdie* (New York: George Braziller, 1994) p. 261.
26 Said, *Politics*, p. 6.
27 E. W. Said, *Peace and its Discontents* (New York: Vintage, 1996) pp. 159–60.
28 E. W. Said, *Culture and Imperialism* (New York: Vintage, 1993) pp. 309–10.
29 Said, *Culture*, p. 303.
30 Akhtar, *Be Careful*, p. 37.
31 E. W. Said, *Representations of the Intellectual* (New York: Pantheon, 1994) pp. 88–9.
32 Said, *Peace*, pp. 74–84.

33 Said, *Culture*, pp. 39–41.
34 Over the past few years, Said has been working on a memoir of his early life. See Said, 'Between Worlds', *London Review of Books*, 7 May 1998, pp. 3–7.
35 See N. Gole, 'The Gendered Nature of the Public Sphere', *Public Culture*, 10.1 (1997) 61–81.
36 'Pawn in a wider game', *The Observer*, 4 July 1993, p. 23.
37 A. Cockburn, 'Turks Fry, Rushdie Peeved', *The Nation*, 26 July 1993, p. 126.
38 Rushdie, *Imaginary*, p. 426.

13
Creative Border Crossing in New Public Culture

Lambert Zuidervaart

The Immigrant Children at Union School

We come from Bratislava and Wroclaw,
Budapest and Prague, Minsk and Tulcea:
a veritable United Nations in my kinder-
garten class. Our halting English
frustrates the teacher but never ourselves – we know what we're trying to say.
We color and paint and draw and listen
to a story read aloud about a missing
princess and the poor peasant boy who
chooses to brave horrific dangers
in order to find her. All the girls
want to be the princess, all the boys
want to be the peasant. I just want
to be here in America, in Ohio,
in Cleveland, living on Salem Avenue
four houses from my grandparents,
and walking to Union School every
morning holding my grandfather's
right hand. In other words, I want
nothing more. But maybe three things:
to be smart enough to read English
and brave enough to scold that princess
for getting lost and kind enough not
to make fun of the girl from Hungary

> with the bright red ribbon in her hair
> who always draws her cats with eight legs.
>
> Linda Nemec Foster[1]

The American poet Linda Nemec Foster grew up in a Polish Catholic neighbourhood of Cleveland, Ohio. Her poems are steeped in the stuff of everyday life – 'halting English', 'a story read aloud', the walk to school 'holding my grandfather's right hand'. I know her through my work at the Urban Institute for Contemporary Arts (UICA) in Grand Rapids, Michigan, a community-based arts centre where she has chaired the volunteer committee that organises readings, workshops and other public literary events. For more than fifteen years she has travelled the state of Michigan teaching young people the wonders of poetry. Both her writing and her teaching display commitments to artistic authenticity and social responsibility that arise in part from her religious background.

A few years ago UICA sponsored Foster's grant proposal to the Arts Foundation of Michigan for a poetry project on the themes of cultural heritage and ethnic identity. While creating a collection of new poems about her Polish background, including the one above, Foster spent three days at a local public school serving primarily Hispanic and African-American students. She wanted to help the students write poetry about their identity and heritage. Foster's experience at the school offers clues to a new kind of literary public sphere.

Picture the scene at Hall Elementary School in the spring of 1996. The fourth- and fifth-grade students are shy, maybe a little scared. They've never tried to write autobiographical poetry before. But as Foster's infectious smile and hearty laugh fill the room, memories and experiences begin to take shape in words on the students' papers. Words of hope and fear, of joy and sorrow, of loneliness and community, of violence and peace. Words both true to the students' lives and socially significant.

When Foster arrived on her third day, the local news media were out in full force. The day before a teenager had shot at a bus outside the school, sending glass flying and striking terror into young hearts. Eleven-year-old Kenya Sturdivant writes the following 'I Am' poem:

> I am from America and Kenya
> I wonder how long I am going to live
> I heard a gun shot yesterday

> I seen News 8
> I want the violence to stop
> I am from America and Kenya
>
> I pretend to take away violence
> I feel sad and happy
> I touched my brother
> I worry about friends and family
> I cry when I think of my grandmother
> I am from America and Kenya
>
> I understand why the world is like this
> I say the world could be better
> I dream there was no violence
> I try to make my friends stop violence
> I hope my kids won't have to live like this
> I am from America and Kenya[2]

I first heard this poem at a public reading in UICA's main gallery. Families and friends sat with the students. Many had never visited an arts centre before. All listened proudly as one by one the students came forward to read their poems. Local radio and television stations recorded the event. I had not heard about the shooting incident when I listened to Kenya reading her poem. But one did not need to know details to be moved by an eleven-year-old girl reciting, 'I hope my kids won't have to live like this / I am from America and Kenya'.

Might not this story provide a new image for what Jürgen Habermas calls 'autonomous public spheres'? Several non-profit organisations and government agencies play a role: a community-based arts centre, a private arts foundation, a state cultural agency, a tax-supported school and public broadcasters. Commercial media and publishers also contribute by covering the event and by writing about Foster's work with school children and publishing her poetry. The key, however, lies in the commitment of a professional writer to interact with amateurs in her field and with the general public. Equally important is the fact that the public in this case is not a homogeneous slice of the middle class, but rather a rich mixture of classes, ethnicities, religions, and educational backgrounds – 'a veritable United Nations'. Together Linda Nemec Foster's ethnic heritage, public schooling and religious faith give rise to a deep commitment to interactive border crossing in the creation of culture.

Such a commitment does not find ready support within the isolated spaces of the academy and the professional art world. Nor does it come easily to religious groups more concerned to maintain their own status and traditions than to learn from others, even though traditional religions can foster such a commitment to social responsibility. The public culture of the new millennium will look quite different from the middle-class enclaves that many literary and religious institutions have become. To prepare for institutions that embrace diversity and participation, scholars need to develop a new understanding of both the autonomy and the public character of 'autonomous public spheres'.

Both Habermas and Theodor W. Adorno, whose paradoxical modernism casts long shadows over Habermas' social theory, understand autonomy in such a way that literature and the other arts are rendered more or less irrelevant for contemporary public culture. Both theorists forge a strong link between art's societal autonomy, as a differentiated system centred on autonomous artworks, and human autonomy, as rational self-determination. Adorno isolates the arts from public culture, while continuing to insist on the political significance of the import of authentic works of art. Habermas suggests the relevance of the arts for public culture, while isolating the import of specific works from those spaces where they could have political influence. Hence neither Adorno nor Habermas has an adequate account of the role of the arts in struggles for liberation and recognition. Yet it is precisely within such struggles, within their 'ethical-political discourses' and public interventions, that much vital and provocative contemporary art arises.

One wonders whether other ideas might serve better to illuminate the public dimension of contemporary art and literature. Specifically, I want to consider the ideas of authenticity and social responsibility that are so important to the work of contemporary artists such as Linda Nemec Foster. Although linked to the notion of autonomy, which I do not wish to abandon, these ideas remain closer than autonomy does to the inside perspectives of practising artists and political activists. 'Autonomy' calls attention to systems and products; 'authenticity' and 'social responsibility' call attention to practices and interactions.

New genre public art

Foster's interactive poetry project is one example of what Suzanne Lacy calls 'new genre public art', a recent artistic development that raises significant questions about the meaning and validity of authenticity as an artistic ideal. Such art may include literature, music, dance, film, visual art or various generic interactions. According to Lacy, new genre public art 'uses both traditional and non-traditional media to communicate and interact with a broad and diversified audience about issues directly relevant to their lives'. Unlike older forms of public art, new genre public art 'is based on engagement' and involves a high degree of collaboration. It aims at social intervention, and it has a highly developed 'sensibility about audience, social strategy, and effectiveness'.[3] Whereas detractors take the emphasis on social intervention as evidence that new genre public art is not art at all, I take it as a sign that artists themselves have come to question modernist notions of authenticity and have begun to replace them or revise them in favour of a new emphasis on social responsibility. Artistic practices have arisen whose apparent aim is to empower a community or to promote a social cause rather than to give unique expression to an artist's personal experience or vision. I don't have the space to give many examples in detail, but let me call attention to a few, in the hope that readers know about these projects or others like them. My examples do not represent the full range of contemporary art, but they call attention to a field within contemporary art that raises questions about the ideal of artistic authenticity.

The first project is called *Womanhouse*. It grew out of the Feminist Art Program begun by Miriam Schapiro and Judy Chicago at the California Institute of the Arts in Valencia. Over several months in 1972, the two artists and their students, joined by several women artists from Los Angeles, converted an empty, dilapidated house that was to be torn down into what Charlotte Streifer Rubenstein describes as 'a repository of the fantasies, frustrations, and nightmares of women'.[4] Rubenstein portrays the results as follows:

> When the public walked through the various rooms they found themselves in another world, a world of female psychological content. A bathtub was filled with sand into which a female figure seemed to be sinking. ... The kitchen ceiling was covered with fried eggs made out of plastic that also resembled breasts. In a bedroom a woman ... sat endlessly painting her face with makeup, hour after hour. A mannikin was stuck fast in a linen closet, trapped in the sheets and pillow cases. According to news reports, some women walked through the rooms and burst into tears, overwhelmed by a sudden sense of the futility of their own lives.[5]

By all accounts, the project caught the imagination of the public and constituted a profound consciousness-raising experience for the artists and their students.

Another project is *The Great Wall of Los Angeles*, begun in 1976 and still unfinished. Under the direction of Judith Baca, hundreds of teenagers have been hired and taught over many summers to create one of the world's largest murals in a flood control channel of the Los Angeles River. The mural provides an alternative history of California, portraying the struggles and contributions of people who are often left on the margins of official histories: indigenous peoples, immigrant minorities and women. One commentary notes that the monumental logistics for this project include 'co-operation from the Army Corp of Engineers, the city, local politicians, teachers, anthropologists, teenage gang members and the criminal justice system, among others. Its strategy aims at political activism and education through art'.[6]

The third project I want to mention is *The Dinner Party*. This was a huge multimedia collaborative installation involving hundreds of women and several men, directed by Judy Chicago. Lasting over five years, *The Dinner Party* installation employed traditionally feminine crafts in order to build a provocative and loving memorial to the contributions women have made to culture and history. Other collaborative projects of more recent years include the AIDS Quilt, displayed for the last time in the fall of 1996 on the Washington Mall in the United States capital, and Jim Hubbard's photography project for homeless children called *Shooting Back*.[7] All such projects break with a modernist fixation on the individual form of an artwork. Some of them also challenge closely related concerns about the prestige and marketability of the work in question. Of primary importance is not the aesthetic purity or commercial success of the finished product, but rather the degree to which the ongoing project supports and empowers the lives of its participants, from the parent of an AIDS victim to the children at Hall Elementary School. New genre public art emphasises community, collaboration and social commitment, and it involves a striking shift in the way people view and practise the arts. Therefore, it is being accompanied by gradual changes in how schools, museums and art organisations describe their tasks and try to accomplish them. This commitment to empowering a community initially appears incompatible with the modernist emphasis on personal and artistic authenticity. This tension needs to be explored.

Authenticity

In *The Ethics of Authenticity*, political philosopher Charles Taylor argues that the modern notion of authenticity is a valid moral ideal and attempts to rescue it both from reactionary critics of contemporary culture who disparage authenticity and from progressive advocates who fail to articulate its moral source. Following the lead of literary critic Lionel Trilling, Taylor suggests that modern artistic works are an especially crucial location for envisioning and contesting this moral ideal. If, as Taylor argues, the moral ideal of authenticity must be rescued from both reactionary critics and progressive advocates, then perhaps the artistic ideal of authenticity needs a similar retrieval. Such a retrieval might help us interpret recent emphases on community, collaboration and commitment, despite their seeming incompatibility with the notion of artistic authenticity.

Taylor describes the 'moral' ideal of authenticity as a commitment to personal originality. It is the imperative to be 'true to oneself'.[8] By calling this a moral ideal, Taylor means that it is 'a picture of what a better or higher mode of life would be', such that it offers 'a standard of what we ought to desire' (p. 16). As he elaborates later: 'Being true to myself means being true to my own originality, and that is something only I can articulate and discover. In articulating it, I am also defining myself. I am realizing a potentiality that is properly my own. ... This is the background that gives moral force to the culture of authenticity, including its most degraded, absurd, or trivialized forms' (p. 29). Although some contemporary forms of culture might make the pursuit of authenticity seem either amoral or immoral, Taylor argues that the dialogical character of human life and the inherent demands of authenticity itself can prevent the ideal from collapsing into mere narcissism and egoism.

As Taylor indicates, the 'moral' ideal of authenticity is not unrelated to notions of authenticity that figure prominently in modern art and modernist aesthetics. I say 'notions', in the plural, because at least three different concepts can be linked to 'authenticity' in the vocabulary of modernist aesthetics. The first concept has to do with authenticity of performance, in the sense of being faithful to the original artwork. This is the concept musicians employ when they talk about using 'authentic instruments' for the 'authentic performance' of, say, Baroque music. The second concept has to do with the authenticity of the artwork itself, in the sense that the work is original, unique and genuine – not derivative, not replaceable and not a forgery. The third concept has to do with authenticity in artistic practices, in composing, writing, painting and the like. This is the expectation that the artist should make something that is true to his or her own experience or vision. One writer expresses the expectation as follows:

> We expect of the best art that it will avoid the clichéd response, the prevailing stereotype, the derivative plot, the predictable pattern of events, the all too familiar viewpoint, the 'academic' style. Authentic artists are supposed to have their own style and viewpoint; we look to them to 'make it new', to use their unique perspective and experience to confront us with the ambiguous and unexpected. When they succeed, their work offers a model of the alert and critical mentality required for a life lived according to the ethical ideal of authenticity.[9]

Of these three concepts – authenticity of performance, of the artwork, and in artistic practices – I believe that the third has been the most influential in shaping an artist's self-understanding. Moreover, it is the concept of authenticity in artistic practices that most closely parallels Taylor's 'moral' ideal of authenticity, as the passage just quoted indicates. Hence I emphasise the expectation of authenticity in the artist's making of art products, and for that I use the term *artistic authenticity*. Artistic authenticity is the expectation that each artist should be true to his or her own personal experience or vision when engaging in artistic practices.

On one side, then, we have the 'moral' ideal of being true to oneself and one's own originality, as articulated and discovered for oneself. On the other side, we have the expectation of the artist's making art that is true to the artist's own vision, and doing so in ways that are original, unique and possibly unexpected. Perhaps the connection from one side to the other is stronger than a mere parallel. Perhaps, as Taylor sometimes suggests, the one is a metaphor for the other, such that we cannot interpret the 'moral' ideal apart from practices and institutions that enact the artistic ideal – and also the other way around. On that hypothesis, a shift within or away from the artistic ideal would be significant for an interpretation of the 'moral' ideal. At this point, however, Taylor's account comes up short, for his references to the arts do not go beyond the modern period, and he has little to say about artistic practices and self-understandings of the past few decades, such as new genre public art and its concern with social responsibility.

Social responsibility

The notion of social responsibility is as complex as it is diffuse. Often people equate it with moral or ethical responsibility. But I want to claim that social responsibility indicates a more comprehensive idea. To say of artists that they have a social responsibility is not simply to say that as individuals those people who happen to be artists ought to be moral and ethical in their persons and their conduct. This would not delineate what is specific to the idea of social responsibility, since as individuals such people would have the same moral and ethical responsibilities as anyone who is not an artist – for example, being honest or treating others with respect. The social responsibility of artists pertains to the specific tasks, expectations and choices that confront them in their capacity *as* artists. Three concepts enter this idea of social responsibility, namely, trustworthiness, accountability and responsiveness.

In the first place, the artist is called to be trustworthy with respect to the tasks of social imagination, advocacy and critique. People become artists by virtue of certain gifts, training and positioning in a society. With such gifts, training and positioning comes a calling to employ these on behalf of society by undertaking the tasks with which artists are entrusted. Second, the idea of social responsibility contains a significant component of accountability. Merely undertaking the tasks of imagination, advocacy and critique is not enough. By entering upon such tasks, artists raise the expectation that they will actually make contributions to society, contributions that are significant and worthwhile and that non-artists would be less likely to accomplish. In that sense, artists are socially accountable not only to themselves but also to their neighbours, to society as a whole, and to that to which they give their ultimate allegiances.

Third, socially responsible artists are responsive as they try to make contributions to society. By themselves, the tasks of social imagination, advocacy and critique, and actually contributing to society, are incomplete. An artist could do all of this but nevertheless miss certain opportunities, ignore certain issues, and avoid certain situations, all of which deserve attention. In responding to a social context, the artist cannot avoid choosing various methods, approaches and partners, and she or he is answerable for the quality of these choices. Hence the social responsibility of artists encompasses their trustworthiness with respect to the work they do, their accountability for the outcome of their efforts, and their responsiveness within the creative process.

Not even the artist who denies social responsibility can escape this calling. Consider, for example, the following comments by the painter Georg Baselitz: 'The artist in not responsible to anyone. His social role is asocial; his only responsibility consists in an attitude to the work he does. There is no communication with any public whatsoever. The artist can ask no question, and he makes no statement; he offers no information, and his work cannot be used. It is the end product which counts, in my case, the picture.'[10] Referring to these and later comments by Baselitz, Suzi Gablik observes that they harbour 'the personal and cultural myth that has formed the artist's identity in the modern world: the myth of the solitary genius whose perfection lies in absolute independence from the world'.[11] For all that, however, Baselitz does not deny altogether the fact of responsibility. Rather, he restricts this responsibility to 'an attitude to the work' such that 'it is the end product which counts'. On the view expressed by Baselitz, to be trustworthy as an artist is to be devoted to the end product; to be accountable is to make sure that the end product counts; and to be responsive is to pay complete attention to what the artwork requires. Such devotion, dedication and attentiveness, highly demanding as they are, are meaningless, however, when they become untethered from the idea of social responsibility, as happens in what Patricia Catto has called 'bad modernism'.[12] That is why the notion of artistic authenticity, so central to the modernist credo, needs to be rescued from the absurdities to which some advocates have pushed it.

Creative tension

When properly understood, and when pursued as valid ideals, not as poor rationalisations for either threadbare elitism or self-serving populism, artistic authenticity and social responsibility are not incompatible. Rather, they constitute a creative tension in which neither ideal can be fruitfully pursued in the absence of the other. Let's look at this tension in each direction, first from responsibility to authenticity, and then from authenticity to responsibility.

A new emphasis on social responsibility brings out hidden aspects of artistic authenticity and helps prevent it from collapsing into aesthetic solipsism. In his retrieval of the moral ideal of authenticity, Taylor argues that subjectivation is irreversible. By subjectivation Taylor means the historical movement whereby more and more decisions, understandings and practices centre on the human agent and not on some external reality. Yet it makes a big difference, Taylor says, whether the *manner* of action or the *matter* of action becomes centred on the self. Properly understood, moral authenticity has to do with the *manner* of action, not its *matter* or content. In fact, when people begin to think that the matter of art – its goals and meaning – can be derived only from the individual self, and not from nature or society or the divine, then artistic authenticity becomes both incoherent and unattainable as a moral ideal.

It seems to me that an all-too-common view of artistic authenticity makes precisely that sort of mistake. People who expect artistic practices to be authentic frequently slide from the legitimate claim that artists should be true to their personal visions to the incoherent claim that each artist must be the only source of this vision. The latter claim is incoherent both because artistic practices are inescapably dialogical and because one cannot have a personal vision apart from the larger contexts (societal, cultural, environmental) that help make such a vision personal.

Properly understood, artistic authenticity concerns the manner in which the artist uncovers, expresses, criticises and reappropriates a personal vision, and this understanding implies that the artist is responsible for doing these things in ways that are genuinely significant. As Taylor indicates in the ethical context, judgements about significance can be made only in the context of something larger than the individual self. The aesthetic solipsist cannot achieve authenticity in art. Both authenticity and artistry imply what Taylor describes as 'openness to horizons of significance' and 'self-definition in dialogue' (p. 66). Artistic authenticity should not be pitted against social responsibility but should be regarded as necessarily embedded in the social context the artist is called to address. The expectations of originality, uniqueness and novelty that give texture to the ideal of artistic authenticity gain their force from the assumption that such qualities are necessary for artistic practices to be significant in a society such as ours.

Similarly, the modern notion of artistic authenticity helps disclose hidden dimensions to the contemporary emphasis on the artist's social responsibility and helps prevent this emphasis from expanding into uncritical collectivism. A tendency toward uncritical collectivism might well be the dark side of the otherwise salutary emphasis on social responsibility. Lacy observes that new genre public art gives artists new roles as educators, myth makers and social healers. With these new roles comes a new sense of integrity. 'Integrity,' she writes, 'is based not on artists' allegiances to their own visions but on an integration of their ideas with those of the community'.[13] I suspect that many artists would find such a statement worrisome. Quite apart from the difficulty of identifying 'the community', the statement could easily be interpreted to mean that artists should simply voice what the group desires, so that artists no longer need to examine, challenge and rearticulate the group's needs and aspirations. On such an interpretation, any notion of the artist's personal integrity would be abandoned. Although Lacy does not endorse such a position, her pitting communal integration against authenticity raises the spectre of uncritical collectivism.

In contrast, but in conjunction with much of Lacy's positions, I want to suggest that the new emphasis on social responsibility necessarily feeds upon the ideal of artistic authenticity, even when the latter is regarded as an impediment to social responsibility. To take on the tasks of educator, community builder and social healer in the manner of Linda Nemec Foster, the artist must have a vision, for example, of what needs to be learned, where the community is fragile, and how suffering and oppression must be countered. Moreover, if the artist is to address these matters as an artist, and not simply as a teacher, social worker or political leader, her vision must be discovered and articulated in genuinely artistic ways. Were these aesthetic expectations simply forgotten, and were the manner of artistic practice simply derived from the social matters to be addressed, then the legitimate call to social responsibility would easily slide into a repressive demand for communal conformity, as if only the community or society at large can establish the manner in which artists should do their work. But such a demand would be incoherent, both because artistic practices are inescapably autonomous relative to other practices and because one cannot pursue social responsibility as an artist apart from the art institutions and organisations that frame the artist's position and self-understanding.

Properly understood, the social responsibility of the artist concerns not only the matter of the art work but also the setting and impact of the artwork, and this understanding implies that the artist is personally responsible for interacting with others in ways that contribute to beneficial social transformation. Judgements about beneficial social transformation cannot be delegated to the community or to society at large, however. They must be made by artists themselves, sometimes in conflict with the community or society. The social conformist will not achieve social responsibility in the arts. Both sociality and responsibility imply the ability and commitment to take a personal stand, even at the risk of offending those with whom one seeks to collaborate. Social responsibility in the arts should not be pitted against artistic authenticity, but should be regarded as inescapably linked to the creative freedom the artist is called to nurture and exercise. The emphases on community, collaboration and commitment that inform current discussions of social responsibility gain their force from the assumption that those features are necessary for artistic practices to be authentic in a society such as ours.

Authentic co-responsibility

To this point I have concentrated on the creative tension between authenticity and responsibility within the artist. Without downplaying the reality of this tension, I wish to stress its creative potential in the making of contemporary art – how each is required in order for the other to flourish. The development of new genre public art reveals, however, that social responsibility in the arts does not accrue to artists alone. If art is indeed dialogical and interactive, as the practitioners and theorists of new genre public art claim, then social responsibility also rests with the artists' collaborators, audiences, critics and the public at large. The work of social imagination, advocacy and critique cannot occur in a vacuum. And if this is so, then perhaps the ideal of authenticity needs to be applied to audiences as well, especially to audiences that are no longer regarded as the passive consumers of a finished product.

The importance of ascribing social responsibility to audience members, and not only to artists, emerges from some implications of contemporary emphases on community, collaboration and commitment. On the one hand, the emphasis on community gives artists responsibility for speaking from, for and to a relatively cohesive social group, while helping to construct and reconstruct that group. The emphasis on collaboration gives artists responsibility for listening to, inspiring and working alongside others on a shared project. The emphasis on social commitment gives artists responsibility for understanding, addressing and helping to change oppressive situations and structures. On the other hand, no one can be a community spokesperson and builder, a project facilitator or an agent of social change unless other community members, project participants and social activists also assume responsibility for the process and its outcome.

It is a little more difficult to ascribe the ideal of authenticity to audience members. The difficulty arises from a double tendency to link authenticity with the making of art products and to remove the audience from the process of art production. Two different questions arise: first, whether it would make sense to expect authenticity on the part of traditional audiences, and, second, whether authenticity can plausibly be demanded of non-traditional audiences in their roles as collaborators, volunteers and public participants.

Concerning the first question I argue that, despite appearances to the contrary, we do expect a certain degree of authenticity on the part of traditional audiences. Mindless consumption and expert resistance are both incompatible with the normative role of the traditional audience. What Adorno describes as 'good listeners', for example, are expected to give themselves to the music, to be open to that which they do not immediately understand or appreciate, and to make up their own minds about the music's quality.[14] Good listening requires precisely those marks of an 'alert and critical mentality' that artistic authenticity is supposed to model for the ethical ideal of authenticity.[15] Although good listeners or viewers or readers are not engaged in the productive practices of composing, painting or writing, and hence cannot be expected to *make something* that is true to their own vision, yet they do *make something of* the artistic product, and in that capacity they can be expected to be true not only to the work but also to their own experience. Because of the latter expectation, even traditional art is dialogical, such that neither the artist nor the audience has the final word concerning the meaning and quality of an artistic product. Whereas bad modernism violates such dialogue by discounting the audience's contribution, post-modern consumerism, particularly as fostered by the culture industry, violates the dialogue by trivialising the artist's contribution. On both sides such violations of dialogue often happen in the name of an individuality – 'I'm just expressing myself', 'I know what I like' – which, ironically enough, cannot be authentic.

But what about non-traditional audiences? Is authenticity plausible as an ideal for people whose involvement occurs primarily as collaborators, volunteers and public participants? To begin with, we must recognise how complex the role of the audience becomes in new genre public art. In her essay 'Debated Territory: Toward a Critical Language for Public Art', Lacy portrays the audience 'as a series of concentric circles with permeable membranes that allow continual movement back and forth'. In this non-hierarchical image, the centre is occupied by the primary originators of the creative work – usually the artists. The next circles out from the centre represent first the primary collaborators or co-developers, then the volunteers and performers, and then the immediate audience (many of whom, like veterans and their families visiting Maya Lin's Vietnam Veterans Memorial, bring 'a deep level of experiential engagement'). The outer two circles indicate first the media audience of newspaper readers, television viewers and attenders of documentary exhibitions and then the 'audience of myth and memory' for whom the artwork becomes part of ongoing community life.[16] Lacy's point is that, depending on the circle they occupy at a certain time, audience members have different degrees of responsibility for the outcome. Moreover, they can easily move from one circle to another or occupy several at once.

Accordingly, the question about authenticity requires a more precise formulation. If different audience members have different degrees of responsibility for a dialogical art process, and if the level of their participation is fluid and dynamic, then at what levels can we plausibly expect their participation to be authentic? To answer this we need to acknowledge that the newer audience roles frequently shade into artist roles, so that the relevant concept of authenticity often has more to do with artistic production than with audience interpretation. At the same time, the role of the artist has become more highly interactive, so that artistic authenticity has as much to do with the quality of the artist's empathy, reporting, situational analysis and consensus building as with the originality, uniqueness and novelty of the artist's modus operandi. Lacy describes the new 'interactivity' as involving a continuum of artist positions from experiencer and reporter through analyst and activist.[17]

Still, the core intuitions of authenticity in art remain relevant for all of the newer audience roles, often in the context of a shared vision or experience. The sharing occurs both between creative leaders (artists) and creative participants (audience members) and among the members of a group or community or public on behalf of whom people embark upon a creative process. To be authentic in one's participation means that, relative to one's level of participation, one makes the emerging vision or experience one's own. 'Making it one's own' means not only that one embraces it in one's own manner but also that the creative process receives the benefit of one's own dedication, openness and critical judgement toward that which is being given birth. The reverse side to this, as Lacy's language suggests, is that the audience, too, is responsible for the creative process and its outcome.

Bringing together the notions of authenticity and social responsibility, then, both with regard to artists and with regard to audiences, we can say that new genre public art at its best provides us with experiences and metaphors of authentic co-responsibility in the creative process. On the one hand, such art refuses to divorce the creativity with which artists discover and express and test their personal visions from the social obligations they have by virtue of their gifts and training and positioning in society. On the other hand, new genre public art at its best refuses to exempt audiences from the double expectation of authenticity and social responsibility as they participate in the creative process. Hence, contrary to Adorno, it is not simply the authenticity of the artwork itself that complements social responsibility. Instead, relationships of complementarity hold between the mutual authenticity and social responsibility of both artists and their audience.

Such relationships require a revision in Critical Theory's account of the public dimension of the arts. On Habermasian lines, the relevance of art for public culture must proceed along the nexus of lifeworld, civil society and public spheres. But Habermas regards art as a specialised system for taking up matters of veracity. Despite some attempts to link art and literature with the political public sphere, Habermas' underlying view of art's societal autonomy already marginalises art with respect to the centres of money and power – the economic and administrative systems – and leaves those centres immune to the alternatives and critiques expressed and enacted in art. The implications of artistic import for structural transformation are left untheorised, partly because the project of structural transformation has faded from view. Habermas holds out the hope that different areas of society can undergo internal transformation, but he seems to have given up the notion of a society-wide transformation linked to fundamental change in the economic system. Hence he writes at one point that 'democratic movements emerging from civil society must give up holistic aspirations to a self-organizing society, aspirations that also undergirded Marxist ideas of social revolution. Civil society can directly transform only itself, and it can have at most an indirect effect on the self-transformation of the political system...'.[18] Artists and audiences can be as authentic as they want – it won't make much real (economic, legal and administrative) difference anyway.

By way of contrast, new genre public art encourages us to regard artists as community members who make crucial contributions to a cultural environment that is itself essential to the well-being of all communities in contemporary society. Since all of us live within the cultural environment, however, and since artists have special gifts and tasks in the care of this environment, the relationship between artists and their public must be one of directed co-responsibility: co-responsibility, because all of us have a stake in the environs we inhabit; directed, because some of us – the artists – have special contributions to make to the care of that environment. It is in conflicts over the quality and future of the cultural environment that the tension between authenticity and responsibility acquires its greatest creative potential.

Religion and new public culture

New genre public art also challenges traditional religions to engage in creative border crossings. The child in Linda Nemec Foster's poem wants to read English, to scold the princess, and to be kind to a stranger. Traditional religions could learn from this child, who embraced such aspirations in a religious context. Three fundamental requirements of a new public culture are open communication, recognition of each community's claim to authenticity, and the pursuit of social responsibility beyond one's own clan, sect or nation. It will not be enough for religions to speak their old familiar languages. It will not do for religions to help people hide in the forests of fixed gender, ethnic and economic roles. Nor will it suffice for religions to restrict their interaction with others to random acts of kindness. To help sustain a new public culture, and to be part of that culture, traditional religions will need to learn from contemporary art how to encourage creative border crossing.

Fortunately, innovative leaders and groups within Judaism, Islam, Christianity and other religions have already begun this process, just as some contemporary artists partially derive their commitment to cross-cultural conversation from generous and dialogical impulses within traditional religions. In contributing to a new public culture, traditional religions will slowly and painfully shed modernist shackles of both fundamentalist and liberal sorts, giving up modernist attempts to secure their authority by force as well as modernist attempts to privatise the content of their own traditions. It will not be enough for religious believers to criticise the sourness of a culture of authenticity gone bad: the pursuit of authenticity turns into narcissism and egoism partly because traditional religions offer inadequate vision for addressing contemporary concerns. Neither will it be enough for religious believers to strike the pose of society's social conscience: one reason why writers and visual artists seek new ways to pursue social responsibility is because the social ministries of religious institutions have proved inflexible and hypocritical.

There is no easy road to a public culture in which both artistic authenticity and social responsibility flourish. Many different institutions and communities will need to contribute. Writers and other artists who have genuine concerns about religion will need to 'scold that princess for getting lost'. Adherents of traditional religions who care deeply about literature and the arts will need to be 'kind enough not to make fun of the girl ... who always draws her cats with eight legs'. In the process, although from different spaces and in different ways, these creators of culture, so often at odds in the past, will come to speak a common tongue, the polyglot language of a new public culture.

Notes

1 L. N. Foster, 'The Immigrant Children at Union School', unpublished manuscript, 1997. Used by permission of the author.

2 *A Poetry Sampler on Two Themes*, prepared by the Fourth and Fifth Graders of Hall Elementary School, L. N. Foster (ed.) (Grand Rapids, Mich.: 1996), with support by a grant from the Arts Foundation of Michigan, in conjunction with the Michigan Council for the Arts and Cultural Affairs. Kenya Sturdivant's poem also appears in 'Poetry in Motion', a story by T. F. Hamilton in *The Grand Rapids Press*, 3 April 1996, pp. C1–C2.

3 S. Lacy (ed.), *Mapping the Terrain: New Genre Public Art* (Seattle: Bay Press. 1995) pp. 19–20.

4 C. S. Rubenstein, *American Women Artists* (New York: Avon, 1982) p. 406.

5 Ibid., p. 411.

6 Lacy, *Mapping the Terrain*, p. 202.

7 *Shooting Back: A Photographic View of Life by Homeless Children*, J. Hubbard (ed.) (San Francisco: Chronicle Books, 1991).

8 C. Taylor, *The Ethics of Authenticity* (Cambridge: Harvard Univ. Press, 1992) p. 15. Subsequent references to this text will be noted parenthetically.

9 P. Taylor, 'Authenticity and the Artist', in *A Companion to Aesthetics*, D. E. Cooper (ed.) (Cambridge: Blackwell, 1992) p. 29.

10 Quoted by S. Gablik from the catalog of Baselitz's exhibition at the Whitechapel Art Gallery in London in 1983, in 'Connective Aesthetics: Art after Individualism,' in Lacy, *Mapping the Terrain*, p. 77.

11 Ibid.

12 Ibid.
13 Ibid., p. 39.
14 T. W. Adorno, *Introduction to the Sociology of Music*, E. B. Ashton (trans.) (New York: Seabury Press, 1976) pp. 5–6.
15 P. Taylor, 'Authenticity and the Artist', p. 29.
16 Lacy, *Mapping the Terrain*, pp. 178–80.
17 Ibid., pp. 173–7.
18 J. Habermas, *Between Facts and Norms: Contributions to a Discourse Theory of Law and Democracy*, W. Rehg (trans.) (Cambridge, Mass.: MIT Press, 1996) p. 372.

14
Storytelling, Suffering and the Public Sphere

Colin Jager

O generations of freedom, remember us, the generations of the vision.

> Inscription on the Memorial to Irish Freedom
> Parnell Square, Dublin

The sad irony of this inscription is that the generations of freedom to whom it is addressed have yet to be born. For they, or we, are partly a generation of freedom, while remaining also and of necessity a generation of vision. Freedom – always partial and imperfect where it exists at all – remains bound up with vision. And violence (as the memorial reminds us) is never far from vision.

Is it possible to conceive of a public sphere free from violence? This is the question I will address with the help of Hannah Arendt. I begin with Arendt's distinction between the public and private realms and Seyla Benhabib's interpretation of these categories. Arendt valued the public sphere, the place of contestation, that she associated with the Greek world; for her, public life ideally remains separate from the private realm, which is a place of mere necessity, devoted to maintaining the physical body. According to Benhabib, we can follow Arendt in thinking of the public sphere as a place of contestation and hence of potential pain, or we can allow the concerns of the private into the public realm and work to create a public sphere based on association and potential solidarity. Benhabib thus emphasises what she calls Arendt's 'reluctant modernism': those elements of her thought that move away from a sharp distinction between public and private and toward association and solidarity. And yet – this is the conviction that motivates this essay – history tells us that we cannot simply exchange one for the other. The poignancy of my epigraph springs, I think, precisely from the realisation that vision never modulates easily into freedom. The monument's inscription, the very fact of its existence, links vision indissolubly with bloodshed and sacrifice, while imagining freedom as a peaceful realm beyond violence, a place of harmony and solidarity for which the 'generations of the vision' sacrificed themselves. Yet we are not that generation of freedom. We have not shed the burden of vision and history, for history is never simply behind us. What the eighty bloody years since the Easter uprising have taught us, if anything, is that the coming of freedom is always delayed and that hopes for a peaceful transition from vision to freedom, agon to association, revolution to democracy, are forever marred by the reality of a world in which there is more than one vision and in which continued sacrifices in the name of vision bring us no closer to peace, or to freedom. To whom is the monument addressed, then? We must conclude that it is to us who remain somewhere between vision and freedom, forced by our own monuments to acknowledge the history that continues to infect our present.

If agon and association, vision and freedom, inevitably bleed into each other, we cannot talk realistically about one simply replacing the other. This essay argues that Arendt's work is crucial in this regard because it teaches us that movement from an agonistic Greek public to an associative modern public is accomplished only at the cost of dis-placing the distributive violence of the Greek world onto a figure of suffering. The necessity of such suffering is the element that Benhabib, with her emphasis on the ideal communicative community, misses. Highlighting suffering therefore helps us to understand Arendt: the suffering figures scattered through her work are the only way to make sense of her crucial notions of storytelling and forgiveness. More generally, highlighting suffering helps us understand what is at stake in any utopian theory of the public sphere: envisioning the transition from an agonistic public sphere, defined by its relationship to violence, to a non-violent associative public sphere of peace and communicative ethics is impossible without acknowledging those who pay the price for such a passage. Freedom, if it does come, comes at a terrific cost – and there is no guarantee that it will still be here tomorrow.

Agonism and associationism

Arendt draws the distinction between public and private most clearly in *The Human Condition*. She describes the Greek *polis* as a place of action and speech 'from which everything merely necessary or useful is strictly excluded'.[1] The *polis* is a public place of freedom and equality where the fundamental concern of the citizens is to talk with one another. It is the space of politics, the showplace of courage and the preserver of all that is noble in human life. The private realm, or household, is the inverse of this: it is a place of unfreedom and inequality, dedicated to the realm of necessity and the demands of the body, a place where one is 'primarily concerned with one's own life and survival' (p. 36). For Arendt, the greatness of the Greek world consisted in the ability of its citizens to negotiate the passage from household to *polis* and back again, to shuttle continually between freedom and necessity, and to rest from the labours and dangers of public citizenship within the comforting environs of the household. But this ability no longer characterises modernity. 'In the modern world', she writes, 'the two realms constantly flow into each other like waves in the never-resting stream of the life process itself' (p. 33). In the modern world public and private bleed into each other, giving rise to a new form of human life that Arendt terms 'the social'. A realm that is neither public nor private, the social excludes the possibility of action because it replaces the values of individuality with certain kinds of behaviour that tend to normalise its members (p. 40). Rather than the sharp contrast between the free *polis*, where men strove to distinguish themselves, and the unfree household, dominated by the common needs of the body, the rise of the social presents us with a homogenised world in which action has been reduced to behaviour and statistical uniformity lends itself to the manipulations of a totalitarian state (p. 43).

It is no surprise that feminist thinkers have given Arendt bad marks for accepting this distinction between public and private. Arendt's apparent preference for the Greek *polis*, where only male citizens have access to public power, while women remain with slaves and non-Greeks in the realm of bodily necessity, runs directly counter to the main thrust of feminist theorising over the past twenty years. At the height of second-wave feminism, Adrienne Rich called *The Human Condition* a 'lofty and crippled book' that 'embodies the tragedy of a female mind nourished on male ideology', while Jean Bethke Elshtain implied a similar masculinist bias when she complained that Arendt was 'enraptured with heroes who died young'.[2] More recently, however, as feminist theory has turned away from an overt rejection of the public/private distinction and toward theorising a model of politics and political action, feminists have turned to Arendt's categories with renewed interest. As I noted earlier, this revisionary project has been taken up most thoroughly by Seyla Benhabib.

Like much of her other work, Benhabib's interpretation of Arendt is indebted to the thought of Jürgen Habermas and the notion of a communicative ethic. In her earlier work Benhabib adopts a rather easygoing vision of community, such as the new model of social organisation that she envisions at the conclusion of her *Critique, Norm, and Utopia*: 'The community of needs and solidarity is created in the interstices of society by those new social movements, which on the one hand fight to extend the universalist promise of objective spirit – justice and entitlements – and on the other seek to combine the logic of justice with that of friendship'.[3] This sounds very nice, but one suspects that the painful process of achieving such a community has not been adequately acknowledged. Here and elsewhere Benhabib spends most of her time justifying the communicative community and very little time actually describing the means by which we might get there. Peter Uwe Hohendahl makes what I take to be a similar point when he notes that Benhabib relegates 'history and historical questions to the background'. For Benhabib, Hohendahl suggests, a theory of the public sphere cannot be grounded in history but must instead be anchored in abstract principles as the only viable way to negotiate questions of the common good.[4]

In a more recent critique of Habermas, Benhabib suggests that communicative theory focus not on consensus itself but on the way that consensus is established. She wants to shift the burden from consensus 'to the idea of an ongoing moral conversation'.[5] Yet, ironically, her emphasis on procedure once again has the effect of cleaning up and dehistoricising the public space of debate. She suggests that 'we view discourses as a procedural model of conversations in which we exercise reversibility of perspectives either by actually listening to all involved or by representing to ourselves imaginatively the many perspectives of those involved',[6] but she gives little attention to the method by which we might develop this enlarged mentality, or to the ways that historical experience might enable or constrain such development. Coming to a consensus may involve very painful compromises; even achieving the sort of community in which the communicative ethic can operate may require the sacrifice of individual desires and dreams – perhaps of individual life itself. Yet these facts disappear in the picture of mutually enjoyable conversation that Benhabib paints. In her ideal community, there are no victims, and there is no history.

The desire for a victim-free public sphere is certainly understandable, but it constrains Benhabib's understanding of Arendt. Benhabib identifies two competing models of public space in Arendt's thought: the 'agonistic' and the 'associational'. In the former, Benhabib claims, 'the public realm represents that space of appearance in which moral and political qualities are revealed, displayed, shared with others. This is a competitive space, in which one competes for recognition, acceptance, and acclaim'.[7] Arendt, of course, identifies this public space with the Greek *polis*; Benhabib doesn't hesitate to criticise it for being antimodern and for privileging 'the predominantly male experience of death through war and domination'.[8] Arendt's associational model, says Benhabib, is the more modern of the two, since it recognises that a strict separation between a comforting private sphere devoted to necessity and an agonistic public sphere devoted to action is no longer an accurate description of the modern world, where the two categories are constantly merging and recombining. Arendt's associational model of public space, writes Benhabib, 'emerges whenever and wherever men act together in concert'.[9] She goes on to argue that this model is more conducive to a feminist politics, since 'in entering the public realm women seem to be bringing with them a principle of reality into this sphere, namely the necessities which originate with having a body, and which from Arendt's point of view have strictly no place' in the agonistic public sphere.[10] Thus the procedural model of public space allows us to integrate facets of human experience that the agonistic model leaves out. Benhabib's choice of association over agon is therefore a strategic one, since it implies that personal issues important to women (reproductive freedom, domestic violence) be accorded a public hearing. 'The defense of the more modernist conception of politics', she concludes, 'found in [Arendt's] associative model, and the defense of the entrance of women into the public sphere is closely related'.[11]

By turning Arendt's theories to feminist use, Benhabib reverses her negative characterisation of the rise of the social. While for Arendt the social realm was harmful because it flattened the distinction between public and private life, in Benhabib's hands feminist concerns ride into the political sphere on the coattails of a hybrid society. Benhabib's redescription of the Arendtian social as an unavoidable necessity of modern life has the virtue of pulling Arendt's thought toward a modern conception of political action and making it more amenable to contemporary concerns. But, while this rejuvenation of the social may be a step forward, Benhabib's rejection of the agonal model has an important consequence. What Arendt's 'Greek' conception of public and private highlights is the difficulty of passing from one to the other, the potential for violence that lurks in such a passage. By declaring that we no longer need concern ourselves with such a passage in the modern world, Benhabib effectively removes violence from the modern public sphere.

Bonnie Honig makes a similar point in her deconstructive interpretation of Arendt when she notes that Benhabib accomplishes her redescription of the public realm only by 'excising agonism from her thought'.[12] Honig's point, I take it, is that by drawing a sharp distinction between the agonistic and associational models of public action Benhabib misrepresents both the reality of present politics and the historical continuum within which such a politics has its being. Honig herself emphasises the disruptive and performative side of public action. Living and acting together, *in the modern as much as in the Greek world*, can lead to disagreement, pain, and even death. Indeed, a normative political model that seeks to bring disagreement under the umbrella of communicative rationality fails to account for the central role of conflict within a necessarily pluralist democracy. In her most recent work on Arendt, Benhabib appears to take the historical dimensions of her argument more seriously. She notes, for instance, that 'while the ideal of the sovereign public collectively deliberating about the common good is a regulative ideal as well as a constitutive fiction of democracy, historical, social, and institutional developments show the need to qualify this ideal'.[13] While this seems like the right direction, Benhabib's 'historical, social, and institutional developments' remain firmly within the realm of general principles and norms rather than particularities. That is, she strives to develop a normative model of public debate that remains, in theory, open to historical and social valences – but she doesn't show how such openness would alter the norm itself. Benhabib's refusal to consider norm and history as reciprocally related ultimately winds up denying the reality of potential antagonism. Yet as Chantal Mouffe has recently argued, facing democratic politics means facing the antagonism that lurks within social relations.[14] Doing away with such antagonism in the name of consensus, as attractive as it may seem, denies the reality of the historical achievements and disasters on which we stand. A workable model of free public association, assuming such a thing can exist, does not appear within a historical vacuum but rather rests on the bodies of those who sacrificed themselves (and were sacrificed) for what was then only a vision. Any contemporary political model must include the stories of such sacrifices and such visions, or risk abstracting itself from the historical conditions that gave it birth.

While Benhabib may be correct in identifying both an agonistic and an associational model of the public in Arendt's thought, it is by no means clear that Arendt herself thought of the distinction as very important. It seems clear, in other words, that Arendtian politics are characterised by both agonism and associationism. Certainly the public sphere is potentially violent simply because it permits dissent. Self-exposure, writes Arendt, is the primary characteristic of the Greek *polis*; to appear in public is to risk exposure to the censure of everyone else: 'Whoever entered the political realm had first to be ready to risk his life, and too great a love for life obstructed freedom' (p. 36). Consequently, for Arendt, if we are to envision a viable public space that has as its goal the betterment of human life through debate and disagreement, we must be willing to risk exposure by acting and speaking before our peers. This realm of public appearance establishes a shared reality because 'everything that appears in public can be seen and heard by everybody' (p. 50). None the less, this shared reality is also a space of acting in concert: the space of appearance, while it offers no promise of agreement, does suggest that human plurality need not preclude the possibility of communicative action – a commonality constructed by learning how each of us sees the world differently and becoming, in a phrase Arendt picks up from Kant, a 'citizen of the world'. In keeping with this communicative ethic, Arendt notes that the public space of appearance has no core values, no transcendental truths or pre-made contracts. Its values are constructed in *ad hoc* fashion by the participants: 'the reality of the public realm relies on the simultaneous presence of innumerable perspectives and aspects in which the common world presents itself and for which no common measurement or denominator can ever be devised' (p. 57). In her *Lectures on Kant's Political Philosophy* Arendt expands on these earlier hints from *The Human Condition* by presenting Socrates as a model of both the agonistic and communicative thinker:

What [Socrates] actually did was to make public, in discourse, the thinking process – that dialogue that soundlessly goes on within me, between me and myself; he performed in the marketplace the way the flute-player performed at a banquet. It is sheer performance, sheer activity. ... He became the figure of the philosopher because he took on all comers in the marketplace – was entirely unprotected, open to all questioners, to all demands to give an account of and to live up to what he said.[15]

This description accords nicely with Honig's version of the agon: Socrates is unprotected, performing in the marketplace, disrupting the ideas of the Athenians. Yet Arendt shortly goes on to blend Socrates' agonistic performance with a notion of communicability that sounds much more like Benhabib's ideal. 'Unless', she writes, 'you can somehow communicate and expose to the test of others whatever you may have found out when you were alone', critical thinking itself will disappear. 'Critical thinking' of the sort that Socrates practised, Arendt concludes, 'implies communicability'.[16]

It is not at all clear, therefore, that Arendt thought of agonism and performance as fundamentally different from communication and association. Socrates makes his thought public 'in discourse': a discourse that is at once an unprotected agonistic performance and an effort at communication. What matters for Arendt, after all, is not so much the superiority of one model of public discourse to another but the very fact of publicity itself. Once we recognise this, we can understand that Socrates' discourse, a blend of agon and association, is the metaphorical equivalent of the literal passage between household and *polis* that Arendt identifies in the Greek world. Effective critical thinkers bring their conclusions into the public space, where they are tested, debated, modified, rejected, in an atmosphere that alternates (depending upon its historical and cultural context) from association to agon and back again.

Storytelling

This arrival of ideas in the public square is what Arendt calls *storytelling*. By providing a discursive passage, storytelling is the key to recovering a vibrant public/private relation in the wake of the modern rise of the social. Telling stories about ourselves transfers private experiences into the public sphere, and if we are being authentic we disclose ourselves in this process. In constructing such narratives 'men distinguish themselves instead of being merely distinct; they are the modes in which human beings appear to each other' (p. 176). It is important to understand that this space of appearance is not a comfortable one – there is every possibility, as I intimated earlier, that one may be mocked, shouted down or beaten as the result of self-disclosure. At the same time, storytelling is a model of communication for at least two reasons: those who mock and beat also operate within the public sphere and therefore appear to their peers as the mockers and beaters they are. Hence they are in turn possible objects of violent treatment and possible subjects of stories. In addition, the very notion of a story implies the existence of an audience, and this audience has the power to evaluate the storytellers and their stories critically. Thus, by telling a story we necessarily enter a public realm full of potential relations characterised by multiple avenues of communication. Finally, this realm need not look like the Greek *polis*; the power of storytelling, and its distinctively modern character, creates a viable public space of appearance in even the most private settings. In this sense, hope for modern society rests in our abilities to tell good stories, since good stories counteract the homogenising effects of the social realm and reinscribe a vibrant space of public/private interaction that is home to both agon and association.

It is not, however, always possible for stories to achieve this utopian relation; at times they seem fated to remain a private moral enterprise. When the moral public sphere is perverted or disintegrates entirely, one must withdraw into the private sphere to preserve moral integrity: 'The truth of the matter', Arendt writes of the Holocaust, 'is that only those who withdrew from public life altogether ... could avoid becoming implicated in crimes'.[17] The great difficulty in living under dictatorial regimes, she points out, is the absurd reversal of ordinary morality: criminality becomes the law, while a moral act becomes a crime. Usual moral values like obedience become morally reprehensible. Because criminal acts appear so normal under totalitarianism, we must derive an ethical sense that transcends the norms of the regime from somewhere else. On the evidence of human history, Arendt rules out the possibility that we possess innately such a sense. On the evidence of the Holocaust, she rules out the possibility that we can rely on human institutions to endow us with such a sense. Those few individuals, then, who did resist the Nazi moral order must have done so on other grounds. Arendt suggests this possibility:

they asked themselves to what extent they would be able to live in peace with themselves after having committed certain deeds; and they decided that it would be better to do nothing, not because the world would be changed for the better, but because only on this condition could they go on living with themselves ... they refused to murder, not so much because they held fast to the command 'Thou shalt not kill', as because they were unwilling to live together with a murderer – themselves.

Making a judgement of this sort, she continues, requires only the habit of 'living together explicitly with oneself ... of being engaged in that silent dialogue between me and myself'.[18] This is storytelling on the private level: we refuse to capitulate to totalitarian regimes because we will be unable to live with the story we must tell to ourselves about ourselves if we do capitulate. In the absence of a viable space of public appearance, private moral storytelling requires that we think of ourselves as constituting that space of appearance, and that we sit in judgement upon whatever of ourselves is revealed there.

It remains unclear how these two forms of storytelling – the private and the public – are related. Is the public kind generally enough to preserve an ethical society, and the private sort only necessary in periods of extremity? Or should the two work together at all times? The connection itself is not adequately explored by Arendt. The two levels must be related, however, since the act of stepping into the light of the public world is surely preceded by private rehearsals. And if we understand storytelling as the modern equivalent of the Greek passage between household and *polis*, then what Arendt values in the act of storytelling is precisely the ability to negotiate the pathways between differing spheres. In her account of Anton Schmidt, a German soldier who supplied the Jewish Underground with forged papers and military trucks, Arendt implicitly suggests that even under conditions of totalitarianism, public and private storytelling are related. When Schmidt's story was told at the Eichmann trial, Arendt writes that

> A hush settled over the courtroom. ... And in those two minutes, which were like a sudden burst of light in the midst of impenetrable and unfathomable darkness, a single thought stood out clearly, irrefutably, beyond question – how utterly different everything would be today in this courtroom, in Israel, in Germany, in all of Europe, and perhaps in all countries of the world, if only more such stories could have been told.[19]

Arendt is obviously resorting to the language of appearance here; the 'sudden burst of light' recalls her description of the light of the public realm. Telling Anton Schmidt's story in the courtroom is an act of public storytelling. But since her wish that 'more such stories could have been told' means in effect 'if only there had been more people like Anton Schmidt', Arendt is evidently thinking also of the private kind of storytelling: if only more people had told themselves the proper story about themselves and decided, like Anton Schmidt, not to live with a murderer.

The example of Anton Schmidt suggests a dialectical relationship between public and private storytelling. Anton Schmidt told himself the right story, and this enabled him to act, to appear in public as a compassionate actor. Such a public appearance, especially under conditions of totalitarianism, is very dangerous: he was executed by the Nazis after five months. Yet Schmidt's story and actions also become the subject of *another* story, a story that re-enacts Schmidt's entrance into public by appearing 'like a burst of light' in the Jerusalem court-room. The first time that Anton Schmidt steps into public, he does so as a person of vision acting within a present reality. The second time Anton Schmidt steps into public, he does so as a historical figure and an image of the way that history invades the present: the story of his life becomes a historical marker for the way things might have been if more such stories could be told.

Suffering

As storytelling becomes historical, we glimpse its relationship to suffering. 'Because', writes Arendt in *The Human Condition*, 'the actor always moves among and in relation to other acting beings, he is never merely a "doer" but always and at the same time a sufferer. To do and to suffer are like opposite sides of the same coin, and the story that an act starts is composed of its consequent deeds and sufferings' (p. 190). Even in the best of circumstances, acting implies suffering because we are always involved in a complicated network of social relationships; the actions of others may cause us to suffer, and our actions start chain reactions that ripple through the social network and may harm others or even unpredictably rebound upon ourselves. Actions, in this sense, are irreversible, for we cannot undo what we have done. Consequently action implies suffering, and in the figure of the sufferer we can begin to glimpse the relation between public and private storytelling. Even in a public realm where agon is minimised, our public acts and public stories inevitably produce private instances of suffering: pain or personal discomfort are the inescapable outcomes of our participation in the realm of appearance. Once we have experienced such damage, once public appearance is transformed into the private experience of suffering, the very existence of the public space of disclosure is threatened. Suffering is a threat to politics: if all who suffer withdraw from public to nurse their wounds, public space itself will disappear, with dire results. For Arendt, the public is the realm of autonomy and of action, the place where humans are temporarily liberated from the necessities of nature. So withdrawing from the public sphere means sacrificing our freedom and subjecting ourselves to the predetermined demands of bodily necessity. When that happens, unjust regimes can easily colonise the political. Thus we should never willingly vacate the public space of appearance. And yet living in public for any length of time makes us vulnerable to the actions of others, and it is inevitable that we will eventually have to withdraw from the harsh light of the public. What we need, then, is a way to re-enter the political arena and begin its difficult work anew.

Here Arendt introduces a new and vital term into her political theory: forgiveness. In order to reconstitute politics, says Arendt, we need to practise forgiveness. For the sake of the continued existence of the free public realm we must make it possible to re-enter the political arena, and therefore we must learn to forgive others for the wounds we suffer, and we must in turn be forgiven for the suffering we have caused: 'without being forgiven, released from the consequences of what we have done ... we would remain the victims of its con-sequences forever' (p. 237). Beginning as a private moral action that moves outward into the public sphere, forgiveness reverses the trajectory from public into private enacted by suffering, interrupting the economy of resentment and drawing the individual out of her own private world and back into the public world of doing.[20] But such forgiveness lasts only until the next wound is given or received; bringing ourselves again into the harsh light of the public arena is a form of forgiving work that is never permanent but 'needs to be reproduced again and again' as each new day dawns, as we commit once again to reforming and restarting the public realm by forgiving and being forgiven (p. 139). Constant renewal motivated by faith in the moral necessity of the political realm is therefore crucial to its maintenance. Arendt calls this renewing act of forgiveness *natality*: 'the new beginning inherent in birth' which is new precisely 'because the newcomer possesses the capacity of beginning something anew, that is, of acting' (p. 9). As suffering and forgiving actors, we are each, in a sense, born anew every day.

My description of Arendtian forgiveness as defined by a movement from private to public should make it clear that I am drawing parallels between three separate parts of her thought: the passage from private to public and back again characteristic of the Greek *polis*; the way that storytelling figures this same passage by creating a space in which private concerns are spoken publicly; and finally the cycle of suffering and forgiveness that is an inevitable dynamic of human association. The important difference between the *polis* and these latter two is that while Arendt describes the *polis* as a place free of private concerns, both story-telling and forgiveness describe a more dialectical relation between public and private. Telling stories means that we allow our private concerns to burst into the sphere of public debate, and the act of forgiveness requires that we say, in effect, 'I forgive you for this hurt *X* that you have visited upon me', and that we enact this in some public way. In both forgiving and telling stories, then, the gulf between public and private is repeatedly crossed. Arendt imagines such crossing most unforgettably in figures like Anton Schmidt, who are wounded and suffering, who are the victims of a regime of unfreedom, but for whom storytelling and suffering, and the telling *of* suffering, momentarily construct a vision of a better order. In this sense figures like Schmidt become living embodiments of the monument with which we began this investigation. Earlier I used the metaphor of bleeding to describe the reciprocal relations between public and private characteristic of storytelling and forgiveness, but the presence of a suffering figure like Anton Schmidt suggests that the metaphor has a literal component as well. This becomes especially clear when Arendt turns in *The Human Condition* to an archetypal example of suffering.

Jesus

'The discoverer of the role of forgiveness in the realm of human affairs', writes Arendt, 'was Jesus of Nazareth. The fact that he made this discovery in a religious context and articulated it in religious language is no reason to take it any less seriously in a strictly secular sense' (p. 238). Both Arendt's introduction of Jesus as the 'discoverer' of forgiveness and her subsequent qualification are crucial to under-standing her idea of the public sphere. In keeping with the former, she describes Jesus as a teacher of forgiveness, a political actor in the public realm. Those pages of *The Human Condition* in which she speaks of Jesus are full of praise for his radical message: that we are required to forgive each other before God will forgive us, that forgiveness signifies a new beginning, that vengeance is not our province. Like Anton Schmidt, Arendt's Jesus is both a storyteller and a figure whose story is a burst of light in the midst of darkness. What Arendt *doesn't* mention is that, like Anton Schmidt, Jesus was killed for his message and his example. Strangely, Arendt's 'strictly secular' account of Jesus divorces his message from the events of his life, paradoxically ignoring her own dictum that suffering and forgiving go hand in hand. For although she holds that suffering is the precondition of the act of forgiveness, her account of Jesus never mentions his suffering and thus elides precisely those things that explain – theologically – his message of forgiveness: that he is the sacrificial lamb, that only his suffering and death can take away (forgive) the sins of the world.

Arendt's reasons for deflecting Jesus into the secular realm are easy to identify. In *The Human Condition* she argues that the emergence of Christianity in the ancient world was disastrous for politics because it introduced notions like the sacredness of each human life, granting dignity to the enslaved and the downtrodden. With Christianity, the private realm displaced the public world of politics and relegated it to a necessary nuisance: 'Political activity, which up to then had derived its greatest inspiration from the aspiration toward worldly immortality, now sank to the low level of an activity subject to necessity. ... It is precisely individual life which now came to occupy the position once held by the "life" of the body politic' (p. 314). The Christian reversal of the very values Arendt held so dear means that it is not surprising that she would strive to secularise her own account of Jesus. At the same time, this secularisation is accomplished only by cleaning up Jesus, wiping away the marks of his suffering. A strictly secular interpretation of Jesus, after all, fails to offer any plausible explanation for his message of forgiveness.

What would a more satisfactory Arendtian account of Jesus look like? First, I think it would celebrate the crossing and re-crossing of public/private boundaries while acknowledging the distinctiveness of these realms. Such a celebration need not run counter to Arendt's theories. While Christianity may have subverted the radical bifurcation between private and public that Arendt celebrates in the Greek *polis*, her work on storytelling and forgiveness contains an implicit acknowledgement that, as Benhabib suggests, 'the public space is essentially porous'.[21] Or, to return to my metaphor, public and private necessarily bleed into one another, and such bleeding is figured in every instance of storytelling, in every dialectic of suffering and forgiveness. Far from being a capitulation to unfreedom, acknowledging this dialectic contains seeds of a radical politics. Elshtain suggests that Jesus remains important for political theory because of his 'insistence that the realm of necessity, the nonpolitical or subpolitical realm, is not a despised forum for human endeavor ... but, simply and profoundly, that place where the vast majority of human beings find their homes and must be allowed to live with dignity and purpose'.[22] Against Arendt, Elshtain argues for the political significance of Jesus: bringing the conditions of necessity into the light of the public is a political act whose consequences Arendt did not appreciate, since she saw there only the destruction of public action. As I suggested above, however, Arendt herself opens the possibility of such a politics in her theories of storytelling and forgiveness. Thus, Elshtain's use of Jesus as a model of politics is not only more consistent than Arendt's interpretation of Jesus but also more consistent with Arendt's own theories of storytelling and forgiveness, and in substantial agreement with the present state of feminist theory. I should emphasise, though, that any public sphere modelled on this understanding of Jesus would not be a utopian community debating issues of public and private import under the guidance of communicative rationality. The dialectic of suffering and forgiveness is truly a dialectic: forgiveness begins by acknowledging suffering, and the community that re-forms itself around this dialectic carries with it the memory of suffering.

The second element (and it flows inevitably from this dialectic) would highlight Jesus' suffering. At the centre of Arendt's political theory is not, I think, an analytical distinction between public and private but rather a collection of figures, those whom she sometimes calls men in dark times: Rosa Luxemburg, Karl Jaspers, Anton Schmidt – and, perhaps, Jesus of Nazareth. These are not simply manly heroes who died young, as Elshtain claims; they are, or can be, suffering and forgiving figures who model for us the passage between public and private worlds, who stand as monuments to the difficulties of such passages. Telling the stories of these figures serves as a kind of remembrance or memorialisation. It makes explicit the suffering that lies at the foundations of community, and it highlights the degree to which a community must learn to ask forgiveness of its victims. Here again the story of Jesus serves as an appropriate model, since the point of the gospel narrative, as Rene Girard has argued, is to make suffering a public issue by acting it out: forcing it from hiding, driving it out into the open, writing it down.[23] To write a political theory that captures this same impulse was, I believe, Arendt's ultimate goal. This theory aims to walk the difficult line between erasing suffering (under the guise of unfettered communication) and getting caught permanently in its web (as with scapegoating, for instance). It accomplishes its delicate balance with equal measures of suffering and forgiving – and it tells the story of these acts so well that they become bursts of light in the darkness. Such a theory might well be worth practising.

Santayana's adage that those who forget the past are condemned to repeat it captures the pragmatic sense of such a theory. Beyond this, however, Arendt's theory of storytelling may offer something like the possibility of redemption. Every public sphere, every political change, generates its own victims. Learning to ask their forgiveness is both the most humane and the most radical response we can have to this inevitability – humane, because forgiveness expands our community and exemplifies the 'reversibility of perspectives' that Benhabib idealises; radical, because seeking forgiveness disrupts our community by adding new members with different needs and desires. This addition means we must change our story, add another chapter to the history of suffering and forgiving that constitutes a community. For us, perhaps, it remains to remember suffering, to tell its story, and to wait for tomorrow, when – forgiven – we may live and act anew.

Notes

1   H. Arendt, *The Human Condition* (Chicago: Univ. of Chicago Press, 1958) p. 25. Subsequent references to this text will be noted parenthetically.

2   A. Rich, *On Lies, Secrets and Silence: Selected Prose 1966–1978* (New York: Norton, 1979) pp. 211–12. J. B. Elshtain, *Public Man, Private Woman: Women in Social and Political Thought* (Princeton: Princeton Univ. Press, 1981) p. 58.

3   S. Benhabib, *Critique, Norm, and Utopia: A Study of the Foundations of Critical Theory* (New York: Columbia Univ. Press, 1986) p. 352.

4   P. U. Hohendahl, 'The Public Sphere: Models and Boundaries', in *Habermas and the Public Sphere*, C. Calhoun (ed.) (Cambridge: MIT Press, 1992) p. 101.

5   S. Benhabib, 'Afterword: Communicative Ethics and Current Controversies in Practical Philosophy', in *The Communicative Ethics Controversy*, S. Benhabib and F. Dallmayr (eds) (Cambridge: MIT Press, 1990) p. 346.

6   Ibid., p. 363.

7   S. Benhabib, 'Hannah Arendt and the Redemptive Power of Narrative', *Social Research*, 57 (1990) 167–96.

8   S. Benhabib, 'Feminist Theory and Hannah Arendt's Concept of Public Space', *History of the Human Sciences*, 6.2 (1993) 97–114.

9   Benhabib, 'Hannah Arendt', pp. 193–4.

10   Benhabib, 'Feminist Theory', p. 98.

11   Ibid., pp. 103–4.

12   B. Honig, 'Toward an Agonistic Feminism: Hannah Arendt and the Politics of the Body', in *Feminist Interpretations of Hannah Arendt*, B. Honig (ed.) (University Park: Pennsylvania State Univ. Press, 1995) p. 156.

13   S. Benhabib, *The Reluctant Modernism of Hannah Arendt* (London: Sage, 1996) p. 209.

14 C. Mouffe, 'Deconstruction, Pragmatism and the Politics of Democracy', in *Deconstruction and Pragmatism*, C. Mouffe (ed.) (London: Routledge, 1996) p. 9.

15 H. Arendt, *Lectures on Kant's Political Philosophy*, R. Beiner (ed.) (Chicago: Univ. of Chicago Press, 1982) pp. 37–8.

16 Ibid., p. 40.

17 H. Arendt, 'Personal Responsibility Under Dictatorship', *The Listener*, 6 August 1964, p. 186.

18 Ibid., p. 205.

19 H. Arendt, *Eichmann in Jerusalem: A Report on the Banality of Evil* (New York: Penguin, 1963, 1991) p. 231.

20 On this point see M. A. Orlie, 'Forgiving Trespasses, Promising Futures', *Feminist Interpretations of Hannah Arendt*, p. 347.

21 Benhabib, 'Hannah Arendt', p. 194.

22 Elshtain, *Public Man, Private Woman*, p. 63.

23 R. Girard, *Things Hidden Since the Foundation of the World* (Stanford: Stanford Univ. Press, 1987) p. 181.

Index